THE GERMAN PEOPLE OF NEW ORLEANS,
1850-1900

THE GERMAN PEOPLE OF NEW ORLEANS, 1850-1900

BY

JOHN FREDRICK NAU

DOCTOR OF PHILOSOPHY

Mississippi Southern College
Hattiesburg, Mississippi

LEIDEN
E. J. BRILL
1958

TO MY FAITHFUL WIFE, JOHANNA LEONORA,
WHO INSPIRED ME IN THE WRITING OF THIS
WORK AND WHO WAS INSTRUMENTAL IN ALL
I HAVE ACCOMPLISHED, THIS VOLUME IS
LOVINGLY DEDICATED.

TABLE OF CONTENTS

ACKNOWLEDGMENTS

Acknowledgment is hereby made to the many individuals who either directed the author to valuable materials in the writing of this dissertation or placed privately owned materials at his disposal. Particular gratitude is expressed to the staff of the Howard Tilton Memorial Library of Tulane University, New Orleans, Louisiana, and the staff of The Library of the University of Alabama. The author is also deeply appreciative of the assistance given by Adolph Flasdick, custodian of the Archives of the Deutsches Haus, New Orleans, Louisiana, by Rose M. Oliver of the Louisiana State Museum Library; by Fay Schultz and Helen Burkes of the Department of Archives of the New Orleans Public Library; and by John L. Rettenmeier.

In the preparation of the manuscript the author is indebted to Arthur G. Nuhrah, instructor of History at Tulane University, New Orleans, Louisiana, who offered technical assistance and who carefully proofread the dissertation; to several of my colleagues at Mississippi Southern College of Hattiesburg, Mississippi; and to Johanna L. Nau, the author's wife, who assisted in the work of preliminary typing of the manuscript.

Above all, the author expresses his thanks to Professor Robert D. Ochs, who patiently and understandingly directed the writing of the dissertation and gave invaluable counsel which has assisted the author greatly in the writing of this work; and to Robert H. Wienefeld, head of the Department of History of the University of South Carolina, who carefully read and corrected the second draft of the dissertation and gave much needed direction to the completion of the work.

PREFACE

The story of European migration to the New World and the establishment of immigrant homes has enchanted the minds and hearts of many, since the element of pathos and the unusual, so deeply inherent in the experiences of migrating peoples, has always appealed to the imagination of man. Particularly at the beckoning of North America, millions of Europeans left kindred and loved ones to seek a new life in its vast regions and in its glorious opportunities. A great number of writers, historians and novelists, have consequently turned to this particular field to bring interesting and instructive accounts of the toils and triumphs of the European immigrants as they came to establish their new home in a new world.

The general background of this dissertation, *The German People of New Orleans, 1850-1900*, lies in that century in which European migration to the United States reached its zenith. More than five million German immigrants alone crossed the Atlantic for a venturesome journey to America to find political, religious, and economic freedom and the opportunity to work and plan for a better future. The direct focus and purpose of the work is to relate the activities and achievements of the comparative small, yet highly expressive, group of German immigrants of New Orleans, Louisiana, which gave its brain and brawn, its heart and hands, to build a great American city and to leave its mark indelibly in its way of life. It is the story of a people who, in spite of the climate to which they were unaccustomed and of the predominant Latin culture of the French and Spanish who had founded the city and molded its early pattern, adopted New Orleans as their home, building their churches, schools, theaters, and social and benevolent societies, and contributing to the economic strength and cultural progress of that city during the last five decades of the nineteenth century.

As early as 1721, three years after the founding of New Orleans by the French, Germans cast longing eyes upon the better life promised in Louisiana. They were encouraged by John Law, a notorious Scotch financier operating in France, to leave their unhappy state in Germany to find happiness and prosperity in his land concession on the lower Arkansas River, which had been pictured to them as a paradise "flowing with milk and honey." This invitation was especially welcomed by those who lived in the Rhineland and the Palatinate, who had suffered most from the ravages of the Thirty Year's War (1618-1648) and from the vindictiveness of Louis XIV.

These immigrants did not fare well in the Arkansas River valley. When they learned of the bankruptcy of John Law and of his flight from France, and were forced to rely upon the mercy of the Indian for food and protection, they decided to return to their homeland. Having come to New Orleans about 1725 seeking passage to some European port, they were offered a stretch of rich alluvial land on the right bank of the Mississippi River about twenty-five miles above the town by the colonial government under Bienville.

This colony of German settlers, known as the German Gold Coast, received an influx of countrymen at various times, both from Europe and from the English colonies in North America. As the number increased, some turned to New Orleans, first for the sale of their garden vegetables and then to find the opportunity to exchange country life for city dwelling. These Germans, together with those who were continually coming in greater number from the old world, formed the nucleus of the German element in the city. By the mid-1830's a goodly number of Germans called New Orleans their home. The group continued to grow in number and in influence, the story of which is related in the pages of this history.

A number of writers have presented varied studies of the life and activity of the German element in New Orleans and Louisiana. Chief among these was J. Hanno Deiler, who especially wrote much about the early Germans in Louisiana, but who also left a record of the Germans' churches, schools, newspapers, and the *Deutsche Gesellschaft*. To him the writer of this dissertation is greatly indebted. Others have considered the German element of Louisiana and New Orleans in their political activities during particular periods of Southern history, in their theater activity, and in their educational endeavors.

The present work has as its chief purpose the presentation of an economic and social history of the German people in New Orleans in the latter half of the nineteenth century in which all of the information offered in these varied works together with that gathered from the German newspapers of the period, the records of minutes of congregations and German societies, and interviews with older members of the German element are brought together to present a full and vivid history.

Besides this, the dissertation presents another purpose, one which is accomplished not by design or intention but solely by letting the record speak for itself. Most individuals know New Orleans as a city of French, Spanish and American culture exclusively. Considerable surprise is manifested when one ventures to suggest that other Europeans besides the French and Spanish have had a part in the forging of New Orleans life, among these the immigrants from Germany. Here is a record of their achievements and contributions which ought to remove any doubts. Likewise, on a larger scale, if one looks over the works treating the origin, history, and accomplishments of the American nation, to ascertain what part the descendants of the millions of German immigrants took in the development of the country, he rarely finds more than a short mention.

Sometimes we see in American newspapers in the larger cities, which are compelled to flatter their many German subscribers, a few words of praise. The well-educated American is likely to acknowledge the thrift, steady habits, the learning and skill of the Germans, but very rarely do we find mention made of the profound social, ethical, scientific, even political, influences the German element exercised during the last two centuries. While the situation has changed markedly in other sections of our land, the Germans' part in building an important city in the lower Mississippi valley has to a great extent been overshadowed by the predominant work of the French and Spanish. Again and again the writer, in pursuit of his research, met individuals who were personally acquainted with a number of Germans of the last decades of the nineteenth century of whom it was said, "These are the men who helped to make New Orleans a city of commerce, industry, and business. They built New Orleans." To give them their deserved recognition, and to add valuable information to the historical records of New Orleans and Louisiana, the work was written.

CHAPTER I

IMMIGRATION OF GERMANS TO THE NEW WORLD

Nineteenth century Europe was a continent of political strife and turmoil, of economic stringency and famine, and of social and religious confusion, which sparked a "Voelkerwanderung" comparable to the mass movement of Asiatic humanity in the second millenium before Christ.[1] It was then that immigrants from every nation in Europe sought an asylum in the New World, with the United States of America harboring the greatest number.[2] From 1840 to 1860, more than two million Irish immigrants were driven by hunger and political and religious discrimination to this country. Likewise the Germans, over five million during the century, came from a fatherland torn by war, intolerance, and oppression to the country that offered each immigrant a new start with new hopes and new opportunities.[3]

These German immigrants of the nineteenth century came in three distinct waves. The first occurred just after the Napoleonic wars. At that time Europe, seething under the tyrannical reaction of the Congress of Vienna, moved steadily toward, and into, revolution. In 1817, a student group of Jena University arranged a gathering of all the *Burschen-schaften* at the Wartburg Castle, to celebrate the fourth anniversary of the Battle of Leipzig and the tercentenary of Luther's *Thesis*. The gathering proved the first public protest against the settlement of 1815. Two years later, a mentally unbalanced theological student murdered the dramatist, Kotzebue, an agent of Alexander I of Russia. The reaction to these outbursts of liberalism was the acceptance of the Carlsbad Decrees by nine principal German states. The German states had been frightened by Metternich.[4] Yet, the fatal year came in 1820, when revolts

---

[1] Joseph Ward Swain, *The Ancient World-Empires and City-States of the Ancient Orient and Greece Before 334 B.C.* (New York, 1950) I, 132-33.

[2] J. Hanno Deiler, *Die Europaeische Einwanderung nach den Vereinigten Staaten* (New Orleans, 1897), 2 ff.

[3] Matthew A. Pekari, "The German Catholics in the United States of America," *Records of the American Historical Society*, XXXVI (1925), No. 4, 349. It is estimated that between the years 1820 and 1900 some 5,010,147 Germans came to America. *Ibid.* Rachel Davis Du Bois Emma Schweppe, *The Germans in American Life* (New York, 1936), 57.

[4] Frederick B. Artz, *Reaction and Revolution*, 1814-1832 (New York, 1934), 140-41.

against the system occurred in many European countries, and continued until the early 1850's. It was in January, 1820, that a company of Spanish soldiers mutinied and proclaimed the Constitution of 1812. [1] During the same year, King Ferdinand IV of the Kingdom of Naples, yielding to the general clamor, agreed to convert his state into a limited monarchy after the Spanish model. The revolutionary fever spread. Portugal, after a liberal uprising, adopted a constitutional system. Greece, fighting for independence against a decaying yet autocratic Turkish Empire, finally gained her independence and autonomy at the Peace of Adrianople. An aroused French people were preparing for revolution against the despised Bourbon monarchs. [2]

Germany and Central Europe were not stirred as perceptibly by the revolutions of the 1820's and 1830's as other sections and countries in the west, south, and east, due to Austria's influence in the Diet. Their lot in life was, however, no better. In fact, in some respects their suffering was more acute due to the ravages of the Napoleonic Wars and the famines that followed in their wake. In 1817, Germany experienced one of the severest famines in her history, particularly in the Rhine provinces. In Baden, Württemberg, Alsace, Palatinate Hessen, and the Rhine Province, the price of bread rose to twenty-six cents a pound and many ate cooked weeds to keep from starving. [3] Such conditions, together with political and religious oppression, hastened the departure of thousands of German sufferers from their fatherland. [4]

The decrees provided that the *Burschenschaften* and the gymnastic societies be dissolved, and that inspectors for each university and censors for the press be appointed, both of which provisions strengthened the power of the secret police.

[1] "The Constitution of 1812 was composed of successive decrees and resolutions which developed the new Liberal program. Its fundamental planks included: sovereignty of the nation, conjointly with the king; constitutional monarchy; separation of the powers of the state; .... equal rights between Peninsular Spaniards and Spanish subjects in America; .... political freedom of the press, which, however, remained subject to the former censorship in religious matters; submission of the King to the *Cortes* with respect to his marriage .... abolition of torture; .... recognition of human rights; means of amending the constitution; .... accelerated development of public education; abolition of the Tribunal of the Inquisition ...; .... establishment of a direct single tax; ...." Rafael Altamira, *A History of Spain — From the Beginnings to the Present Day* (New York, 1949), 537-38.

[2] Artz, *Reaction and Revolution*, 149-160; Ferdinand Schevill, *A History of Europe* (New York, 1947), 453-54, 457, 460-63.

[3] J. Hanno Deiler, *Geschichte der deutschen Gesellschaft* (New Orleans, 1897), 36-38; Louis Voss, *Die Deutschen in Louisiana* (Detroit, 1929), 48.

[4] Walter O. Forster, "Settlement of the Saxon Lutherans in Missouri, 1839-1847," (Washington University, Ph. D. Thesis, 1942), 274. The adoption of the Prussian Union of 1817, an attempt of Fredrich William III to establish an evangelical national

Within the midst of such a strife-torn Europe, the great Goethe, cried: "America, thou hast it better!" [1] In America there was no enforced service in the army, taxes were negligible, and so great was the government surplus that Congress was actually troubled by what to do with it. In America immigrant peoples who had lived under extortionate taxes, rents, and tithes, and had been harassed by government spies, soon learned that government cost little and interfered little with citizens. No wonder that an observer who asked German immigrants why they were going to America received from all of them the same answer: "There is no king there." [2] The United States of America became a haven for these distressed, oppressed, and troubled Europeans, among whom were large numbers of Germans, who saw in that country the land that "flowed with milk and honey." [3] Finding that no white man in America acknowledged a master made the United States even more attractive to them. Seeing farm hands and housemaids sitting at the table with their employers and American women not accustomed to field drudgery; hearing their own rejoice, "There are no estates whose owners can take the last sheaf from their dependents and then turn them out to beg"; and believing the claim, "Neither is my cap worn out from lifting it in the presence of gentlemen"; these immigrants pictured the United States as the land of opportunity, of freedom, and of a new life. [4]

With such an America awaiting them, millions of German immigrants came, floating down American rivers, crossing the prairies in ox-carts and covered wagons, helping to swell the population of North America to the very edge of the Pacific Ocean. [5] In 1817, 16,000 people left Württemberg alone to find refuge and relief in other parts of the world, especially in the United States. Thirty thousand Germans left Mainz for passage

---

church comprised of Lutherans, Reformed, and Evangelical, caused much religious confusion and led to persecution. This persecution also caused many Germans to leave their homeland to migrate to the United States. John Henry Kurtz, *Church History* (New York, 1890), III, 178; Charles M. Jacobs, *The Story of the Church* (Philadelphia, 1925), 369-70; Lars P. Qualben, *A History of the Christian Church* (New York, 1935), 385; Forster, "Saxon Lutherans in Missouri," 274.

[1] Leland D. Baldwin, *The Stream of American History* (New York, 1952), I, 610; *Goethes Werke* (Hamburger Ausgabe, 1948), I, 333. These words are taken from the poem, *Den Vereinigten Staaten.*

[2] Baldwin, *The Stream of American Hictory*, I, 610.

[3] J. Hanno Deiler, *Die Ersten Deutschen am unteren Mississippi* (New Orleans, 1910), 9-10.

[4] Baldwin, *The Stream of American History*, I, 610.

[5] Schweppe, *The Germans in American Life*, 57.

to Holland with America as their ultimate goal. [1] It was this post-Napoleonic wave of immigration which increased the system of "redemption" whereby many German immigrants, to pay for their passage from a nation torn to pieces by French invasions, bound themselves to service for a period of years after arriving in their new paradise. [2] The greater number of these immigrants were bound to the captain of the ship for their passage to America. On arrival in the port of entry, merchants were on hand to purchase the services of the immigrants who contracted their labors for periods from three to eight years. During that time they received no salary, only lodging, food and clothing. Their lot was a rather hard one. [3]

Louisiana and New Orleans received their share of these politically, socially, and religiously harassed German immigrants. On March 6, 1818, the Dutch ships, *Emmanuel Juffer Johanna* and *Johanna Maria*, discharged 597 German redemptioners at New Orleans, who worked on the soil of Louisiana for several years. [4] From 1820 to 1850, 53,909 German immigrants entered the port of New Orleans. [5] The greater number of these were redemptioners. After they were freed, many of them turned to New Orleans as their home in the New World. By the mid-1830's there were about 7,000 Germans living in the city. [6]

The second wave of immigration began in the early 1840's and continued

---

[1] Deiler, *Geschichte der deutschen Gesellschaft* 36-38.

[2] Robert T. Clark, Jr., "The German Liberals in New Orleans (1840-1860)," *Louisiana Historical Quarterly*, XX (1937), 137.

[3] J. Hanno Deiler, *Zur Geschichte der Deutschen am unteren Mississippi* (New Orleans, 1901), 4.

[4] Deiler, *Geschichte der deutschen Gesellschaft*, 36-38. Deiler stated, "these 597 Germans were the remainder of 1,100 that had been placed on the three ships. The others died enroute due to sickness, or, because of fever and confusion jumped overboard."

[5] *Ibid.*, 39-40.

[6] Founded by Bienville in 1718, and until 1762 it remained a French city. In the latter year it passed into Spanish hands and so remained until 1801, when Spain not unwillingly restored it to its original owners. In 1803, it finally came into possession of the United States by what was known as the Louisiana Purchase. *Progressive New Orleans*, published by the Young Men's Business League (1895), 13. This booklet is in the T. P. Thompson Collection, Alabama University Library, Tuscaloosa, Alabama In 1800, New Orleans had a total of 9,650 inhabitants which was more than six times as large as Pittsburgh, more than twelve times as large as Cincinnati, fifteen times as large as Louisville, and ten times as large as St. Louis. Arthur H. Moehlenbrock, "The German Drama on the New Orleans Stage," *Louisiana Historical Quarterly*, XXVI. (1943), No. 2, 368.

until the outbreak of the Civil War. [1] By this time central Europe was also perceptibly steeped in political strife and bitterness. In Italy, Joseph Mazzini, the leading spirit of the revolutionary government of Rome, was fighting unsuccessfully for the establishment of a republic, assisted admirably by the gallant Garibaldi. In Hungary, Louis Kossuth and Gorgei, fighting for independence from the Austrian Empire, were overcome by the combined forces of the Austrians and Russians; and by August, 1849, the movement for Hungarian independence came to a tragic close.

Germany also was rocked by revolution. When King Frederick William III of Prussia died in 1840, his successor, Frederick William IV, faced a new generation of subjects who let it be known in no uncertain terms that, while it approved of the efficient administration maintained by the state, it did not intend to let itself be excluded any longer from a share in legislation. This condition led to friction and strife between king and people, which ultimately restored the supremacy of Austrian power in German affairs with the reestablishment of the old Germanic Confederation in 1850 and gave new life to the system of reaction with all its attendant abuses and miseries. With it all, German hopes for liberalism had been shattered. [2]

Besides these political upheavals, there were other conditions that added to the misery of the German population. In the Silesian weaving districts unemployment was a serious problem. The hard winters, the failure of crops, and accompanying famines in the years 1845 and 1846, plagued the people no end. Misery was stalking through every street and visiting every middle class home throughout Germany. Then came the cry of gold from the land of California. This proved another strong incentive for Germans to leave their homeland of trouble and sorrow for the land that promised riches for those that would venture. [3] All of these conditions were important factors in establishing immigration records during the years of the second wave. [4]

These German immigrants were no longer merely of a peasant class, but included a very large number of well-educated political refugees.

---

[1] Robert T. Clark, Jr., "The German Liberals in New Orleans," *loc. cit.*, XX (1937), 137-38.

[2] Robert C. Binkley, *Realism and Nationalism*, 1852-1871 (New York, 1935), 131-32; Carlton J. H. Hayes, *Modern Europe to* 1870 (New York, 1953), 670-71.

[3] J. Hanno Deiler, *European Immigration* 1820-1900 (New Orleans, 1907), 4-5. A lecture delivered before the Germanistic Society of Chicago, December 16, 1907.

[4] J. Hanno Deiler, *Die Europaeische Einwanderung nach den Vereinigten Staaten* (New Orleans, 1897), 4; Deiler, *European Immigration*, 6.

Among them came trained engineers, physicians, druggists, chemists, and technologists, seeking opportunities in the new land.[1] Of these opportunities wrote a certain Joseph Eder:

> We have not seen a single man begging, for here everyone who can must work.... America does not say: 'Eat what we give you or starve' but 'Lazy fellow, work or die.' ... Not a single house is locked here at night, everything is open, yet you do not hear that anything has been stolen.... Tailors and cobblers earn two dollars ... a day without board. But everyone must first know his trade. Painters do well. They earn three dollars a day. If a cabinet maker has been here long enough to know his way around, he can earn three dollars a day. Carpenters earn three dollars a day, but it is hard to stand the work in summer on account of the great heat .... foods are not as expensive in fact cheaper than in Bavaria. It is also good that one can do what one wishes without asking anyone. A person need do no more than hang up his sign. If he has a business which does not please him, he need only change his sign and start something else. A fortune is not necessary for this. An artisan who has no more than his tools can work independently. A person wishing to marry need do no more than take along another man to the minister and to be married there—that finishes the matter. Here you do not hear of affairs of single people who know each other for years and then get children, as happens in Germany. When two have met who love each other they are married. And if they do not have enough to run their own home, they board at first. They must work, however, and soon they will have enough to run their own household.

> Now, my dear friends, I have written you the pure truth, and if perhaps one of you wants to come to America, let him by no means be deterred by the many hardships of travel that he must endure. Once you are here all that is forgotten and you certainly do not regret it.[2]

New Orleans received its share of these trained people, as well as many

[1] Albert B. Faust, "German Culture Influences in American Life," *The Concord Society of America Year Book 1928* (Detroit, 1929), 8-9. Foremost of all were the German engineers. Roebling, suspension bridges and manufacturer of steel cable; Fink, railroad engineer; Sutro, tunneling of mines; Baron Stiegel and Peter Hasenclever, foundries; Mathieson and Hegeler, zinc plate; Foerderer-Pfister and Vogel, Schieren, Groetzinger, Schmidt, Schoellkopf in textiles; David Tannenberg and Steinway and Sons, musical instruments; Bausch and Lomb (Rochester), optical instruments; Prang, Bien, Gugler, Hoen, lithography; Hecker (flour), Ziegler (baking powder), food products; Heintz, Lutz, Schramm, pickling; Anhaueser, Busch, Pabst, Seipp, Ehret, Uihlein, Ruppert, brewing. *Ibid.*

[2] Karl J. R. Arndt, "A Bavarian's Journey to New Orleans and Nacogdoches in 1853-54," *Louisiana Historical Quarterly*, XXIII (1940), No. 2, 492-93, 495.

penniless German immigrants. [1] Among those that came were doctors, lawyers, journalists, musicians, engineers, dentists, artisans, and business men. The brewing trade was gradually monopolized by Germans. Draymen in the city were Germans. Metal workers were Germans. Streetrailways were built by German engineers, who also drew up and carried out the plans for the New Orleans waterworks. [2] German architects built many of the houses of the non-German elite. [3] Many of them were politically German nationalists inspired with the humanitarian views of Herder, the nationalistic ideals of Fichte, and the revolutionary doctrines of Young Germany. As a more highly educated group, they were prepared to compete in many fields with the native Americans. [4]

In 1850, New Orleans was a thriving port town with a population of 116,375, of whom 11,425 were Germans, not including the children born of them in their newly-adopted country. This very active German colony received about 126,006 German immigrants during the first five years of the 1850's, with the peak year, 1854, bringing 40,006 to the city. [5] By 1860, the city had grown to 174,491 of whom 10,689 were free colored and 13,385 were slaves. [6] At the same time there were 24,614 Germans in the State of Louisiana, the greater number of whom lived in the city of New Orleans. [7]

During the entire period from 1840 to 1860, New Orleans was enjoying

---

[1] *One Hundred Years in New Orleans, Louisiana-Centenary Souvenir, Redemptorist Fathers* (New Orleans, 1944), 10-11. According to the records of the German Society of New Orleans 227, 247 Germans made their entry between 1848 and 1858, of which almost 60,000 remained. The yellow fever cut down almost half of these. The majority of the survivors were young people. Robert T. Clark, Jr., "The German Liberals in New Orleans," *loc. cit.*, XX (1937), 137-38.

[2] Albert Stein, engineer from Duesseldorf drew the plans for the New Orleans waterworks. This was in 1844, but the building was not begun until 1849. He also built the waterworks at Richmond and Lynchburg, Virginia; Nashville, Tennessee; and Mobile, Alabama, and the Appomattox Canal at St. Petersburg. J. Hanno Deiler, *Geschichte der New Orleanser deutschen Presse* (New Orleans, 1901), 7.

[3] *One Hundred Years in New Orleanser, Louisiana*, 10-11.

[4] Robert T. Clark, Jr., "The German Liberals in New Orleans," *loc. cit.*, XX (1937), 137-38.

[5] J. D. B. De Bow, *The Seventh Census of the United States 1850* (Washington, 1853), 468; *Souvenir of the Eightieth Anniversary of the German Society of New Orleans* (New Orleans, 1927), n.p.

[6] J. D. B. De Bow, *The Eighth Census of the United States 1860* (Washington, 1864), 195.

[7] *Ibid.*, 196. Of this number there were 399 from Austria, 3, 621 from Bavaria, 4, 685 from Baden, 1, 006 from Hesse, 155 from Nassau, 2,739 from Prussia, 889 from Württemberg, and 11,120 not specified.

extraordinary growth and prosperity. Not only did the population of the city increase by 44.9 per cent but its industrial output exceeded the quarter million dollar mark. [1] Hustle and bustle was in evidence everywhere. One casual reporter stated:

> We have never seen so many people pressing into our city, as there are at present. All the States and the country parishes seem to be represented in our city. The weather is mild, balmy and spring-like, and everybody seems to be smiling and happy. The ladies trip along our streets, as beamingly and gracefully, as so many dear, graceful fawns, gliding over a velvet sward. Chartres street is refulgent, from early morn to dewy eve—Canal glitters with silks, satins, and velvets; and Camp street radiates with all the hues of autumn. Altogether, New Orleans is at present a very gay—it is, at all times, a pleasant place. [2]

The city was also a thriving port. It was fifth in population in the nation, exceeded only by New York, Philadelphia, Baltimore, and Boston. Other river and lake ports were trailing her in size. Brooklyn was only four-fifths as large; Saint Louis, seven-eighths; Cincinnati lacked one twenty-fifth of her number; while Louisville, Chicago, Buffalo, and Pittsburgh had a population number ranging from a mere forty to fifty thousand. [3] At the same time it ranked very high with all the ports in the world, its receipts from the interior alone amounting to nearly $ 97,000,000 in 1850. [4] Its port was filled with steamboats, flatboats, schooners, and brigs. Its wharves were piled high with rows of cotton, bags of salt, and merchandise of all kind. [5] It was the hub of a triangular trade. Raw materials from the lush Mississippi Valley came through the city and in return manufactured goods came from Philadelphia, Pittsburgh, and Baltimore. Some trade developed with Mexico. The value of produce received at New Orleans from the interior increased from $ 22,065,518 in 1830 to $ 185,211,254 in 1860. By 1860, sixty per

---

[1] William R. Merriam, *Abstract of the Twelfth Census of the United States 1900,* (Washington, 1902), Part I, 437. Henry Rightor, (ed.) *Standard History of New Orleans, Louisiana* (Chicago, 1900), 516.

[2] New Orleans *The Daily Delta,* January 6, 1850.

[3] De Bow, *The Eighth Census of the United States-1860,* 90, 195, 225, 297, 381; George E. Waring, *Report on the Social Statistics of Cities* (Washington, 1887), Part II, 256. Kendall states that New Orleans was the fourth largest city, with Boston fifth. John S. Kendall, *History of New Orleans* (New York 1922), I, 202.

[4] Kendall, *History of New Orleans,* I, 202. Some held the port to be the fourth largest in the world, with only London, Liverpool and New York ahead. Thomas C. Johnson, *Life and Letters of Benjamin Morgan Palmer* (Richmond, 1906), 173.

[5] New Orleans *Daily Picayune,* April 1, 1853.

cent of the value of the goods received was attributable to cotton. [1]

This city was also the port of entry for immigrants on their way to the West of the United States. [2] The great Mississippi River became "eine Voelkerstrasse nach dem Westen" and New Orleans the second largest port of immigration. [3] An observer wrote in 1853, when 36,000 Germans landed in this port city:

> A large immigrant ship just arrived with a load of steerage passengers. Their style of beauty proclaimed them German, and if that was not sufficient to ensure conviction the grunting gutturals of their language, their meershaums and picturebook clothing would have been conclusive. Little fraus and frauleins built on the six by five principle, waddled around the deck or climbed on the bulwarks and surveyed with prodigious leaden eyes the land of promise. On the levee a large number of older emigrants from the fatherland assembled, who with stentorian lungs and beaming countenance called to the new comers. [3]

After 1857, however, only those immigrants landed in New Orleans who intended to go to Texas. [5] This was due to the linking of New York with the West by railroad. [6] And even this traffic fell off after the United States government deepened the harbor of Galveston, so that vessels drawing eighteen feet could reach its wharves. Consequently, both the North German Lloyd and the Hamburg-American Line withdrew from the port of New Orleans and sent their steamers from Hamburg and Bremen to Galveston. [7]

The third and final wave of German immigration to the United States in the nineteenth century began about 1864 and continued to the middle of the 1890's after which time it slackened considerably. From 1870 to 1895 over two and three quarter millions of Germans arrived. [8] The year

---

[1] New Orleans *Item*, June 10, 1952, Transport Section, 1.

[2] Louis Voss, "Die Letzten Sechzig Jahren," *Concord Society of American Year Book 1928* (Detroit, 1929), 52.

[3] Deiler, *European Immigration 1820-1900*, 9.

[4] New Orleans *Daily Picayune*, April 1, 1853.

[5] Deiler, *European Immigration 1820-1900*, 9.

[6] Voss, "Die Letzten Sechzig Jahren," *loc. cit.*, 52.

[7] Deiler, *European Immigration 1820-1900*, 9.

[8] Edward Alsworth Ross, *The Old World In The New* (New York, 1914), 66. The author presents the following table: Immigration from Germany, Netherlands, and Switzerland.

1861-65	242,500	Civil War in the United States
1866-70	577,600	
1871-75	532,700	
1876-80	220,200	Hard Times in the United States
1881-85	1.031,500	Militarism and Over-population in Germany
1886-90	548,200	
1891-95	432,600	

of greatest migration to the United States was 1882, when 250,630 Germans left their homes to seek a new life in America. [1] Of these, more and more were industrial workers, and fewer and fewer were peasants. Very rarely an intellectual or a man of substance appeared for admission to the United States. After 1882, the number of German immigrants rapidly subsided. The lowest ebb, in 1898, brought only 17,111. [2]

Varied reasons compelled these Germans to leave their homeland in such numbers that this final wave of immigration broke all previous marks. At this time, the great trans-Atlantic steamer lines, the North German Lloyd, the Hamburg-American Line, the Compagnie Génerale Transatlantique of Havre and several English lines, went all out to find business in the transportation of European immigrants to the United States. These, together with the American railways, which had received land grants and wanted their territories settled, and such states that had lands to give away, threw a whole network of agencies over Europe, and their agents distributed glowing descriptions of America and invited emigration from Europe. [3]

To these steamship and railroad agents, the most successful of all propagandists must be added the letters of those who had already found their fortunes in America. Such letters on reaching Europe were not only read in the families but also were passed from house to house, everywhere increasing discontent with existing conditions, turning toward America the eyes of everyone who was striving to better his condition, and in this way recruiting emigrants. If such a letter contained money to pay the traveling expenses of the members of the family or relatives, then not only were these alone enthusiastic about going to America, but also others joined them; and instances were abundant where whole communities prepared to depart for America. [4] Even after Civil War days, glowing reports of the gay life of the city were published throughout Germany to attract the attention of those dissatisfied with their lot in life. One of these reports was written by a German visitor to the city in the year 1869. He wrote:

> New Orleans awakens as soon as the sun disappears behind the horizon and the cool of the evening sets in. Orchestral music is played in many places and happy throngs mass themselves on the broad dance floors.

---

[1] Samuel P. Orth, *Our Foreigners* (New Haven, 1921), XXXV, 141.
[2] *Ibid.*, 141.
[3] Deiler, *European Immigration 1820-1900*, 7-8.
[4] *Ibid.*, 8.

Window shoppers, theater goers, and restaurant visitors crowd the scenery. Everywhere is gaiety and laughter. Everyone is happy, refreshing himself from the week's work and obtaining new strength. [1]

The great wars in 1864 and 1866, [2] which led to the annexation of Hanover, Schleswig-Holstein, Kur-hesse, Nassau and other territories by Prussia, and the convulsions into which the German states were thrown before they were welded into one nation through the Franco-Prussian War of 1870-71 added to the flow of German immigrants to the United States during that period. [3] Prussia introduced in these newly-acquired territories universal compulsory military service which again caused tens of thousands to leave their fatherland. After 1866, the same system was also introduced in the southern states of Germany. How great the effect of this law was may be seen from the fact that in the ten years from 1881 to 1891 there were annually 18,000 convictions in the courts of Germany for violating the law of compulsory military service. Many of these violators eventually came to the United States. [4]

Other disturbing factors contributed to the mounting number of immigrants pouring into the United States during this third wave. Bismark's effort to control education by the power of the state led him into furious conflict with the Catholic Church. [5] The demands of the Social Democratic party, which in 1877 polled a half million votes, were checked by special laws prohibiting publications, meetings, and associations aimed at the subversion of the social order. [6]

After 1885, however, the number of immigrants steadily declined, reaching the lowest point in 1898. [7] This was caused partly by the successful attempt of Bismark to remedy the conditions of the working classes of Germany. He said in 1884, "Give the workingman the right to work so long as he is healthy, assure him of care when he is sick and maintenance when he is old ... then if the state will show a little more Christian

---

[1] W. E. H. v. W., *Sechs Monate in Amerika* (Oppeln, 1869), 154.

[2] Binkley, *Realism and Nationalism, 1852-1871*, 262-270.

[3] Albert Bernhardt Faust, *The German Element in the United States* (New York, 1909), I, 586; Deiler, *European Immigration 1820-1900*, 11.

[4] Deiler, *European Immigration*, 11.

[5] Bismark, *The Man and The Statesman, The Reflections and Reminiscences of Otto, Prince Von Bismark*, trans. under supervision of A. J. Butler, (New York, 1899), II, 135-154.

[6] Carlton J. H. Hayes, *A Generation of Materialism, 1871-1900* (New York, 1941), 185; Walter Phelps Hall and William Stearns Davis, *The Course of Europe Since Waterloo* (New York, 1947), 358.

[7] Faust, *The German Element in the United States*, I, 586.

solicitude for him, the Socialists will sing their songs in vain." [1] In 1883, 1884, and 1885, laws insuring workmen against sickness and against accidents were enacted; in 1889 there followed one for insuring the aged and the disabled. [2] In the same period, the United States government moved to restrict immigration for the first time in its history. This first Federal immigration law of 1882 merely provided for the exclusion of convicts, of lunatics and idiots, and of persons likely to become a public charge. This policy was later gradually extended in a series of acts to cover the exclusion of polygamists, prostitutes and white slavers, persons suffering from loathsome or dangerous contagious diseases, epileptics, alcoholics, anarchists, and advocates of violence. Also in 1885, legislation forbidding importation of contract labor of any race was enacted. [3] These measures affected the flow of German immigration after this time.

As in the first and second waves of German immigration to the United States, so also in the third, New Orleans continued to receive a number of Germans. However, the newcomers did not increase the numerical strength of the German element, for after 1860 this group remained rather constant. The 1870 records showed that there were 15,239 Germans in the city compared to 8,845 French, 212 Swedes and Norwegians, 960 Spaniards, 936 Cubans, 668 Swiss, and 254 Austrians. [4] In 1880, there were 17,475 Germans in Louisiana with 13,944 living in New Orleans. [5] The next twenty years showed a definite drop with the 1890 census reporting 11,338 and the 1900 census only 8,733. [6]

---

[1] Hall and Davis, *Europe Since Waterloo*, 359.

[2] Hayes, *A Generation of Materialism, 1871-1900*, 212-13.

[3] *Restriction of Immigration* compiled by Edith M. Phelps in *The Reference Shelf* (New York, 1924), I, 34-35.

[4] Francis A. Walker, *The Statistics of the Population of the United States compiled from the Original Returns of the Ninth Census* (Washington, 1872), 357. These government figures might be very conservative. Reports of the Commissioner of Immigration estimated the number of Germans in Louisiana at this time at 60,000 of whom 30,000 were said to live in New Orleans. Robert T. Clark, Jr., "Reconstruction and the New Orleans German Colony," *Louisiana Historical Quarterly*, XXIII (1940) No. 2, 501 n.

[5] J. Hanno Deiler, *Germany's Contribution to Population of New Orleans with Census of German Schools* (New Orleans, n.d.), 5. Deiler takes issue with the Government Census of 1880 by stating that there were 25,000 bona-fide residents of New Orleans that were born in the German Empire. He also claims that there were in New Orleans in 1880 62,075 persons who had a German father, and 57,650 persons who had a German mother.

[6] Deiler, *Geschichte der deutschen Gesellschaft*, 50; Robert P. Porter, *Report on Population of the United States at the Eleventh Census* (Washington, 1895), 630; William R. Merriam, *Twelfth Census of the United States*, 1900 (Washington, 1901), Part I, 757.

During these decades of high immigration New Orleans was merely a way-station for the greater number of new comers, including the Germans, who were on their way to Texas, Arkansas, California, and other points North and West. [1] Records of the German Society for these years showed that 118,094 were assisted to reach Saint Louis, 39,372 to reach their destination on the Ohio River, and 21,838 to reach Texas. [2] Preferring the water route up the Mississippi River and the Ohio to the tedious overland-journey from the Atlantic ports, they poured into the Mississippi Valley and the West through New Orleans. Undoubtedly, the more fertile lands and more temperate climates were beckoning them away from New Orleans. Since the city and area also presented a French and Spanish atmosphere, many of the German immigrants were motivated to go into those areas where the concentration of Germans was more prominent. [3]

The population of New Orleans continued its climb upward until by 1900 it had reached the mark of 287,104 inhabitants. [4] This meant an increase of over 100,000 in the forty year period. During the four decades the German population of the city decreased, ultimately predicting the fate of this energetic and expressive group of foreigners in the midst of this growing American metropolis. Before this people wrote their "swan-song", however, they had carved a memorable niche in the hall of achievements in this city.

---

[1] J. Hanno Deiler, *Germany's Contribution to the Present Population of New Orleans* (New Orleans, 1886), 3.

[2] Louis Voss, *History of the German Society* (New Orleans, 1922), 81-2.

[3] Deiler, *Germany's Contribution to Population of New Orleans*, 3; interview, December 27, 1952, with John Rettenmeier, New Orleans resident who came from Germany to the city in 1885.

[4] Merriam, *Twelfth Census of the United States*, 104.

CHAPTER II

NEW ORLEANS—A NEW HOME FOR THE GERMAN

In the 1850's, New Orleans was a city described as "five hours' walk long and three hours' wide." [1] It was a sea port in which one could see endlessly sailing vessels and steamboats coming in and going out every day. The sight was almost unbelievable. [2] In this teeming port city dwelled a diversified population of 20,200 Irish, 11,425 Germans, 7,522 French, and 2,670 English and Scotch, together with other nationalities, making a metropolitan center of over a hundred thousand inhabitants. [3] The commercial business of the city was concentrated on the levee; and the levee was one of the show places to which strangers were taken to give them some idea of the city's immense commerce. It seemed to have impressed the visitors for many declared that they had never seen anything like it. The levee of the river was the storehouse for the great Mississippi Valley. Along the wharves lay steamships two or three deep, for the wharfage was not sufficient to accommodate all the vessels loading at the port. All was action. The very water was covered with life. It was one of the most active commercial centers of the New World. [4] Together with its industrial output of agricultural implements, iron foundries, lumber, leather, boots and shoes, and soaps and candles, the city offered each immigrant a great opportunity for a new start in a new home. [5]

But all things were not rosy. It was reported that New Orleans was "one of the dirtiest and consequently one of the sickliest cities in the nation." Sanitary arrangements in the "Acropolis of the South" were incredibly primitive. The sewage system consisted of open gutters,

[1] One hour amounts to about three miles.
[2] Karl J. R. Arndt, "A Bavarian's Journey to New Orleans and Nacogdoches in 1853-54," *loc. cit.*, XXIII (1940) No. 2, 492.
[3] *One Hundred Years in New Orleans, Louisiana*, 5; *Progressive New Orleans*: Young Men's Business League, (1895), 9; De Bow, *The Seventh Census of the United States, 1850*, 474.
[4] Rightor, (ed.), *Standard History of New Orleans*, 569. In 1850, a total of 2,673 ships both of United States and foreign registry with a tonnage of 931,509 tons cleared for New York; at the same time 1,131 ships with 487,690 tons cleared for New Orleans. New Orleans was second in tonnage to New York. *Index to Executive Documents* (Washington, 1850), 313-14.
[5] Rightor, (ed.), *Standard History of New Orleans*, 516.

into which filth was emptied. Stagnant water from constant rains collected, and millions of mosquitoes flourished there. [1]

It was also a city of immorality, "a perfect hell on earth." [2] Decent citizens believed that nothing could ever put an end to the murders, manslaughters, and deadly assaults till it was made penal to carry arms. Likewise, the ever-present bar rooms, cocktails, mint juleps, gambling houses, and political discussions completed the den of vice and crime. [3]

At the very height of German immigration to New Orleans in the early fifties, the city was in the midst of the darkest ten years of her history. In 1853, 1854, and 1855, the cemeteries had received over thirty-five thousand dead, victims of cholera and yellow fever. [4] There were so many dead to be buried that it was necessary to employ chain gangs in the different cemeteries to do the interments. The regular corps of sextons was not sufficient. These grave-diggers had to work from early morning until late at night, but it was impossible to finish the work. In one instance, seventy-one bodies were left unburied in one cemetery alone. The mayor was called upon to try to get the workers to finish the burials before leaving the cemetery. Only after extra pay and a supper were promised was the work completed. The burials were performed in a very careless manner, for the coffins were put down no lower than the level of the ground and covered like potato ridges. These long, shallow ditches were dug wide enough to entomb many corpses. [5] People became so accustomed to the sight of death that on clear days, when an epidemic of a mild character prevailed, strollers would walk in the shade of the trees of the cemetery. They enjoyed the cool breezes and appeared to be having a happy time while eighteen or twenty interments were going on. In 1853, while burials were being conducted within the cemeteries and the corpses were piled high in pyramids, old women stood outside selling ice cream, candy, and other confections. Flies that swarmed in the cemetery lighted on their wares, and were mildly brushed away.

---

[1] "Tulane vs Tropics" *Newsweek* (August 3, 1953), 46; New Orleans *City Guide* (Boston, 1938), 29.

[2] Kendall, *History of New Orleans*, I, 231.

[3] *Ibid.*

[4] George W. Cable, *Dr. Sevier* (Boston, 1885), 10. It was sometimes called "Bronze John," "The Saffron Plague," and "The Knight with the Orange Plume," by inhabitants, who in a stoic way even joked about it. B. J. Krieger ,*Seventy-Five Years of Service* (New Orleans, 1923), 30.

[5] Thais Emelda Kaiser, "Yellow Fever in 19th Century New Orleans," (Master's Thesis, Tulane, 1941), 66.

People on their way to interments bought the wares without any qualms, or at least with no visible repugnance. [1] And as soon as the allotted span for the fever had run its course, people flocked back into the city in great numbers to participate in amateur theatricals and minstrel concerts. Practically overnight, great activity in building began anew. The city seemed almost to forget its terrible catastrophe and the business of living took on a fresh start. People who had walked about for several weeks with bags of camphor, ammonia, garlic, or asafoetida around their necks, were again buoyant. [2]

Into such a city came the thousands of German immigrants. Work could be found for every German who desired work, and thus the means of livelihood were available. [3] But like America as a whole, New Orleans was not the imagined land that "flowed with milk and honey." While the immigrant had suffered indescribable hardships crossing the ocean, his suffering did not end with his landing. The first enemy he encountered was his own poverty, having left Europe with no worldly goods or having lost what little he had enroute; his contracted sickness (and there were many that arrived desperately ill) which called for immediate medical attention; and the vultures of his own nationality who dragged him off to boarding houses and jobs with the intention of swindling him. [4] These difficulties, especially that of poverty, forced the German immigrants to settle in the outlying sections or in the poorer districts of the city. [5]

In 1850, New Orleans was divided into three municipal districts. Each part extended from the Mississippi River to Lake Pontchartrain. The first municipality included the section from Canal Street to Elysian Fields Avenue; the second included the area from Canal Street to Felicity

---

[1] *Ibid.*, 68.

[2] *Ibid.*, 72-3. Yellow fever epidemics raged in New Orleans in the years 1853, 1867, 1878, 1897. In these years the scourge was most pronounced and devastating. Max Heller, *Jubilee Souvenir of Temple Sinai 1872-1922.* (New Orleans, 1922), 27-29. The greatest number of deaths in any one day was 283, of which 239 were from yellow fever. This occurred on the 22nd of August, 1853. The greatest number of deaths from the fever in any one month was in August, 1853, amounting to 5,189, or by adding the unknown, 5,242; by adding all the deaths, 6,235, an average exceeding 201 per day, about nine every hour, one every six or seven minutes for a whole month. Bennet Dowler, *A Tableau of the Yellow Fever of 1853* (n.p., 1854), 30.

[3] Deiler, *Geschichte der deutschen Gesellschaft*, 67.

[4] *Souvenir of Eightieth Anniversary of German Society*, 75. Baldwin, *The Stream of American History*, 609.

[5] *New Orleanser Deutsche Zeitung*, June 31, 1898.

Street; and the third included the section from Elysian Fields to the Saint Bernard Parish boundary. [1] The Germans settled particularly in the municipality that stretched from Esplanade to Elysian Fields, which, because of the great number of Germans living there, became known as "Little Saxony." [2] Those who did not move into this area found a welcome in the city of Lafayette or in the village of Carrollton. [3] A goodly number also moved to the west bank of the river to find a home in Algiers. [4] In these localities rentals were cheaper than in the heart of the city and it was easier to become a property owner. [5]

While most of the German immigrants crowded into these particular areas, there were some who, having arrived in New Orleans prior to 1850, had already become well established and had acquired a comfortable income. These no longer lived in the poorer sections of the city but had purchased property and had built homes in the better localities. [6] Such were, however, in the great minority.

Another virulent enemy soon faced the incoming foreigner which for a time forced him to believe that his welcome in the New World was questionable. About 1852, a secret oathbound fraternity, with numerous lodges and with conventions which made nominations secretly, attained sudden importance. From the professions of ignorance with

---

[1] New Orleans *Item*, June 10, 1952.

[2] Deiler, *Geschichte der deutschen Presse*, 11; Interview with John Rettenmeier, resident of the area from 1890 to 1906, and residing in New Orleans since 1885, December 29, 1950.

[3] *New Orleanser Deutsche Zeitung*, June 31, 1898. As Lafayette grew in importance, it attracted the overflow of population from its larger neighbor, New Orleans. These new inhabitants were usually people from foreign lands, chiefly Germans and Irishmen. This type of citizen, together with its fine location (present day Felicity Road to Toledano Street), helped to make Lafayette a thriving, growing, busy place, with wharves, shipping, cotton presses, slaughter houses, and business establishments and offices of all kinds. Kathryn C. Briede, "A History of the City of Lafayette," *Louisiana Historical Quarterly*, XX (1937), No. 4, 925. Father Kundeck, a priest of the Redemptorist Fathers, stated that there were from 1,200 to 1,400 German families residing in Lafayette in 1850. *One Hundred Years in New Orleans, Louisiana*, 6. In 1852, the city of Lafayette was absorbed as the Second District of New Orleans. *New Orleanser Deutsche Zeitung*, June 31, 1898. The village of Carrollton was all that portion lying between Toledano and Jefferson Parish and from the River to the Lake. Martin H. Burke, "Discipline in the New Orleans Public Schools," (Master's Thesis, Tulane, 1941), 36. In 1872, the village of Carrollton became the 7th District, rounding out the present boundaries of the city and parish. New Orleans *City Guide*, 34 .

[4] Interview with John Rettenmeier, who in 1887 came to Algiers on the west bank of the Mississippi River, December 29, 1950.

[5] *New Orleanser Deutsche Zeitung*, June 31, 1898.

[6] John S. Kendall, "Old New Orleans Houses and Some of the People who Lived in Them," *Louisiana Historical Quarterly*, XX (1937), No. 3, 810.

which its members met all questioning, they were called "know-nothings."[1] Know-nothingism was also the political exploitation of an instinctive dislike for foreigners. Many native-born Americans found the rising flood of Irish Catholics and Germans most unpleasant and therefore endeavored to check their immigration to the United States. [2] Agitation of this group was also very much apparent in the South and in New Orleans, most of their membership coming from former Whigs. Their platform demanded more severe naturalization laws and the selection of none but natives for office. Within the party was also a large lawless element given to rioting and obstructing foreigners at the polls or any other occasion. [3]

Reaction to the activities of the Know-Nothing party was quite evident in New Orleans. The German newspapers struck out quite vehemently against these anti-foreign agitators and warned Germans in particular to have nothing to do with them but to work against them by exhibiting their value and worth to their adopted country. [4] In May, 1855, after a report of an election riot in Louisville staged by Know-Nothing advocates had reached New Orleans, the Louisiana *Staats-Zeitung*, one of New Orleans German newspapers, screamed, "The Know-Nothings have won more wreaths but not of honor but of shame and disgrace!" [5] And again in October of the same year, it cried, "Our Know-Nothings, or, as they call themselves, reformers, are in truth allies of the devil." [6] By the end of the decade, however, the threat of this group had disappeared in the face of more complex problems which confronted the inhabitants of the South. While New Orleans' native Americans never molested Germans by mob action, the Know-Nothing movement excited the immigrants and kept them closely banded together. [7]

The worst enemy of the newly-arrived immigrant was the scourge of yellow fever that raged at intervals between 1853 and 1897. Especially

---

[1] Faust, *The German Element in the United States*, II, 126 n.

[2] Samuel Eliot Morison and Henry Steele Commager, *The Growth of the American Republic* (New York, 1937) I, 518.

[3] Faust, *The German Element in the United States*, II, 127.

[4] Louisiana *Staats-Zeitung*, May 19, 20, 29, 1855.

[5] *Ibid.*, May 19, 1855.

[6] *Ibid.*, October 7, 1855.

[7] Both Cincinnati and Louisville had riots involving German societies and members of the Know-Nothing movement. Louisiana *Staats-Zeitung*, May 19, 20, 1855; Faust, *The German Element in the United States*, II, 391-94.

severe were the early epidemics in the 1850's. Doctor J. Jones, president of the Board of Health of the city, reported that 1,593 Germans died during the year 1853, and that the nationality of 8,059 of the victims could not be ascertained, thus making it probable that at least 2,000 more must be added to the death-toll of the Germans. [1] Entire families were swept away with sometimes only one survivor left. This was especially the case among the unacclimated foreigners whom the fever struck with greatest virulence and destruction. From July 10 to September 23, 1853, ninety-eight people of the city were buried at the expense of the community: while one hundred and seventeen were said to have been buried at Lafayette. Almost all of them were foreigners, among whom was a goodly number of Germans. [2] These victims were not among the old and feeble but among the comparatively young between the ages of twenty and forty years. [3] As repeated epidemics of yellow fever struck, the Germans of the city continued to be numbered among the victims. [4] When the later epidemics struck, however, they were in a better position to secure proper medical attention, even being able to leave the city during the summer months when the epidemics were at their worst. [5]

The real source of the malignant epidemic of yellow fever being unknown, sundry remedies, some common sense, others downright puerile and laughable, were adopted. City authorities ordered that tar should be burned in the streets, and that cannons should be fired morning and evening. Doctors cupped, bled, starved, and purged patients, dosing them with quinine and sweating them under double blankets in tightly shuttered rooms where fires were kept burning: In contrast with these drastic methods, Negro mammies applied what was called the "Creole treatment". They did not bleed, but confined their ministrations to hot mustard

---

[1] Deiler, *Germany's Contribution to Population of New Orleans*, 3.

[2] Heller, *Jubilee Souvenir of Temple Sinai*, 27.

[3] *The Epidemic Summer List of Interments in all the Cemeteries of New Orleans from the First of May to the First of November, 1853.* Published by the proprietor of the *True Delta*. List in the T. P. Thompson Collection, University of Alabama. (n.p.) In 1853, according to this record, a total of 2,344 Germans died of yellow fever. They were interred in the following cemeteries: Cyprus Grove No. 1, 15; Cyprus Grove No. 2, 527, Odd Fellows' Rest, 6; Charity Hospital, 485; Lafayette, 628; Saint Vincent de Paul, 584; Hebrew on the Ridge, 3; Hebrew Lafayette, 84; Protestant, 5; Saint Louis No. 1, 6; Saint Louis No. 2, 1.

[4] *New Orleanser Deutsche Zeitung*, June 31, 1898.

[5] Minutes of the New Orleans German Society, April 4, 1888. These minutes are kept in the archives of the Deutsches Haus, New Orleans, Louisiana.

footbaths, hot aromatic teas, and castor oil. This gave nature a chance to repair the ravages of disease in a system not weakened by blood lettings and exhausting emetics and purgatives. [1] Some believed that drinking pipe water was the cause of the disease since the newspapers of the day urged that there be no drinking of pipe water. This gave the German beer gardens the opportunity to advertise their ware by exhibiting posters which read, "Drink no water, drink beer!" [2]

Coming into a new land with these accompanying trials and tribulations, the German immigrant was in desperate need of help to establish a new home. Where could he and where did he find help in his newly-adopted home, New Orleans? Some were received by relatives and friends. In fact, they had received the call and the necessary funds to come over from a brother, uncle, aunt, or some other relative who had preceded them to New Orleans. They were met by their loved ones and safely cared for in the protective confines of a very modest home, not owned but usually rented. [3] But what about the great number who arrived penniless, sick, friendless, in need of succour, counsel, and a Samaritan's heart?

There were individual German families that opened their hearts and homes to needy immigrants and gave commendable service to many during the epidemic years. A Mrs. Francis Rickert was remembered for many years for the assistance she gave to immigrants of all nationalities. [4] Some German institutions, like orphanages and old peoples' homes, gave employment to a goodly number in the capacity of gardeners and house servants. [5] But the greatest friend of all German immigrants was the German Society of New Orleans. [6]

---

[1] Thomas Ewing Dabney, *One Hundred Great Years* (Baton Rouge, 1944), 98-99.

[2] New Orleans *Taegliche Deutsche Zeitung*, September 23, 26, 1854.

[3] Interview with Anna Altmann, member of Zion Lutheran Church, who was born in New Orleans in 1853, New Orleans, Louisiana, March 2, 1948.

[4] New Orleans *The Daily Picayune*, January 30, 1899.

[5] Minutes of the New Orleans German Society, November 7, 1888.

[6] Deiler, *Geschichte der deutschen Gesellschaft*, 51-3. In January ,1842, Joseph Cohn in the second number of the *German Courier* pleaded for an organization of Germans in New Orleans to help the shipwrecked passengers of the vessel *Oceana*, which on October 20, 1841, had left Havre, France, with 241 passengers, mostly Germans, and was stranded south of Jamaica on December 3. The Germans at that time gathered at the Firehouse No. 4 on the Old Levee Street near Bienville Street and in short order $ 817.00 and clothes were gathered. But this *Oceana Verein* disbanded after help had been extended these shipwrecked passengers. But repeated calls for an organization were sounded.... The need for sending bread, etc. to Germany because of harvest failure prompted another attempt to form a German Society. Likewise, the need to

The main work of the Society during its first forty years of activities consisted in aiding immigrants upon landing, not only at customs inspection, but in all other matters. The immigrants bound for the North and West were assisted on their way up the Mississippi River, while others who intended to make their home in New Orleans or Louisiana were found employment. The majority of the immigrants landing here took advantage of the services rendered by the agents of the Society free of charge. Needy immigrants received free transportation through the Society and provisions for the rest of the trip. [1] From 1847 to 1887, 118,094 persons were aided in reaching Saint Louis; 39,372 in reaching their destination on the Ohio River; and 21,838 in reaching Texas. [2] Many of the newly arrived immigrants were warned to beware of unsanitary water, to be careful of eating too many fresh fruits, especially oranges, melons, collards, and green cucumbers. They were also warned to watch the sun since they were not accustomed to the heat and to wear light clothing and to wash their bodies each day. [3] Many immigrants who had been misinformed by ship agents in Europe were assisted. Some of these immigrants had been told that it would be easy for them to go to Venezuela by way of New Orleans in spite of the fact that only one boat a year made that run. Others came to New Orleans on their way to numerous other South American countries, having been told it was possible

---

protect German immigrants, to attend to their custom regulations, to gather a list of folks who would invite these German immigrants, to arrange for their departure to other sections of the country, to help find work for some, these were the conditions that prompted the organizing of a society similar to the New York German Society. On April 27, 1847, an announcement appeared in the German newspaper, *The Courier*, inviting all interested Germans to a meeting to be held on May 5, 1847. By May 19 of that year, 397 members had joined the organization and $ 3,075.00 had been gathered in the treasury. On June 2, an election took place. The first officers were: President, Wilhelm Vogel, Consul of Prussia, Hamburg, and Oldenburg; First Vice President, J. H. Eimer, Consul of Austria and Baden; Second Vice President, Dr. E. Authenreid; Treasurer, J. D. Kamper; Secretary, J. F. Behnker; Financial Secretary, A. Schneider. Directors were :George Dirmeyer, F. W. Freudenthal, L. A. Gunst, P. William, M. Schneider, C. V. Voigts, Dr. D. S. Gans, F. Honold, P. E. Huenten, H. G. Schmidt, C. A. Fidler, and J. Schuhmann. *Ibid.*, 52-4; *Program of Third German Day Festival-October 6* (New Orleans, 1912), n.p. This program is in the possession of A. Flasdick, member of the *Deutsches Haus* in New Orleans. The object of the society is to give advice and assistance to German immigrants and other Germans coming to, or residing in, this city, more particularly, to aid them in obtaining employment and to succor those who are in distress. *Berichte der deutschen Gesellschaft 1883-1895*. Portfolio in the *Deutsches Haus* in New Orleans, Louisiana.

[1] *Souvenir of Eightieth Anniversary of German Society*, 81-2.

[2] *Ibid.*

[3] Deiler, *Geschichte der deutschen Gesellschaft*, 68-9.

to reach their destination in this way, even though not a single boat was making that run out of New Orleans. [1]

No task was too menial nor too small for this society of Germans, who themselves had once been immigrants, in behalf of their immigrating countrymen. When a young German Jew, named Bonkowsky, arrived penniless in the fall of 1883 and desired to go to Monroe, Louisiana, the society immediately contacted his brother for the railroad fare and gave the Israelite from Bromberg in East Prussia "protection care." [2] Hermann Nitschmann with his wife and family was the recipient of the society's generosity in the late spring of 1888. Having come from Stettin, Germany, via New York, they had a lot of baggage but only seventy-five cents and had lived for five days—the time it took to come from New York to New Orleans—on bread and water. Their destination was Plaquemine in Iberville Parish to work at a saw mill. In their predicament they found a friend of the friendless and a help to the helpless. The society gave them lodging, food, and drink, and put them on a river steamer, named *Oliver Bierne*, for the journey to Plaquemine. [3] Even when called upon to locate lost articles of immigrants, the society spared neither time nor effort to complete its task. [4] In this manner the German Society of New Orleans rendered a great service to all German immigrants not only in the 1850's and 1860's but throughout the second half of the nineteenth century.

But this was not its only contribution to the immigrant coming to find a new home in New Orleans. Throughout its existence, particularly after 1865, the society served also as an employment bureau. [5] Work was secured for machinists, locksmiths, carpenters, wheelwrights, builders, paperhangers, and gardeners, as well as young business people. [6] Large numbers of job-seeking immigrants just recently arrived found work in railroad construction. They helped to build the Opelousas and Great Western Railroad, the Vicksburg-Shreveport, and the New Orleans-Baton Rouge. Those who were not able to stand the damp climate of the low country sought employment in higher lands working for the Cincinnati-Saint Louis and the Jackson Railroads. [7] Seasonal work in the

---

[1] *Ibid.*, 64; Voss, *History of the German Society*, 77.

[2] Minutes of the New Orleans German Society, October 3, 1883.

[3] *Ibid.*, May 30, 1888

[4] *Ibid.*, October 1, 1884.

[5] *Souvenir of Eightieth Anniversary of German Society*, 82; minutes of the New Orleans German Society, May 28, 1890.

[6] Minutes of the New Orleans German Society, June 2, 1895.

[7] Deiler, *Geschichte der deutschen Gesellschaft*, 67-8.

harvesting of sugar cane and rice beckoned the German, particularly in the months of November, December, and January. [1] Through the efforts of the Society hundreds of Germans found this type of employment, using not only those who lived in and near the city but often those that had come from northern cities and were without any means. [2] After the close of the harvest season many of them came back to town both to spend their money with the local merchants, which helped business very much, and to find a permanent home with members of their nationality. [3] German gardeners and dairyworkers were also in great demand, and any immigrant who was trained in these tasks could find ready employment. [4] German girls also found work quite readily through the help of the Society, especially as domestic servants. It was standard for a woman to receive forty dollars a month with board and lodging. [5]

In rendering this type of service to the Germans of the city and surrounding area, the Society regarded no task too large or too small. For a cabinetmaker, Conrad Heinrich, the Society obtained a saw, plane, and measure for the price of one dollar so that he might do his work; and for Anton Muenster a support was purchased from a druggist, named Bruno Tuma, for seventy-five cents so that he might continue his work without jeopardizing his health. [6] Even when Johann Friedrich Steinecke came from Chicago, saying that he had a sure cure for leprosy, the Society did not regard him as insane or foolish but referred him to the Board of Health, which promised to give him every opportunity to try his cure. [7] Certainly here was a friend of Germans collectively and individually, assisting them to get a foothold and maintaining it in their newly-found home.

Other services were also cheerfully rendered. During the repeated yellow fever epidemics of the period from 1850 to 1900, the Society worked together with other organizations in the city to bring help to the stricken. [8] When destitute German girls frequented dens of vice in the

---

[1] Minutes of the New Orleans German Society, October 3, November 7, December 5, 1883, January 2, February 6, 1884. A typical harvest employment record ran as follows: October, 1883, 330 men used; November, 362; December, 138; January, 140.

[2] *Ibid.*, October 5, 1892.

[3] *Ibid.*, November 2, 1887.

[4] *Ibid.*, May 30, 1888.

[5] *Ibid.*, April 1, 1891; July 6, 1892; May 30, 1888.

[6] *Ibid.*, July 3, 1889.

[7] *Ibid.*, September 4, 1889.

[8] Deiler, *Geschichte der deutschen Gesellschaft*, 73. The "Howard Association" was

vicinity of the levee, the Society rescued some of them and tried to find them other employment.[1] German children sent by their poverty-stricken parents to the river levee to pick up cotton, sugar, and coffee were warned repeatedly not to engage in such activity. When German children arrived without parents and had to be cared for, they were often referred to the German churches, especially those which had an orphan's home. [2]

Not to leave anything undone, the Society also acted as a chamber of commerce. Prospective immigrants were encouraged to come to New Orleans in the fall and winter when work was more plentiful. It answered inquiries from Idaho, Wisconsin, Montana, and other western states, about the advantages of Louisiana's climate, products, and other conditions, often encouraging Germans of that area to come to New Orleans because of its weather and great opportunities. [3] In this way, and in many others, the German Society of New Orleans was a friend in need to every German in finding a permanent place in his newly-chosen home.

In performing this work, the Society encountered many heartaches. Among the immigrants who came to the city in the early 1850's were those who had fled the Revolution of 1848. These men of learning began a political agitation against the South and its practice of slavery, thereby embarrassing many members of the Society who had fully identified themselves with the community, its political philosophy, and its culture. [4] Harsh criticism came from various quarters. Immigrants blamed the Society for overcrowded river steamers charging that there was more desire for profit than to give help. [5] When it was impossible to obtain free or half fare passage on train or river boat, which many immigrants expected of the Society, they became angry and accused the organization of unjust dealing.[6] It was also a common occurrence for New Orleanians, not members of the German Society, to direct unemployed to this group, which overtaxed the effort and forced the decision "to stick strictly to the constitution." [7] In spite of all, assistance was given to over a quarter million people in a span of fifty years. [8]

---

one of these organizations to care for the sick and for the relief of "poor people in time of epidemics." Kendall, *History of New Orleans*, I, 176.

[1] Deiler, *Geschichte der deutschen Gesellschaft*, 83.
[2] Minutes of the New Orleans German Society, April 1, 1885; July 11, 1888.
[3] *Ibid.*, March 7, 1888; February 2, 1887.
[4] Deiler, *Geschichte der deutschen Gesellschaft*, 59-63.
[5] *Souvenir of Eightieth Anniversary of German Society*, 81.
[6] Minutes of the New Orleans German Society, March 5, 1885.
[7] *Ibid.*, September 5, 1883.
[8] *Souvenir of Eightieth Anniversary of German Society*, 82. 179, 304 were aided in

The establishment of a new home in New Orleans for the German immigrants did not, therefore, depend solely on the constant flow of immigration from the fatherland, nor on the abundance of work for all who desired to work. While these factors were of great importance, credit must be given to the many resident German families that opened their hearts and homes to the newly-arrived immigrants; to the eleemosynary institutions that offered jobs with room and board; to the German churches, singing societies, and gymnastic clubs, many of which were organized and developed during this period of the nineteenth century, which gave the immigrant an opportunity to worship God in his accustomed language and to frolic with comrades; and to the German Society which always lent a ready hand to every immigrant to gain a permanent foothold in the city of his adoption. [1] Difficulties which loomed so menacingly at every turn in the immigrant's life were gradually overcome and New Orleans became his home, a home to which he contributed as much or even more than he received, and consequently, assisted in the building of a great American city.

---

reaching their destination, while 72, 690 found employment. Cash given to needy applicants during the first 50 years amounted to $ 17,500.00.

[1] J. Hanno Deiler, *Zur Geschichte der deutschen Kirchengemeinden im Staate Louisiana* (New Orleans, 1894); *Program of The Third German Day*, n.p.

CHAPTER III

THE NEW ORLEANS GERMAN
IN PERIOD OF STORM AND STRESS

At the opening of the second half of the nineteenth century, many political issues were disturbing the thoughts and actions of the American people. Particularly troublesome was the problem of slavery. It was threatening to undermine the nation for the South held tenaciously to the idea that slavery must expand to live; that contracting its area, or admitting that it might be contracted, would mean that the abolitionists had the South on the defensive. This idea was very seriously attacked when California demanded admission to the union with a free constitution, which meant that slavery would be prohibited in California. Were this to happen, slavery would have lost over half the American conquests from Mexico. The temper of the South was steadily rising. [1] John C. Calhoun had foretold the tragic future in his Fourth of March, 1850, words that "unless the majority section were willing to give constitutional protection to the rights and interests of the minority section the South would be forced to seek security in independence." He had little hope that the North would do that for he said that it was "difficult to see how two people so different and hostile can exist together in one common union." [2] The South had a strong, emotional sense of insecurity. From every side—England and New England, Jamaica and Mexico, Ohio and the Northwest, and now California—abolition seemed to be pointing daggers at the heart of the South. And the South played at the game of secession.

With the passage of the Compromise of 1850 the slavery question subsided, but it was not forgotten. *Uncle Tom's Cabin*, published in 1852, served to keep it in the back of people's minds; and Northern abolitionists and Southern "fire eaters" kept the issue very much alive. Then, in 1854, came the most fateful factor in undoing the sectional truce, the Kansas-Nebraska Bill, which repealed the Missouri Compromise and stirred up the question of slavery in the Louisiana Purchase

---

[1] Francis Butler Simkins, *A History of the South* (New York, 1953), 112-114.
[2] *Ibid.*, 189.

territory again. From that day on the country moved irrepressibly toward secession and civil war. [1]

Louisiana and New Orleans were a distinct part of the South and its way of life. Slavery as an institution had been well established on their soil since the days of the French and Spanish governments. [2] Yet it was affirmed that Louisiana would neither lead nor follow in any secession movement. She acknowledged a fealty to the Constitution and regarded her own honor too highly to favor extreme measures before they became the last alternatives. In the light of these conditions, Governor Thomas Overton Moore in his inaugural speech in 1860 declared that "Louisiana had always been moderate and conservative in her sentiments, and her citizens had been loyal lovers of the Union. But Louisiana was something more than a mere state of the Union; she was a Southern slave-holding state, and Louisiana's duty to herself and to her sister slave-holding states might be brought into painful conflict with her devotion to the Union." [3] This division of sentiment was clearly seen in the presidential campaign of 1860, when the vote of the state was divided between Bell and Breckinridge. Breckinridge representing the seceded Democrats received a popular vote of 22,681; while Bell, an old Whig and a slave-holder and strong Union man, received 20,204. [4] Again on January 7, 1861, when the Secession Convention was called, Louisiana sent eighty "secessionists," forty-four "co-operationists," and six "doubtful" delegates. The popular vote of the state was 20,448 for secessionist delegates and 17,296 for co-operationists. [5] However, on January 26, when the final vote was taken by the convention, the cause for secession carried the day by a vote of one hundred and thirteen to seventeen. [6]

Church bells proclaimed the fact in vibrating tones, while the deep voice of cannon announced it more loudly and boldly. From public buildings, hotels, and private buildings, the Pelican flag was hoisted and displayed its ample folds to the breeze. In the streets people met in

---

[1] *Ibid.*, 189-207; William B. Hesseltine, *A History of the South, 1607-1936* (New York, 1936), 376-399.

[2] François-Xavier Martin, *The History of Louisiana* (New Orleans, 1882), 154; Robert T. Clark, Jr., "The New Orleans German Colony in the Civil War," *Louisiana Historical Quarterly*, XX (1937), 995.

[3] Jefferson Davis Bragg, *Louisiana in the Confederacy* (Louisiana State University Press, 1941), 5-6.

[4] *Ibid.*, 15.

[5] *Ibid.*, 26.

[6] Baldwin, *The Stream of American History*, 783.

groups, inquiring about the news and exchanging congratulations or comments upon the important step taken by the people of Louisiana and New Orleans. [1] The fear expressed by Governor Robert C. Wickliffe in 1856 had become a reality.

> I do not wish to speak lightly of the Union. Next to liberty of the citizen and the sovereignty of the States, I regard it as the primary object of patriotic desire. It should be dear to us as a sentiment, and dearer to us for its real value. But it cannot have escaped observation that the hold which the Union once had upon the affection of the South has been materially weakened and that its dissolution is now frequently spoken of, if not with absolute levity, yet with positive indifference, and occasionally, as desirable. [2]

In the midst of such serious political issues the German people of New Orleans were not altogether impassive. In spite of their language difficulties and in spite of their desire to succeed in their newly-adopted homeland, they were confronted by certain problems which could not keep them politically impassive but forced them into the political scene with some measure of activity. [3]

Even before 1850, an interest was taken in the issues of the day. In the presidential election of 1840, the inhabitants of Lafayette showed marked interest in national politics. Among them was a goodly number of Germans who met in a mass meeting on October 9, at the home of Louis Marconi. A Mr. F. Beekman was chosen president of the group, and speeches were made by the Reverend Doctor Miller, by Christian Roselius and by Judge M. Elliott. The speech of the minister was given entirely in German. Several resolutions were also adopted by the assembled Germans. These reflected a dislike for militarism for it was stated that "the establishment of an army of 200,000 men, as recommended by Martin Van Buren, during a period of profound peace is calculated to awaken our liveliest fears and calls for unremitting and determined opposition of every freeman." [4] They also showed the Germans' love of democracy and an interest in the yeomanry of the country, which these believed Harrison, the Whig candidate, would never permit to be trampled upon. [5]

---

[1] Bragg, *Louisiana in the Confederacy*, 32-33.
[2] Charles Gayarre, *History of Louisiana* (New Orleans, 1885), IV, 681.
[3] Jeannette K. Laguaites, "The German Element in New Orleans, 1820-1860," (Master's Thesis, Tulane, 1940), 41.
[4] Briede, "A History of the City of Lafayette," *loc. cit.*, XX (1937) No. 4, 925-26.
[5] *Ibid.*

On May 2, 1846, when the call came for volunteers to serve with General Zachary Taylor at the Rio Grande, of the four regiments formed, the Montezuma Regiment under Colonel H. Davis included four companies of New Orleans Germans under Georg Dippacher with sixty-four men, Karl Wirth with eighty-two men, J. C. Boepler with sixty-two men, and H. Roemer with sixty-five men. Besides these, there were the Jaeger Company, the Jackson Guard, and a cavalry corp known as the Black Hussars. [1] Again in December, another regiment of Louisiana volunteers was organized. In this regiment were two German companies whose officers were Christian Wirth, Joseph Preg, Peter Basterdes, J. S. N. Ogler, Joseph Polozewski, Fred Otto Eichholz, V. H. Lindenberger, Peter N. Terbusch, J. S. Arold, Gustav Heimberger, and Fr. N. Jaeger. [2] During the course of the Mexican war a New Orleans German was promoted to the rank of colonel and commander of a battalion of Louisiana volunteers that saw service under General Winfield Scott. This individual was Karl Fiesca. [3]

By 1850 interest in the political life of the city and nation on the part of the German element of New Orleans seemed to be increasing. This was undoubtedly due to the nature of the new problems to be faced, the manner in which these problems affected the Germans of the city, and the influx of a new element of German immigrants, the Forty-Eighters, who offered the necessary leadership. [4] Despite the fact that many Germans did not even trouble to obtain citizenship, the interest of Germans in national and local political affairs was not wanting.

The agitation of the Know-Nothing party during the 1850's, working fear in the ranks of the immigrant foreigners, gradually forced the greater

---

[1] Deiler, *Geschichte der deutschen Presse*, 7-8. These New Orleans Germans, however, did not enter the field against Mexico since the secretary of war ruled that no soldier with less than one year training should be sent into battle. The Germans of of New Orleans had only six months training under General Gaines. Thus General Taylor in Matamoras ordered the return of the Louisiana-Alabama Regiment. On August 13, 1846, these Germans returned to New Orleans.

[2] Christian Wirth died at Tampico, April, 1847. Many of these Germans lost their lives due to yellow fever and a surprise attack by 1,300 Mexicans at Huazala. Gustav Heimberger was wounded at Huazala. Deiler, *Geschichte der deutschen Presse*, 8-9.

[3] *Ibid.*, 9.

[4] Deiler, *European Immigration 1820-1900*, 5. It was during this period that Germany gave her heart's blood to the United States—tens of thousands of her most intelligent and highly educated men: professors of universities, students of all faculties, editors, ministers, artists, and professional men, all men of high ideals, liberty loving men, who had taken part in the revolution of 1848 and thereby had forever ruined their prospects in their fatherland.

number of Germans into the Democratic party. [1] The *Deutsche Zeitung*, New Orleans' leading German newspaper, appealed to all its readers to accept the "glorious aims of the Party." [2] In an editorial of March 22, 1854, it commented that "the penetration of the ticket of the Natives would be a misfortune for every German, every worker. In order to win the battle against the united power of the Natives (Know-Nothings and Whigs), it is especially the duty of the Germans to stand in the first line for the democratic principles, and as a man, repel every limitation of freedom and recover common sense." [3] Consequently, Germans in the South were encouraged to seek refuge with the Democratic party, and many of them joined for it was the party that spoke "against all fanaticism, condemned the Know-Nothing," and "protected the right of the immigrant." [4] The German press went so far in its praise of the party by asserting that "as long as one boat sails the Mississippi River, so long will the Democratic party defend our rights, the rights of the entire South." [5] The cause of the Democratic party became that of the German element of the city, and as it became more and more politically organized gave its loyal support to the cause of democracy. [6]

On the local scene, the German population took an interest in municipal affairs. A Mr. James C. Kathmann, acting as spokesman for them, asked the board of aldermen in 1853, that meetings be conducted in

---

[1] The Constitution and Ritual of the Know-Nothing party was drawn up by a meeting in New York City in June of 1854. Slight revision and amendments were made by the second National Council which was held in Cincinnati on November 15, 1854. The new party was organized as a secret lodge, with all the paraphernalia of secret signs, grips, secret sessions with sentinels posted, passwords, solemn oaths and ceremonies, and various degrees of membership. The Constitution declared that "the object of this organization shall be to protect every American citizen in the legal and proper exercise of all his civil and religious rights and privileges; to resist the insidious policy of the church of Rome, and all other foreign influence against our republican institutions in all lawful ways; and to place in all offices ... none but native-born Protestant citizens ... and to protect and uphold the Union of these States." A person to be eligible for membership had to be twenty-one years of age, believe in a supreme being, be a native-born Protestant and, in most states, not married to a Catholic. The Protestant clause was disregarded almost entirely in several states in the South, notably Louisiana, Maryland, Alabama, and Mississippi. W. Darrell Overdyke, *The Know-Nothing Party in the South* (Louisiana State University Press, 1950), 37-8.

[2] New Orleans *Deutsche Zeitung*, March 22, 1854.

[3] *Ibid.*, March 22, 1854.

[4] Louisiana *Staats-Zeitung*, August 25, 1855.

[5] *Ibid.*, February 19, 1856.

[6] Robert T. Clark, Jr., "The New Orleans German Colony in the Civil War." *loc. cit.*, XX (1937), 995.

German and not only in French and English. [1] At many Democratic
mass meetings, called to sponsor the political campaign of the party
standard bearers or to express official party protests, the German element
was not only present but took part, if no more than supplying the music
with the presence of a spirited, if not too harmonious, German band [2].
In 1855, F. J. Laiger ran for the office of mayor of Jefferson City on an
independent ticket and solicited the support of his fellow Germans to
elect him. He was elected with a one hundred and sixty-five majority. [3]
Again and again the German newspapers urged the German immigrant
to register and in that way receive the privilege to vote in all elections. [4]
That a goodly number of them gained citizenship in the troublesome
1850's was shown by the Germans uniting in civic clubs, beginning with
the German Society of the Third Municipality organized in 1851. These
societies banded together in 1854 and established a Central Committee
of German Societies. It was composed of representatives from each
district society, and it was to "meet each first Tuesday to discuss conditions of general interest, whether inland or foreign politics." [5] Activities
of this kind proved that the German element of New Orleans was not
passive nor disinterested in political matters but that political responsibility was readily accepted and that German immigrants were learning
well the vital lessons of democracy.

On the national political level, the German was equally as interested
and active during the hectic decade of 1850. In the presidential campaign
of 1852, the Democratic standard bearer, Franklin Pierce, with his running mate, William R. King of Alabama, was victorious over the Whig
candidates, Winfield Scott and William A. Graham. [6] During the campaign the Germans of the city conducted a Democratic meeting to cham-
pion the cause of Pierce and King. [7] Sentiment was, however, divided.
Both the *Deutsche Zeitung* and the *Louisiana Staats-Zeitung* supported
Pierce and King; but a German printer, Franz Beuter, went to the offices

---

[1] New Orleans *Taegliche Deutsche Zeitung*, April 16, 1853. From 1847 to March
1854, this German newspaper was known as *Deutsche Zeitung*; from April 1854 to
1890, as *Taegliche Deutsche Zeitung*; from 1890 to 1907, as *New Orleanser Deutsche
Zeitung*.
[2] Louisiana *Staats-Zeitung*, July 21, 1855.
[3] *Ibid.*, May 25 and 30, 1855.
[4] New Orleans *Deutsche Zeitung*, October 25, 1850.
[5] Laguaites, "The German Element in New Orleans," 45.
[6] Baldwin, *The Stream of American History*, 730.
[7] New Orleans *Deutsche Zeitung*, October 30, 1852.

of the *Staats-Zeitung* and, with the ruse of beginning a religious brochure, bought sixty pounds of German type and later even more. Then, in the midst of the 1852 campaign he published a Whig paper supporting the candidacy of Scott and Graham. [1] Undoubtedly, he thought that there was enough Whig sentiment among the Germans of the city to bring success to his journalistic venture. [2]

The most pressing political problem of the decade centered around slavery and secession. On the question of slavery German feeling was divided, with perhaps more of them opposed to slavery than in favor. The reasons for this were that few Germans owned slaves and few were in competition with slave labor. At the same time, the natural German attitude was anti-slavery. [3] Many, therefore, interpreted patriotism as prompting eternal enmity to the institution of slavery. Some of the old Forty-Eighters braved ostracism and persecution rather than condone the institution. Others left the city with their families because the conditions had become somewhat hostile for them. [4]

One of those Germans whose comments on slavery were most expressive and persuasive was Christian Roselius, an eminent lawyer of the state and city. [5] He viewed slavery with alarm for it presented the danger of twenty white men in a slaveholding parish having the same vote and influence in the State House as one thousand five hundred white persons living in what might be termed a "free soil" parish. Therefore in the light of the proposed constitution of 1854, which contained the provision that "representation in the House of Representatives shall be equal and uniform,and shall be regulated and ascertained by the total population of each of the several parishes of the State," Roselius charged:

[1] Deiler, *Geschichte der deutschen Presse*, 13.

[2] His paper was the newly-restored or resurrected *Der Wahre Republikaner*.

[3] Robert T. Clark, Jr., "The New Orleans German Colony in the Civil War", *loc. cit.*, XX (1937), 995.

[4] Max Heller, *Jubilee Souvenir of Temple Sinai 1872-1922*, 38.

[5] Christian Roselius was born on August 10, 1803, in Thedinghausen, near Bremen, Germany. From 1850 to 1873 he was professor of Civil Law at University of Louisiana in New Orleans (now Tulane University) and was outstanding in his work. He took no part in German life in the city. He hated to visit public places and lived entirely for his studies and family. He always gave advice to Germans, if asked for it. He died on September 5, 1873. Deiler, *Geschichte der deutschen Presse*, 18-19. In 1856, a Doctor Harris attempted to assassinate Professor Roselius. He failed in the attempt. Ellis Diary found in Samuel Lang, "The First Century of the Tulane University of Louisiana," (New Orleans, 1934), Ch. 9, p. 11.

Before this issue all party distinctions will cease. Not a single vote in the city will be cast in favor of a Constitution which contains so infamous a proposition. The city will be united in its resistance, and will have the sympathies and voices of the country who are not insensible to the dictates of justice. The Constitution with such a principle will never be sanctioned— never! never! never ! [1]

He saw in it a political weapon to crush the political liberty of the white non-slave owning citizen. [2]

Perhaps the most ardent advocate of abolitionism was Michael Hahn, a prominent German attorney of New Orleans, one of the greatest figures of Louisiana history in the Reconstruction period, who began the practice of law in 1852 at the age of twenty-one years. [3] During the 1850's his voice was not as provocative as it was during the days of civil conflict. In the campaign of 1860 he voted for Douglas and against secession. By 1863, he had become an ardent advocate of Lincoln. He had always been in favor of emancipation, and after 1862, he tried to convince Southern slave owners that they had nothing to fear economically over the emancipation of slaves and the removal of slavery. He reasoned that

> ... a good field hand was worth in times of peace about fifteen hundred dollars. A fair interest on this sum in most of the Southern states was ten per cent per annum, making one hundred and fifty dollars a year for the services of his slave. He also runs the risk of sickness or death of the slave,

---

[1] Speech by Michael Hahn entitled "What is Unconditional Unionism?" delivered before the Union Association at Lyceum Hall, November 14, 1863 (New Orleans, 1863), n.p. Copy of this speech is in the T. P. Thompson Collection of the University of Alabama. In this speech Hahn quoted the very words spoken by Roselius regarding slavery.

[2] *Ibid.*

[3] Michael Hahn was born in Klingenmuenster, Palatinate, November 24, 1830. He settled in New Orleans. He was trained in law and early entered the political area. In 1862, when New Orleans was taken by the Union forces, Hahn, who had also before the event been opposed to the principles of the Confederacy, founded the Union Association, the purpose of which was to create a Union party in Louisiana. Hahn was elected to the United States Congress in 1863 by this party. He advocated the reorganization of the state on the basis of the abolition of slavery. He founded a newspaper, *The True Delta*, to represent his party's views. At the next election, in 1864, he was made governor of Louisiana by the loyalists of the state. The difficult task of the reorganization of the state's affairs devolved on him, and he had a great share in initiating the movement of the actual emancipation of the slaves. Faust, *The German Element in the United States*, II, 174; Deiler, *Geschichte der deutschen Presse*, 23. *Beruehmte Deutsche Vorkaempfer fuer Fortschritt, Freiheit und Friede in Nord-Amerika* (Cleveland, 1889), 465.

and escape from his involuntary servitude. When there is no slavery ...
the planter can hire a negro for ten dollars a month, making one
hundred and twenty dollars a year, and run none of the risks of the
slave owner, and receive a more willing and cheerful and, therefore,
more advantageous labour. [1]

Should the Negro refuse to work, he suggested that "if all this will
not work well, (that is, laws by the Legislature to have the negro work),
then let the negroes be sent to colonies abroad, where they will cease to
trouble us; and let the plantations be divided into small farms and culti-
vated by white labor." [2] His political ideas on the entire Negro problem
were incorporated in the statement, "I sanction the abolition of slavery;
I sanction the education of the Negro; but I am opposed to their political
and social equality with the white race and oppose the granting of vote
to the negroes." [3] In the light of a later era, this spirited and active
political leader of the New Orleans Germans was possessed with a far
sighted program beneficial to the South. In his day, however, he was
misunderstood, hated and maligned. Undoubtedly, his views on the
subjects of slavery and emancipation fearlessly and openly expressed were
a cause for the hatred that many New Orleanians had for their German
neighbors during the Civil War. [4]

The opposition to slavery did not, however, excite the Germans of
New Orleans to adopt the program of Lincoln as a whole nor to be in
complete sympathy with him. A goodly number of them did agree with
the Republican program, but it was astonishing that the number was
not larger. To many Germans of the city, who asked only to be allowed
to pursue their callings in peace, Lincoln was a firebrand and a cheap
politician, who threatened to cause trouble for no purpose whatsoever. [5]

There were some Germans, however, who were just as enthusiastic
about the need of the institution as those opposed to it. These owned
slaves and therefore sided even with extreme Southerners. Likewise,
wealthier German citizens who did not own slaves leaned heavily toward
pro-slavery sentiments because their income was derived in one way or
another from the proceeds of slave labor. [6]

---

[1] Speech by Hahn, "What is Unconditional Unionism?"
[2] *Ibid.*
[3] Deiler, *Geschichte der deutschen Presse*, 22.
[4] *New Orleanser deutsche Zeitung*, August 2, 1898.
[5] Robert T. Clark, Jr., "The New Orleans German Colony in the Civil War,"
loc. cit., XX (1937), 995.
[6] *Ibid.*

A notable case was that of Philip Peter Werlein, educator and founder of the Werlein music business, which he opened in 1853. He was affiliated with the Democratic party. Before and during the Civil War his sympathies were entirely with the South. [1] About the time war clouds were gathering, young Daniel Emmett, with his minstrel troupe, composed and sang, "I wish I was in Dixie." This song, popularly known as "Dixie," was published by the "House of Werlein," and became the marching song of the Confederate soldiers at the height of the Civil War. While the publication of "Dixie" was in pursuance of Philip's business, it might be said, particularly in the light of the consequences of the war upon his business venture, that it expressed his love and affection for the South and its way of life. [2]

Julius Weiss was a slave owner from 1853 to 1857. Although favoring the institution, he was strongly opposed to any harsh treatment of the negro slave. The sight of whipping slaves and the capture of them by bloodhounds were most repulsive to him. He stated that he "never found it necessary to punish them in such manner." [3] Many Germans felt like the one who wrote, "... it is true, there are many slaves here, but they are all Negroes, who know no better than to be slaves. In Germany, however, there are far more slaves than here, for there all of you are slaves, a few well-to-do people excepted." [4]

Divided sentiment on the slavery problem could also be clearly seen in an incident of August, 1856. A certain C. F. Hennisch accused the *Deutsche Zeitung* of abolitionist tendencies and therefore regarded the newspaper a disgrace for the Germans of the city. Writing to the editors, he charged:

---

[1] Alcée Fortier, *Louisiana* (Century Historical Association, 1914), III, 461.

[2] Undated clipping in the Private Scrap Book of Philip Werlein Company, New Orleans, Louisiana. He was born in Rheinkreisz, Bayern, Germany, on March 30, 1812. At the age of nineteen he came to this country and taught music for a short time, finally settling in Vicksburg, Mississippi, where he opened his first music store in 1842. In 1853, he decided to seek a larger field, opening a store in New Orleans with William Mayo. Because of his loyalty to the Confederacy he and his family were forced to leave the city. During his absence, his stock was seized by Federal troops and sold at public auction. Thus his entire business was ruined. On November 1, 1865, with the few pianos that had been saved from seizure by hiding them, the business was resumed. It is still operating today. Clippings undated in Private Scrap Book of the Company, Canal Street, New Orleans; New Orleans *Times Picayune*, January 25, 1937.

[3] Heller, *Jubilee Souvenir of Temple Sinai*, 37.

[4] Arndt, "A Bavarian's Journey to New Orleans and Nacogdoches in 1853-54," *loc. cit.*, XXIII (1940), No. 2.

4

Gentlemen: The course which your paper has pursued during the last few months has been undoubtedly the cause of disgrace for all citizens of German birth, who are accused of abolitionism by their support of your paper. This state of things shall not continue. I have therefore prepared extracts of your paper to show that it is a nuisance in the South, which should be removed, and (written an article which I hope) is accepted by one of the English presses of this City for publication. If that is done you will perceive that the further existence of your paper is a mere impossibility. But I will not adopt that severe measure without a warning. Now, I propose you first, hoist the democratic banner and publish the whole Democratic Ticket from tomorrow to the end of the canvass; and secondly, defend the democratic principles purely and sincerely. The effect of it will be that the German population be united at the next election in our city. [1]

The *Deutsche Zeitung* answered the accusation by publishing a satirical poem, *Der Kuester und Sein Esel*, [2] in which Hennisch was pictured as an irresponsible person whom no one could believe or trust. [3] In following issues of the paper Hennisch was exposed and ridiculed.

The question whether the moon is inhabited by human beings has been an open question for a long time. It was determined by some that these people must be without heads. He, who can't imagine such human beings, should go to 97 Exchange Place, office of C. G. Hennisch. [4]

The Louisiana *Staats-Zeitung* was inclined to defend slavery and thereby brought upon itself severe criticism from German newspapers of the North, especially one in Albany, New York. [5] In an editorial of September 4, 1855. the *Staats-Zeitung* caustically observed:

It is a moral evil, but our negroes are better off than the working day worker in the North. The South also has no guilt when the load was pressed upon her by the mother country. Who will pay the worth of the Negro? Who will do his work? What shall be done with the freed, unlucky and uncivilized black whom we cannot receive as citizen? Do the abolitionists desire to send him to Liberia? [6]

New Orleans Germans, despite the gravity of local and national political issues, kept a live interest in European developments. Their daily news-

---

[1] New Orleans *Taegliche Deutsche Zeitung*, August 20, 1856. Hennisch was a fellow German residing in New Orleans.

[2] *The Carpenter and His Ass.*

[3] New Orleans *Taegliche Deutsche Zeitung*, August 21, 22, 1856.

[4] *Ibid.*, August 24, 1856.

[5] Louisiana *Staats-Zeitung*, July 24, 1855.

[6] *Ibid.*, September 4, 1855.

papers carried many items dealing with foreign affairs, and attempted to keep alive the fires of liberalism in the hearts of the people. [1] *The Central Union for the Advancement of the Republic in Germany*, organized in the late 1840's, was dedicated to the task of eventually establishing a German Republic in the Fatherland. Funds were gathered among Germans of the city which were sent to leaders of German liberalism in Germany to be used in whatever way they saw fit. Two of the most important of these leaders were Carl Schurz and Gottfried Kinkel. [2] Schurz had escaped from Rastatt fortress and had helped Kinkel to escape from the penitentiary at Spandau near Berlin. At the time the New Orleans money was sent them, they were busy organizing German refugees in London. Expressions of gratitude were sent by these men to the Germans of the city, who in turn promised to raise a sum of three million dollars. This was given up, however, after Kinkel visited the city. The embittered politics of the late 1850's crowded this effort out of the minds of the liberals in New Orleans. [3]

The coming of the 1860's brought memorable events for the state of Louisiana and for New Orleans. The "existing system of domestic servitude, with the right, unchallenged by men, to go and root itself wherever providence and nature may carry it," was being challenged by the Republican party. Politicians and clergymen alike stirred up the fervor and ire of the people with passionate speeches and orations. The "madness of the hour" appealed "to the arbitration of the sword," and soon Americans were not "shrinking even from the baptism of fire." [4] Louisiana seceded January 26, 1861. Civil war had come to New Orleans. [5]

Germans of the city were caught in the maelstrom of war. Rising prices and scarcity of money greatly affected them. [6] Yet, the business

---

[1] *Ibid.*, April and May, 1855.

[2] Carl Schurz, himself a "Forty-Eighter," was a strong advocate of Americanization after coming to the United States. He became an organizer of the Republican party, a Union general in the Civil War, and eventually Secretary of the Interior. Gottfried Kinkel (1815-1882) was a professor of art and cultural history at the University of Bonn. He was an interesting figure in the German revolution of '48; Carl Schurz, *The Reminiscences of Carl Schurz* (New York, 1909), I, 171-172; III, 46 ff; Carl Schurz, *Abraham Lincoln* (New York, 1888), 6-8; Baldwin, *The Stream of American History*, I, 606.

[3] Robert T. Clark, Jr., "The German Liberals in New Orleans," *loc. cit.*, XX (1937), 142-43, 145.

[4] New Orleans *Delta*, December 2, 1860; Kendall, *History of New Orleans*, I, 177.

[5] Robert T. Clark, Jr., "The New Orleans German Colony in the Civil War," *loc. cit.*, XX (1937), 997.

[6] Minutes of St. John Lutheran Church, financial report for the years 1863 and 1864; Anna Hoppe, *Negro Slavery* (St. Louis, 1935), 34-35.

of the city was going its normal way, to judge from the surface. Even the natural gaiety of the city was hard to suppress. There was great rejoicing among the Germans of the city when one of its members succeeded in running the Federal blockade with a shipment of Nuernberg beer, while many of the particular German institutions, such as churches, schools, and theaters, thrived during the days of the war and reconstruction. [1]

Fighting the war against the Union forces was, however, the paramount concern of the people of New Orleans. In this trying venture the German population of the city was divided. There were those of whom it was said that "our large German population is hostile to it (slavery). About all these Dutchmen would be not only Unionists, but Black Republicans, if they dared." [2] Others, in rather large number, looked upon the conflict as purely an American "family" affair and did not take an enthusiastic or active part in it. [3] Besides these, however, were those who supported the cause of the state with their life, their honor, and their property, and voted the National Union ticket, which had as its standard bearer, John Bell, an old Whig and a slaveholder. [4] Their spokesman, stated in an address given before a large crowd on Canal Street on August 1, 1860, that it was his belief that Lincoln and Hamlin were destroying the Union and threatening to rob citizens of their property, and that the Democratic party was too divided against itself to offer any effective resistance. When the die was cast, however, and the South went to war, Roselius served in the Jefferson Parish Mounted Guard. He therefore set an example which many hundreds of Germans of New Orleans followed by joining up with the forces of the Confederacy. [5]

When the firing on Fort Sumter brought on the long-feared flames of war, there was still no specifically German unit larger than a company in the Confederate service from Louisiana. In their recruiting the Germans were hampered by several things: first, their own internal rivalries; secondly, the continuing enmity of a large section of the French and

---

[1] Robert T. Clark, Jr., "The New Orleans German Colony in the Civil War," *loc. cit.*, XX (1937), 1006-7.

[2] Ella Lonn, *Foreigners in the Confederacy* (Chapel Hill, 1940), 34.

[3] Interview with E. W. Kuss, minister of New Orleans since 1888, February 29, 1948.

[4] Deiler, *Geschichte der deutschen Presse*, 20; Robert T. Clark, Jr., "The New Orleans German Colony in the Civil War," *loc. cit.*, XX (1937), 996; Baldwin, *The Stream of American History*, I, 777. Kendall, *History of New Orleans*, I, 232.

[5] Robert T. Clark, Jr., "The New Orleans German Colony in the Civil War," *loc. cit.*, XX (1937), 996-97, 1000.

Anglo-American groups; and thirdly, their lack of "friends at court." [1] Added to these conditions, many of the French and American contingents of the city did not like the idea of Germans commanding troops of any importance. They knew the political inclinations of the Germans in the North and feared that blood might be thicker than water. Finally, the officers of the companies, being generally men of no political influence, found it impossible to get things they needed from the state. Ludwig von Reizenstein [2] told of one German company which deserted because provisions were deliberately withheld by the state authorities and because packages sent them by relatives were appropriated by anti-German officers. [3] Yet, in spite of such difficulties, efforts went ahead to form a number of companies of German soldiers. German Confederate soldiers were grouped in the 13th and 20th Regiments of the Louisiana Infantry, and individual companies were also attached to the 6th, 22nd, 23rd, and 24th Infantry regiments. The 13th Louisiana Infantry had half of its ranks filled with Germans, while the 20th had three quarters, with German officers elected by their own men. This particular Regiment was the closest to a full compliment· of Germans. [4]

The number of Germans who saw service under the Confederate flag was difficult to ascertain. In 1860, the total German population of what became the Confederate States of America was approximately 70,000 of whom more than one-fifth lived in New Orleans. On June 15, 1861, the *Deutsche Zeitung* estimated that of the 14,000 soldiers from Louisiana that had gone to the front, 4,000 were Germans, and a goodly number of these came from New Orleans. [5] German companies were recruited

---

[1] *Ibid.*, 998.

[2] Ludwig von Reizenstein was born in 1829 in Germany. He came to the United States and New Orleans in 1849. He was author of *Die Geheimnisse von New Orleans* in which romance he pictured New Orleans Germans like Prinz Paul von Württemberg, who was staying in New Orleans at that time, and later Governor Michael Hahn, in such a manner that everyone could tell about whom he spoke. This romance appeared in the *Loutsiana Staats-Zeitung* from January 1, 1854 to March 4, 1855. He also wrote *Feuilleton* in the same German newspaper. He was also a student of the physical sciences, ornithologist and zoologist. He was a member of the Entomological Society of Philadelphia and collector of rare insects. In his last years he wrote exclusively for the English press and it was of his favorite that he wrote: *The Fauna and the Flora of Louisiana*. He died in 1888 at the age of 59. Deiler, *Geschichte der deutschen Presse*, 15-17; Louisiana *Staats-Zeitung*, 1854, through the first quarter of 1855.

[3] Robert T. Clark, Jr., "The New Orleans German Colony in the Civil War," *loc. cit.*, XX (1937), 998; New Orleans *Taegliche Deutsche Zeitung*, June 4, 1865.

[4] Robert T. Clark, Jr., "The New Orleans German Colony in the Civil War," *loc. cit.*, XX (1937), 999.

[5] *Ibid.*, 997-1000.

in Louisiana, Georgia, South Carolina, Virginia, and Texas. The *Turner* of New Orleans fought for the South under the command of a former reporter for the New Orleans *Deutsche Zeitung.* [1]

While the overall number of New Orleans Germans serving in the ranks of the Confederate army was not publicized, individuals served the cause of the South well and are therefore remembered. August Reichard was elected and commissioned colonel of the 20th Louisiana Infantry on November 28, 1861. He was a Prussian by birth and was acting Prussian consul at the outbreak of hostilities. In May, 1862, he rose to the rank of Brigadier-General. He fought brilliantly at Shiloh, Murfreesboro, and Chickamauga. When the Federals took possession of New Orleans, his property was confiscated. [2] Leon von Zincken was elected and commissioned major in November, 1861. During the course of the war, he rose to the rank of Brigadier-General. He commanded posts at Marietta and Columbus, Georgia. Von Zincken was especially successful in training recruits, having had military experience in Europe. He was wounded several times in battle, and he had the sad experience and duty of leading Reichard's mangled 20th Louisiana Infantry back to New Orleans in 1865. [3] At the Battle of Shiloh Lieutenant Petz, Captain Mueller, Corporal Wilhelm Baude, Lieutenant Hollermann, Lieutenant von Schellenberg, Lieutenant Rosenbaum, Lieutenant Schneider, and Lieutenant Cobel fought with distinction and bravery. [4] Among the New Orleans Germans who sacrificed and gave much in this bitter conflict were Adolph G. Ricks and the family of Henry Greenwall. The former became vice-president of the Metropolitan Bank of New Orleans, while the latter was the last noteworthy personality in the history of the New Orleans theaters. Ricks enlisted in the service of the Confederacy and served with honor. [5] Greenwall would have enlisted but for the fact that he was needed at home to take care of a large family. However, two of his brothers joined and served gallantly, one as a private soldier

---

[1] Carl Wittke, *Refugees of Revolution-The German Forty-Eighters in America* (Philadelphia, 1952), 222. The *Turner,* see page 88.

[2] Robert T. Clark, Jr., "The New Orleans German Colony in the Civil War," *loc. cit.,* XX (1937), 1001. Andrew B. Booth, *Records of Louisiana Confederate Soldiers and Louisiana Confederate Commands* (New Orleans, 1920), III, 839.

[3] Robert T. Clark, Jr., "The New Orleans German Colony in the Civil War," *loc. cit.,* XX (1937), 1002.

[4] New Orleans *Taegliche Deutsche Zeitung,* April 15, 1862.

[5] *Progressive New Orleans* published by Young Man's Business League (New Orleans, 1895), 30. This copy is in the T. P. Thompson Collection, University of Alabama; Fortier, *Louisiana,* III ,377.

in the 5th Louisiana Regiment and the other in the 10th Louisiana Infantry. One of them ,Philip, was seriously wounded at the battle of Williamsburg. The other, Morris, survived four years of battle and came home at the end of the war uninjured. [1]

In spite of German volunteer groups and the devotion and gallantry with which they fought for the cause of the South, the New Orleans American newspapers were unwilling to concede the existence of any good qualities in the German military organizations. The *Picayune* of May 2, 1861, viciously attacked them. The *Crescent* was satirical. Even the neutral *Delta* said, when the German Society gave the largest single donation to the support of Confederate soldiers' families, that the contribution covered a multitude of sins. [2] The basis for this attitude was undoubtedly the same which made it difficult to organize German companies, namely, the Anglo-French feeling against the Germans often voiced publicly in their newspapers. Yet, the German soldier did his duty to his adopted country and the city of New Orleans. [3]

In April, 1862, the Federal fleet passed the Confederate forts defending the mouth of the river and appeared before New Orleans. It was greeted with a scene of wholesale destruction. All the steamers in the river which could not escape up-stream were set fire to and sent floating down the river in flames, lest they might fall into the hands of the Union forces. [4] The Union troops took the city, and on May 1, 1862, General Benjamin Butler set up federal rule. [5]

In this crisis the Germans of the city again showed mixed reactions. The *Staats-Zeitung* became an enthusiastic advocate of Butler's regime. It urged young Germans to become recruits in Butler's Federal army by stating, "Now comes the opportunity for the strong German arm to help the cause of the Union. [6] "At the same time the *Deutsche Zeitung* set itself in opposition to the occupation forces. Members of German churches in the city observed special days of prayer and thanksgiving when requested by Jefferson Davis, [7] while some of their religious

---

[1] John S. Kendall, *The Golden Age of the New Orleans Theatre* (Baton Rouge, 1952), 583-84.

[2] Robert T. Clark, Jr., "The New Orleans German Colony in the Civil War," *loc. cit.*, XX (1937), 1000.

[3] Robert T. Clark, Jr,. "Reconstruction and New Orleans German Colony," *Louisiana Historical Quarterly*, XXIII (1940), 503.

[4] Rightor (ed.), *Standard History of New Orleans*, 570.

[5] Deiler, *Geschichte der deutschen Presse*, 20.

[6] *Ibid.*, 20.

[7] Minutes of St. John Lutheran Church, June 4, 1861.

leaders and pastors were very reluctant in taking the oath of allegiance required by General Butler. [1] Nevertheless, the silent attitude of the members in the churches, as attested by the proceedings of their church
meetings during these hectic war years, seemed to convey the feeling
that they were not much concerned about the outcome of the struggle
nor the rule inaugurated by the Union forces. [2]

The fortunes of war, however, projected a German-born New Orleanian to the highest office in the State. Early in January, 1864, General
N. P. Banks, who had replaced Butler, proclaimed that a state election
would be held on February 22. He restricted the vote to white men,
twenty-one or older, who had been residents of the state for twelve
months and of the parish six, and who had taken the oath prescribed by
the President in his proclamation of December 8, 1863. Of Louisiana's
700,000 population, only about 125,000 were within the Union lines.
Michael Hahn, who had taken the oath of allegiance to the United States
after the capture of New Orleans, and who under Butler had been
elected to Congress, was elected governor. In winning he polled 6,171
votes and thus became the first governor elected under Lincoln's "ten
per cent rule." [3] As governor he had authority only in that portion of
the state which was controlled by the Northern soldiers. The rest of
the state chose Henry W. Allen as governor. [4] In February, 1865,

---

[1] G. M. Kramer, Lutheran pastor of New Orleans ,related these incidents to the
author, December 10, 1947. Kramer was personally acquainted with Teacher Conzel-
mann of Zion Lutheran School, who told him of their happenings. Heller, *Jubilee
Souvenir of Temple Sinai*, 11.

[2] Minutes of St. John Lutheran Church, 1860-1864; Minutes of Zion Lutheran
Church, 1860-1864.

[3] Dabney, *One Hundred Great Years*, 206. "His inaugural on March 4, 1864, was a
great occasion .... There was no building large enough for the ceremonies, so Lafayette Square was used. The tree trunks were whitewashed, the branches were fes-
tooned with arbor vitae, the walks were spread with fresh shells, and an amphitheater,
with seats rising twenty-five feet above the platform, was built of Maine spruce. The
square was aflutter with flags, and hundreds of Chinese lanterns were hung between the
pillars of City Hall. At sunrise, a hundred guns saluted the return of civil government. By
11 A.M., Lafayette Square and the surrounding streets were packed. To the accompany-
ment of a three hundred piece band, five thousand children lifted their voices in song.
Hahn and Banks spoke, the church bells went mad and fifty guns roared. Parades
throbbed through the streets at night; there was a brilliant ball at the opera house."
Dabney, *One Hundred Great Years*, 207.

[4] Grace King and John R. Ficklen, *A History of Louisiana* (New Orleans, 1893), 235.
Allen had been a soldier under Breckenridge in the famous attack on Baton Rouge.
Shreveport became the capital of that part of the state not in Union hands. New Orleans
was the capital of that part of the state which was held by the Union forces.

Hahn resigned his office as governor to run for the United States Senate. [1]

The difficult task of reorganizing the state's affairs devolved on him, and he had a great share in initiating the movement to emancipate the slaves. [2] In this work he was motivated by an unflinching loyalty to Abraham Lincoln.

> I stand fully and squarely on the platform of Abraham Lincoln ....
> Let him be true in the future as he has been in the past, and whatever he
> in his honest discretion, shall deem good for the preservation of the Union,
> I will approve, and whatever he shall denounce as injurious to the Union,
> I will condemn. ... I am for the Union with or without slavery, but prefer
> it without. I am emphatically an unconditional Union man. [2]

The years between 1865 and 1877, known as the Era of Reconstruction, were the most trying in the political history of New Orleans. It was a period of violence, lawlessness, political agitation, and corruption. [4] Yet it was in this very time that the Germans of the city became more active in the arena of politics. [5]

After the frightful Mechanics' Institute riot on July 30, 1866, [6] Major General P. H. Sheridan branded Hahn as a "political agitator and a bad

------

[1] Robert T. Clark, Jr., "Reconstruction and the New Orleans German Colony," *loc. cit.*, XXIII (1940), 503.

[2] Faust, *The German Element in the United States*, 174.

[3] "What Is Unconditional Unionism?" Speech by Hahn. In the T. P. Thompson Collection, University of Alabama.

[4] New Orleans *City Guide*, 31.

[5] Robert T. Clark, Jr., "Reconstruction and the New Orleans Germany Colony," *loc. cit.*, XXIII (1940), 504.

[6] Dabney, *One Hundred Great Years*, 210-16; Kendall, *History of New Orleans*, I, 307-309. Hahn's fate in the riot as written by a correspondent of the New York *Times* is found in "New Orleans Riot," *The Tribune Tracts*, No. 1. This report is in the T. P. Thompson Collection. This riot grew out of the attempt to draw up a state constitution to enfranchise the Negro. Governor Wells called for an election to fill vacancies in the convention which was to draw up a new constitution since the Constitution of 1864 was regarded to be a creation of fraud and violence and not in any sense the expression of the will of the people of the state. Lieutenant Governor Albert Voorhies and other state officers were opposed to the Governor's move. It was on July 27, 1866, that the Governor had issued the proclamation, the very night a meeting was held in the Mechanics' Institute, where Hahn made a violent speech and A. P. Dostie said that if the convention was interfered with on July 30, "the streets of New Orleans would run with blood." On July 30, twenty-five members met in convention in the Institute. Violence was expected. Members met at twelve noon and adjourned at one P. M. At one o'clock about one hundred persons with fife and drum and the American flag, also partly armed, arrived at the hall. A Negro in the procession fired a shot and rioting began in the front of the building where the convention was held. Police held in readiness by Mayor Monroe arrived. Shots were fired and the mob entered the building. Negroes were killed. Ex-Governor Hahn escaped almost miraculously and among the mortally

man." [1] Consequently, German voters who formerly had been influenced by Hahn and other radical reconstructionists gradually joined the ranks of the Democratic party. At the same time they saw the struggle in Congress between the radicals and moderates over the problem of reconstruction with which they were not in sympathy. These conditions together with the interest manifested by the Democratic party of the city in the German element soon bore fruit. In the election of 1866, both German newspapers, *Die Deutsche Presse* and *Die Deutsche Zeitung*, supported James G. Taliaferro, a conservative Republican, for governor against Henry Clay Warmoth. The *Deutsche Presse* characterized Warmoth as a "carpetbagger par excellence," a man who was not connected with the State by the slightest personal or business interests, and whose chief claim consisted in the fact that during the war he was a judge of a Provost-Marshal's court in New Orleans. Judge Taliaferro was spoken of as a "Republican but an honest Republican." [2]

The conservatives lost in the state race by the election of Warmoth, but the city vote went for Taliaferro. Of greater importance to the Germans, however, was the election of a number of their people on the parish Democratic ticket: W. H. Woelper, clerk of the 7th District Court; H. Bensel, tax collector; F. Schumacher and G. H. Braughn, state senators; F. Forge, Charles Stringer, J. E. Rengstorff, I. Zoelly, and A. Wiltz, state representatives; and H. F. Stuercken and P. Kaiser, aldermen. In this election the Germans voted conservative Republican in the state and Democratic in the parish. It was not at all surprising that the *Deutsche Presse* declared the local victory due to the German vote. It appeared that the Germans of the city had become a conscious minority in the political life of Louisiana and New Orleans. [3]

The German element, almost to a man, refused to have anything to do with the "carpetbag" Warmoth administration. It was too radical for most of them, and they were generally drifting into the rank of the white conservative Republicans who were inclined to make common cause with

---

wounded was Dostie. About forty-eight were killed, all Negroes except four, and sixty-eight severely wounded and ninety-eight slightly. Alcee Fortier, *A History of Louisiana* (New York, 1904), IV, 82-87.

[1] "New Orleans Riot", *The Tribune Tracts* No. 1, 7. This tract is in the T. P. Thompson Collection .Robert T. Clark, Jr., "Reconstruction and the New Orleans German Colony," *loc. cit.*, XXIII (1940), 504.

[2] Robert T. Clark, Jr., "Reconstruction and the New Orleans German Colony," *loc. cit.*, XXIII (1940), 504-05.

[3] *Ibid.*, 504-05.

Democrats. For the same reason they had nothing to do with William Kellogg, S. B. Packard, and J. S. Casey, supporters of the Republican party.[1] This attitude seemed to portend the action to be taken by the Germans of the city in years to come. In the local elections of 1872, there was the largest German representation ever seen on any Louisiana ticket; however, none of the members ran on the Radical ticket but on the Fusion ticket of Democrat and Liberal. [2]

On the local ticket of the Fusion party was the American-born German, Louis Wiltz, running for the office of mayor. Besides him, were Louis Schneider for administrator of finance, Charles Fitzenreiter for administrator of waterworks, H. F. Stuercken for administrator of police, and Peter Schwager, Charles Kummel, and M. Dietrich for the legislature. [3] Wiltz was elected mayor of the city. [4] In spite of the situation in the state and nation, the candidates of the Fusion party were successful in their races and were officially installed into their respective offices. [5]

In the state election of 1872, the Germans of the city also identified themselves with the Fusion party, forming the liberal wing of that group. As liberals of this party, a politically conscious number began to organize themselves early in 1872 for the national campaign. In February, a committee of fifty-one, of whom thirty-one were Germans, was organized with the purpose of building a true reform party along the lines advocated by the Liberal Republicans nationally. [6] Other political elements joined this reform group. The Germans, however, gradually went into the camp of the Liberal Republican party then being formed by Horace Greeley and Carl Schurz, at the same time remaining an integral part of the committee of fifty-one. At a mass meeting held in the Deutsche Company Hall, which was attended by a large number of German fellow-citizens,

---

[1] *Ibid.*, 508.

[2] *Ibid.*, 521.

[3] *Ibid.*, 520-21.

[4] Kendall, *History of New Orleans*, I, 349-50. The new mayor was a native of New Orleans and was in his twenty-ninth year. Among his ancestors were some of the first German settlers in Louisiana. He enlisted in the New Orleans Artillery. He was captain of Company E. Chalmette Regiment, stationed at Fort Jackson, where he and his men were captured in 1862. After the war he began a successful mercantile business. In 1868, he was state legislator. He was also a member of the Board of Aldermen in New Orleans. He was a man of energy, ability, and dauntless courage. *Ibid.*, 349-50.

[5] Robert T. Clark, Jr., "Reconstruction and the New Orleans German Colony," *loc. cit.*, XXIII (1940), 522.

[6] The platform of these liberal Republicans called for withdrawal of troops from the South, civil service reform, and a resumption of specie payments. Samuel E. Mo-, rison and Henry S. Commager, *The Growth of the American Republic* (New York 1942), II, 70.

eight delegates to the Cincinnati convention were elected. In this move the Germans expressed their feeling regarding the movement that was expected to be inaugurated in Cincinnati. [1]

This group of liberals was determined to have nothing to do with Warmoth. They refused to coalesce with the administration forces and therefore elected their own delegates to the national convention. They agreed to permit Warmoth to lead the state's delegation to the convention, but otherwise maintained their aloofness to the end. After having had their minute part in the nomination of Greeley and B. Gratz Brown for president and vice-president respectively, the eight German delegates returned to New Orleans with the remaining one hundred and seventeen liberal delegates, and began campaigning. On November 4, 1872, the election took place in Louisiana, one day prior to election day in all other states of the Union. [2] By November 19, the results of the campaign, as determined by the qualified voters of New Orleans, were tabulated, showing that Greeley had received 23,721 votes and Grant a mere 12,721. [3] Since the Germans formed the main strength of the Liberal party in Louisiana and New Orleans, in spite of their small delegation to Cincinnati, the campaign was a victory for the political thought of the German voters of the city. [4]

In the election of 1876, in which Louisiana cast a decisive vote, for the promise of a withdrawal of Federal pressure, the vote was given to Hayes, who had already been reconciled to defeat. Again it was impossible to say what Louisiana's vote actually was since the returns were undoubtedly doctored to fit the bargain between state and national machines. The bargain was, however, a good one, for it gave reasonable assurance of the end of carpetbag rule. In the meanwhile, the bargain also confirmed the belief of the New Orleans Germans that no faith could be placed in Republicans. With the memory of the Durell scandal of 1872 and the trade of 1876 in mind, the German group became an important part of the Democratic party in a one-party system, in spite of the recognized dangers of a one-party rule. [5] In that way, the liberal

---

[1] Robert T. Clark, Jr., "Reconstruction and the New Orleans German Colony," *loc. cit.*, XXIII (1940), 517-18.

[2] New Orleans *Daily Picayune*, November 4, 1872.

[3] *Ibid.*, November 19, 1872.

[4] Robert T. Clark, Jr., "Reconstruction and the New Orleans German Colony," *loc. cit.*, XXIII (1940), 519; Ella Lonn, *Reconstruction in Louisiana After 1868* (New York, 1918), 156-57.

[5] The disputed election of 1872 showed that the Fusion candidates had been elected. The German party was with the Liberal party which fused with the Democratic ticket.

wing of the Fusion party of 1872 likewise entered the ranks of the Democratic party by the year 1876. Since then, the group has remained solidly Democratic, and is still an important element in the political life of the city. Even the once-radical Michael Hahn made an about-face in politics. Disgusted with the administration's juggling of school funds, he began in 1871 to withdraw from the Radical group. [1]

These Germans were mostly of the middle class, of all trades and occupations. They were substantial citizens and taxpayers whose names were hardly known outside of their own circles, except a few, because they had never moved to take an active part in political matters. But ground down by high taxation, exasperated by the ever-growing mismanagement of public affairs, they came forward in this crisis to try by their own exertions to save what was left to them out of the fruits of their labors. [2] Having also been very well assimilated by the process of Americanization, these energetic German voters were ready to take an active part in the political life of their community. They likewise encouraged the newly-arrived immigrants to become naturalized, to learn the language, and to enjoy the privilege and duty of every American, namely, to take part in political activity. [3]

With this change taking place in the political life of the German people of New Orleans, Federal troops marched out of the city in April 24, 1877, given God-speed by cheering throngs and a hundred-gun salute by the Washington Artillery. It was a great day in Louisiana history for it ended fourteen years of military oppression. [4] It was a memorable time for the German voter who from this day stood side by side with his democratic American friend.

But the Custom House candidates—so called, extreme wing of the Republican party, for it was led by the United States marshal, Packard, who had his office in the Custom House building—declared themselves elected. To make sure the latter decision would hold, William Pitt Kellogg and C. C. Antoine (colored barber), Custom House candidates, brought suit in the United States Circuit Court, presided over by Judge E. H. Durell. To the astonishment of the nation at large, the judge declared the Custom House candidates elected, and his decision was immediately confirmed by the chief beneficiary of the action, President Grant. Kendall, *History of New Orleans*, I, 342; Robert T. Clark, Jr., "Reconstruction and the New Orleans German Colony," *loc. cit.*, XXIII (1940), 515.

[1] Robert T. Clark, Jr., "Reconstruction and the New Orleans German Colony" *loc. cit.*, XXIII (1940), 514.

[2] *Ibid.*, 520; New Orleans *Daily Picayune*, July 24, 1872.

[3] Interview with Anna Altmann, March 2, 1948.

[4] Dabney, *One Hundred Great Years*, 241-42; New Orleans *Item*, June 10, 1952.

CHAPTER IV

THE NEW ORLEANS GERMAN
AND HIS FIRST LOVE—HIS WORK

The physical appearance of New Orleans in 1850 after an all-day rain on February 8, of that year was vividly reported by *The Daily Delta:*

> The elements yesterday frowned. The rain fell steadily from morning to noon, from noon to night. Streets were mire and sidewalks slippery . . . It was a rare day for young ducks! Lake Poydras rose in dudgeon and threatened crevasses to surrounding properties. Little boys—embryo navigators—set their boats on the "muddy profound,' and aping Captain Noah, of the good ship Ark, made adventurous explorations of mud islands and roundstone continents in the depths of the waters. Pedestrians knew not the color of their garments, so besprinkled and bespattered with the prevailing currents of mud in solution—for dandytraps were in wrath and vented it in mortar! . . . .[1]

Mud, silt, and water were everywhere. It was a grand mess which was accompanied by its inconveniences and miseries.

Although no one was aware of it at the time, the commercial life of the city was soon to be in a similar predicament, which was to continue throughout the 1860's. All this in spite of the fact that in the greater part of the 1850's New Orleans was one of the most active and prosperous commercial ports of the world, which was reflected in the gaiety of her life. [2]

While the prosperity of New Orleans in this period grew by leaps and bounds, there were, beneath the brilliant surface, forces operating which were very imperfectly understood at the time, but which menaced seriously the continued importance of the city. Relatively it was losing ground. The vast increase of production which was taking place in the upper and central part of the Mississippi Valley—which ought, according to the reasoning of the New Orleans merchants, logically seek New Orleans—was pouring into other cities. This was due to several reasons. First, New Orleans was concentrating more and more upon the

---

[1] New Orleans *The Daily Delta*, February 9, 1850.
[2] Rightor, (ed.), *Standard History of New Orleans*, 569; New Orleans *The Daily Delta*, March 17, 1850.

handling of a single article. Cotton, she unfortunately was coming to believe, "was king". For the sake of cotton she was neglecting the sugar of Louisiana, the tobacco of Kentucky, the flour of Ohio—in fact, all the products of the Ohio, upper Mississippi and Missouri valleys. Secondly, her position was menaced by the diversion of trade routes resulting from the construction of the Erie, Ohio and other canals. The effect was seen in the cost of the transportation of commodities; as, for instance, of flour. The duration and danger of the trip via New Orleans and the high cost of insurance resulted in an expense to the shipper considerably larger than if he patronized the new interior waterways. Ultimately more serious to her commercial prosperity was the effect of the building of the railroads which was ignored at this time by New Orleanians. Those that were built were expected to supply transportation only to markets where no other avenues were open. Consequently, there was for many years no line connecting the Eastern seaboard with the teeming West. Besides these threatening conditions, there existed the dire need of improving the great river itself. One by one vessels which had made the river famous had vanished, burned or sunk by striking on the snags which were the chief peril of navigation in the Mississippi; and the larger ocean-going vessels could not safely navigate the treacherous passages of the river at its mouth.

Finally, political forces were at work in this period which were inimical to the future welfare of the city. People were trained in the habit of disregarding the law and in depending upon force to carry out their will, whether licit or illicit. [1] These causes, coupled with the ravages of the civil conflict and of political reconstruction, augured evil days for the city throughout the 1860's. [2]

In 1870, however, New Orleans began to eliminate the obstacles which had retarded her economic development during the previous decade. This was particularly true in the field of transportation by rail and water. Railroads had been slow in coming to the city. Only one hundred and forty-three miles of track were in the area by 1860 with most of it belonging to the New Orleans, Opelousas, and Great Western Railroad, but after the war rail mileage increased rapidly. By 1880, four major lines, the New Orleans, Opelousas, and Great Western; the New Orleans,

---

[1] Kendall, *History of New Orleans*, I, 202-04.
[2] New Orleans *City Guide*, 31; Thomas Ewing Dabney, "The Butler Regime in Louisiana," *Louisiana Historical Quarterly*, XXVII (1944), 492, 517-18.

Jackson, and Great Northern; the New Orleans, Mobile, Chattanooga; and the New Orleans-Pacific, were serving the area. By 1883, with the Illinois Central Railroad extending its rail operation into the South, a network of rails connected New Orleans and the Gulf of Mexico with Chicago on the Great Lakes. By 1900, there were ten lines operating in the area with five of them of major importance, connecting the city with all parts of the United States. [1]

In water transportation, the turning point was the year 1874-75, when the jetties at the mouth of the river were begun. After both a canal and dredging to deepen the river passes had failed, Congress allowed Captain James Buchanan Eads to try his jetty plan. [2] It was a great success. Completed in 1879, it afforded a depth of thirty feet in the center of the Channel and opened New Orleans to the largest vessels then afloat. [3]

Transportation within the city was also growing apace. From 1878 to 1880, there were five hundred and sixty-six miles of street, of which four hundred and seventy-two were unpaved; one hundred and forty miles of city railroad track, with three hundred and thirteen horse or mule cars; and sixty small passenger coaches on the steam lines to Carrollton, West End, and Spanish Fort. [4]

These improvements in rail and water transportation contributed greatly to the industrial development of the city. While still predominantly a merchants' town up to 1883, the city's industrial life was quickening. In 1870, there were five hundred and fifty-four factories with a combined capital of $ 5,429,140, employing 4,411 hands whose wages amounted to $ 1,204,254 annually and the value of whose products was $ 8,450,439. In 1880, the figures had risen to nine hundred and fifteen factories with $ 8,565,303 capital; 8,404 hands employed; $ 3,717,557 in wages; and $ 18,808,909 the value of products. By 1890, the number of factories had climbed to 2,152 with a capital investment of $ 22,865,000. There were 23,504 hands employed earning in annual wages $ 10,392,604. The value of the products manufactured amounted to $ 42,770,519.

[1] New Orleans *Item*, June 10, 1952, Section on Transport, p. 3, 5, 9, 12. Kendall, *History of New Orleans*, I, 189.

[2] James Buchanan Eads (1820-1887) was an American engineer. He built the jetties at the mouth of the Mississippi River and also designed and built the Eads Bridge across the Mississippi at St. Louis. He was the first American to receive the Albert medal. This medal was given by the British Society to encourage arts, manufactures, and commerce. *The World Book Encyclopedia*, V, 2155.

[3] Rightor, (ed.), *Standard History of New Orleans*, 573-74.

[4] Dabney, *One Hundred Great Years*, 280-81.

This increasing industrial development continued with the approach of the new century for in 1895, while the number of factories did not increase appreciably, the capital investment had doubled since 1890 and employment in these industries had increased by an additional 11,000[1].

Such industrial growth, coupled with a rising tide of commercial activity which had its best year in 1890-91, when the total value of commerce in the New Orleans area amounted to $ 531,764,118, made the South, and especially New Orleans, a good country for the Germans. [2]

In such a setting extending over fifty years filled with prosperity and with privation, the Germans of New Orleans made their mark achieving individual success and building a leading metropolitan area of the United States. They broke new roads and then kept on, even though the beginning did not promise them good returns. As tradesmen they were adventurers. Being satisfied with small profits in the beginning, they became rich. They stuck to their trades, and thus, through patience, overcame native competition. The objects were to make money; to advance trade; to serve the guild; and to improve the methods of a particular branch of business. [3]

The Germans coming to New Orleans early took an active part in the business and professional life of the city. This was particularly true of the great number of professionally trained men who came in the wake of the European revolutions in the late 1840's. Among them were doctors, lawyers, journalists, actors, musicians, dentists, engineers and architects. [4] As early as March, 1852, Doctor von Poellnitz, a German physician, organized a union of German doctors of the city. The purpose of this union was to handle the patients only according to nationally-accepted practice; to protect the patient against quackery; and to give new German doctors assistance to get a start in their practice. All German doctors were invited. Meetings were held each Sunday evening from eight till ten in the home of Doctor von Poellnitz. [5] All of these men were competent, having received their medical training in European medical centers.[6]

---

[1] *Progressive New Orleans*, 19; Rightor, (ed.), *Standard History of New Orleans*, 537.

[2] Rightor, (ed.), *Standard History of New Orleans*, 576; New Orleans *The Daily Picayune*, February 13, 1890, 4.

[3] Faust, *The German Element in the United States*, II, 469-70.

[4] Robert T. Clark, Jr., "The New Orleans German Colony in the Civil War," *loc. cit.*, XX (1937), 993.

[5] New Orleans *Deutsche Zeitung*, March 30, 1852. Physicians who signed the advertisement were: Langenbecker, Leisnig, Maas, Poellnitz, and Wetzel.

[6] Louisiana *Staats-Zeitung*, September 25, 1855.

Some of them engaged in specialized medicine, but most of them were general practitioners who kept offices in neighborhood drugstores, made house-calls and thus often endeared themselves to every member of the family. [1] Assisting the doctors in caring for the health of the German population was a goodly number of German apothecaries. They handled all kinds of medicinal goods, even importing them from Germany, France, and England. [2] Together with these guardians of the health of the people were the German barbers. Benedict Rehm opened a barber shop on Bienville Street near Marais. He not only advertised expert haircutting but also careful blood letting, teeth extractions, and the like. [3]

The legal profession among the Germans in the 1850's was well represented by men like Christian Roselius and Michael Hahn. Both of these jurists have left an enviable record which was an inspiration to later jurists in the city, such as Charles F. Buck, Charles F. Buck, Jr., George Walshe, G. G. Kronenberger, W. H. Seymour, P. J. Kraemer, H. Heidenhain, Paul Reusch, and many others. [4]

Christian Roselius, reaching the height of his fame in the 1850's, had come to New Orleans in 1820. Due to his poverty he was forced to apprentice himself for several years. In the meantime he was studying law and was admitted to the bar at the age of twenty-five Much of his money went into a law library containing the works of all the German jurists and political thinkers. His vast knowledge of German legal philosophers at a time when the works of these savants were virtually unknown in America won esteem from Daniel Webster, who sought him as a law partner in the 1830's. [5] The Law School of the University of Louisiana, organized in 1847, had this eminent German jurist as professor of Civil Law. [6] It was said of him that, except for Edward Livingston, there was no more profound scholar in civil law than Christian Roselius. [7] While at the height of his reputation and influence, he played a vital part in the two decades of litigation over John McDonogh's will, follow-

---

[1] *Ibid.*

[2] *Ibid.*

[3] *Ibid.*

[4] New Orleans *Taegliche Deutsche Zeitung*, January 1, 1884; *New Orleanser Deutsche Zeitung*, May 1, 1898.

[5] Christian Roselius, "Collegiate Education," McCaleb (ed.), *The Louisiana Book*, editor's introduction, 149; interview of Arthur G. Nuhrah with Mitchell Franklin, W. R. Irby Professor of Law, Tulane University, June 10, 1951.

[6] Rightor (ed), *Standard History of New Orleans*, 250.

[7] Christian Roselius, "Collegiate Education," McCaleb (ed.), *loc. cit.*, editor's introduction, 149.

ing the Scotsman's death on October 26, 1850. He and Randell Hunt were instrumental in saving the bequests made by McDonogh for public education in New Orleans and in Baltimore. [1] Besides his outstanding public service, he was one of the kindest and most generous men of his time. He was always ready to give advice to his fellow Germans, even though he did not associate himself with the German organizations of the city, and in spite of his large income left no great fortune because of his philanthropy. [2]

Michael Hahn came to New Orleans as a lad in the company of his mother, who died of yellow fever shortly after coming to the United States. Being a talented youth, he attended high school and then studied law under Roselius. He entered the practice of law in 1851. At the age of twenty-two he was a member of the school board and later became its president. After a hectic career in the period of Reconstruction, he moved to his plantation in Saint Charles Parish, where he founded Hahnville. Here he was beloved by all. He held many offices—school director, member of the legislature from Saint Charles Parish, police juror, director of the United States Mint, district judge, and congressman of the United States from the Second Louisiana Congressional District. He died in Washington on March 14, 1886, an old and poor man, a suicide. [3]

A number of Germans were musicians and actors, and by leading the Turner and Singing Societies in song and amateur stage productions helped to foster and advance these cultural activities among the Germans. These music teachers also visited the homes of both Germans and Americans to teach the new generation. According to Henry Drueding, leading German musician and organist of New Orleans, all musicians of note in the nineteenth century were trained in Germany. Among them were A. J. Hoffmann, Joseph Engel, Carl Weiss, and Hanno Deiler. [4]

Preachers were also well represented among the professionally-trained. Ernest Berger conducted private instructions at the Odd Fellow's

---

[1] Ficklen, *History of Reconstruction in Louisiana*, 18.

[2] Mrs. S. B. Elder, "The Germans in Louisiana History-Their Splendid Work in Colonization," *Souvenir of the Eightieth Anniversary of the German Society of New Orleans* (New Orleans, 1927), 64; Deiler, *Geschichte der deutschen Presse*, 18-19. For Roselius' viewpoints in political issues see chapter 3, page 58 of this thesis.

[3] Deiler, *Geschichte der deutschen Presse*, 21-24. For a discussion of Hahn's activities in the days of reconstruction in Louisiana, see chapter 3, pages 59 ff. of this thesis. Some have doubted the suicide angle claiming he died a natural death.

[4] A. B. Faust, "German Cultural Influences in American Life," *loc. cit.*, (1929), 15; Interview with Henry Drueding, June 13, 1953. For a discussion of cultural activities see Chapter 6.

Hall on Lafayette Street, not only in religion but also in languages, particularly French, German, and English. His tuition fee ranged from two dollars an hour to three dollars. [1] Most clergymen were engaged, however, in gathering congregations of German-speaking people and building houses of worship. Better known among these in the 1850's and 1860's were Henry Hiestand, who organized the first German Protestant congregation; [2] Christian Sans, who laid the early foundation of the first German Evangelical Church in the heavily-populated Third District of the city; [3] J. H. Kleinhagen, who pastored Zion Lutheran Church and also the Clio Street Church; [4] Brother J. H. Hollander, who was lay preacher of Saint John Evangelical Church and later pastor of the First German Presbyterian Church on First Street. [5] Most of these religionists were free lancers not affiliated with an organized church body.

The teaching profession was followed by a goodly number of the cultured Germans of the city. They found employment particularly in the many private schools maintained by individuals and churches. [6] Perhaps, one of the most interesting of these schools was the one founded by the Ueber Brothers, John and Jacob. These pedagogues conducted the Ueber school from 1850 until 1901. At the time of General Butler's authority in New Orleans, the school was crowded beyond its capacity. The attendance on one day, by actual count, was two hundred and seventy-nine pupils. When the brothers celebrated their fiftieth anniversary in the teaching profession, it was estimated that more than 3,000 pupils, among whom were some of the most prominent citizens in the city, had passed through its halls. [7] Likewise Gustav Eckhardt and G. M. Zinser, by conducting classes in English, assisted many a German immigrant adult to learn the language of his adopted land. [8]

The years from 1850 to 1870, however, drew more Germans into the

---

[1] Louisiana *Staats-Zeitung*, September 25, 1855.

[2] J. Hanno Deiler, *Zur Geschichte der deutschen Kirchengemeinden* 21.

[3] G. J. Wegener, *Geschichte der St. Paulus Gemeinde* (St. Louis, 1890), 10.

[4] Minutes of Zion Lutheran Church, August 26, 1849; July 2, 22, 1848.

[5] Minutes of St. John Lutheran Church, May 21, 1853; W. Robinson Konrad, "The Diminishing Influences of German Culture in New Orleans Life Since 1865," (Master's Thesis, Tulane University, 1940), 20.

[6] Deiler, *Zur Geschichte der deutschen Kirchengemeinden*; Beryl M. Hoffman, "German Education in Louisiana," (Master's Thesis, Tulane University, 1939).

[7] Konrad, "Diminishing Influences of German Culture," 37-8; Hoffman, "German Education in Louisiana," 47-8.

[8] Louisiana *Staats-Zeitung*, September 25, 1855.

field of business and industry than into the professions. New Orleans seemed to be a good place for the German merchant, small business man, and small industrialist. The one business which seemed to have a particular fascination for the German was the restaurant-boarding house. Many of these were found in all parts of the city, serving the people not only as places of recreation and rest but also as rendezvous, especially for the newly-arrived German immigrant who felt himself strange and otherwise lonely in his new surroundings. At 243 Bienville Street was the restaurant, Zur Fliege. An inviting and attractive sign read, "For good German sausage come to Die Fliege." Here also was sold that tasty and nourishing Frankfurter Bratwurst and Braunschweiger liver sausage. [1] Johann Lockert operated the restaurant "Zum Schwan." [2] Joseph Fabacher's Coffee, Beer, and Boarding House between Chartres and Exchange Alley was one of the most popular places of them all. But there was also John Mueller at 117 Royal Street, who offered his services to the German public. His boarding house prices were exceptionally reasonable. Opposite the French Theater on Orleans Street was Krost's Beer Parlor, where many an after-theater drink was enjoyed. Charles E. Seeliger offered food and drink at the Kossuth House on Royal Street ,while the Anderson White Hall Coffeehouse on St. Louis Street offered bowling recreation and rooms for bachelors only. [3] Leaving the heart of the city and approaching the uptown river area, Heinrich Wolfskul on the corner of Third and Water Streets and the Stevedore's Exchange and Coffee House operated by R. von Weinmann offered the best in food, drink, and lodging. [4]

A closely related work was the restaurant and hotel business. Mathieu Vonderbank was one of the best known with his establishment at 126-130 Common Street, which was a pleasant rendezvous for many Germans. Joseph Voegtle operated a saloon on the corner of Poydras and St. Charles and the Cosmopolitan Hotel on Royal Street near Canal. John Schmitt served warm meals and oysters any style from six in the morning until eight at night at 143 Gravier Street just two doors from St. Charles Street. Charles Mattern, better known to all Germans as "Charlie," served lunches and refreshing beer at the Columbia Beer Hall at Exchange Alley and Customhouse. But the most popular places were Valentine

---

[1] *Ibid.*, January 23, 1856.
[2] *Ibid.*, February 7, 1856.
[3] *Ibid.*, September 25, 1855.
[4] *Ibid.*, January 10 and 12, 1856.

Merz's establishment on St. Charles, purchased by Conrad Kolb and operated under that name from that time on, and the fabulous eating place of Laurence Fabacher on Royal Street. The Fabacher was first organized in 1880 on Gravier Street near Magazine, but a few years later was moved to Royal Street. In 1887, the young Laurence purchased the business from his father. It was not long before the Fabacher Restaurant became famous throughout the country and helped to establish New Orleans as a culinary center of the world. Besides these well-known eating and drinking places, hundreds of smaller and larger saloons and restaurants were operated by Germans of the city. [1]

Among the business men were contractors handling all building materials and encouraging commercial and private building ventures. Early in the period Otto Knoop and F. Kuntz became interested in this work and established a business that was to last throughout the last five decades of the nineteenth century. [2]

A cigar business operating under the name of Philip D. Mayer and Son; a soap works owned by J. H. Keller and covering two squares of ground at Felicity, Josephine, and Front Streets, with a total output of $ 200,000 a year in 1900; and Reis's Ironmongery on Tchoupitoulas Street near the St. Mary's market, were only three of the more successful business ventures of New Orleans Germans in the 1850's. [3]

The great majority of Germans, however, had no financial resources to get a start in a business venture. In fact, most of them were in desperate condition and eager to find any kind òf work in order to keep body and soul together. In such circumstances, most New Orleans Germans offered what each possessed, a strong body and sturdy will to work. This meant that most Germans became laborers. [4] Work was found on the river front loading and unloading ships, constructing and repairing levees, and after Civil War days in seasonal occupation in the sugar cane fields of south Louisiana and elsewhere. Records of the German Society of

---

[1] *Souvenir of the Eightieth Anniversary of the German Society*, 21, 57; *Official Text Book of the Twenty-Sixth American German Choral Union Festival* (New Orleans, 1890), rear page advertisement; *Progressive New Orleans, 1895*, 52, 55; *Louisiana ,Its Builders and Its Industries* (Louisiana, 1924), 97; *New Orleanser Deutsche Zeitung*, August 31, 1902.

[2] *Ibid.*, March 23, 1858.

[3] Rightor, (ed.), *Standard History of New Orleans*, 522; *Souvenir of the Eightieth Anniversary of the German Society*, 43; New Orleans *Deutsche Zeitung*, November 29, 1853.

[4] Minutes of the New Orleans German Society, 1850-1863.

New Orleans revealed that plantation operators sent their requests for workers to toil in the fields at the time of planting and harvesting promising transportation, board and lodging, and a monthly cash salary of $ 20.00. Some of these calls for workers came as far away as Mississippi. [1]

There were enough workers to warrant the organization of a branch of the Allgemeiner Arbeiter Bund. This association was originally founded in Philadelphia and had branches in thirty cities. It cost ten dollars to join and one dollar a month for dues. In return, the member was given aid in sickness, accident, or loss by fire. An old-age pension of two hundred fifty dollars a year was granted, and widows and orphans were provided for. [2] Besides this workers' organization, the Louisiana German Draymen's Association was organized in 1854, which was one of the largest. According to the act of incorporation, its object was to take care of the widows, provide for and educate the orphan children of its members, and diffuse a spirit of benevolence and mutual charity. As a part of its work, it built a mausoleum in Greenwood Cemetery for the use of its members. [3]

Some Germans, however, because of their excellent training in a trade, were successful in setting themselves up in their particular specialty. Heinrich Oterson was a paperhanger; Heinrich Hille, a tailor. Edward Stein was a portrait painter, who guaranteed the likeness of his portraits. He also instructed in free hand drawing and painting for reasonable charges. [4] Theodore Lilienthal was one of the pioneers in photography and one of the leading artists in New Orleans. His studio was located at 121 Canal Street. Lilienthal employed twenty-one males and three females. [5] Jacob Lees operated a mortuary and livery stable on Front Levee between Montegut and Clouet, while Madame Schleiniger busied herself with offering instruction in all kind of needlework and embroidery to the daughters of all families "who ought to know this fine art." [6]

Particularly impressive was the number of Germans engaged in wholesaling. In this business was George Jurgens, Edward Goetz, Henry

---

[1] *Ibid.*

[2] Laguaites, "The German Element in New Orleans," 35.

[3] *Ibid.*, 34-5.

[4] Louisiana *Staats-Zeitung*, September 25, 1855.

[5] John E. Land, *Per Illustration of New Orleans-Its History, Commerce, Industry-1881-82* (New Orleans, 1882), n.p. This pamphlet is found in the T. P. Thompson Collection, Alabama University Library.

[6] Louisiana *Staats-Zeitung*, September 25, 1855.

Lochte, H. Zuberbier, P. W. Dielmann, William B. Schmidt, F. M. Ziegler, J. M. Schwabacher, E. F. Del Bondio, Fred D. Becker, Gustave Beck, A. M. Felt, and H. Theurer.[1] Perhaps, the largest and most successful of these was the organization of Schmidt and Ziegler located at 49-55 South Peters Street. Not only was this firm interested in domestic trade and markets but also in foreign trade. The company's ship, *Margaret*, made regular trips to Jamaica laden with American goods and returning with goods of the tropics.[2] Competing quite successfully, Zuberbier Wholesale Grocers and Commission Merchants maintained a good stock of more than $ 300,000 in their spacious building fronting on Peters and Fulton Streets.[3] In fact, most of these men were very successful in their business ventures, which motivated a goodly number of them to enter the world of finance in the city. William B. Schmidt was a director of the Canal Bank and president of the Teutonia Insurance Company, as well as an active partner in certain insurance organizations. H. Zuberbier was president of the Germania Savings Bank and of the Germania Insurance Company.[4] Jacob Hassinger was president of the Germania Savings Bank after the days of Zuberbier. Emile F. Del Bondio was director of several banks. Albert P. Noll was president of the Teutonia Insurance Company succeeding William B. Schmidt. P. W. Dielmann was a director of the Metropolitan Bank and of the Germania Insurance Company, while Morris Schwabacher was a director of the Germania National Bank. A. G. Ricks was president of the Metropolitan Bank. Besides these, there were G. Adolph Blaffer, cashier of the Germania Savings Bank, and Eugene F. Buhler, president of the Teutonia Bank. All of these were but a few of the many German business men who became associated with various financial institutions of the city.[5]

Although practically every profession was represented among the Germans, the crafts were more predominant since the German immigrants

---

[1] *Souvenir of the Eightieth Anniversary of the German Society*, 51-53; *New Orleans and The New South* (New Orleans, 1888), 87-122; Land, *Per Illustration of New Orleans-Its History, Commerce, Industry*, 69-152.

[2] *New Orleans and The New South*, 80; New Orleans *Taegliche Deutsche Zeitung*, February 8, 1883.

[3] Land, *Per Illustration of New Orleans-Its History, Commerce, Industry*, 69.

[4] *New Orleans and The New South*, 80, 88.

[5] *New Orleans and The New South*, 87; *Souvenir of the Eightieth Anniversary of the German Society*, 51; *New Orleanser Deutsche Zeitung*, August 31, 1902. The newspaper material is in the form of a pictorial supplement, now in possession of Henry Kraak of New Orleans.

of the 1870's to 1890's were not as intellectual as their compatriots of the 1850's and 1860's. [1] While there were several outstanding doctors and lawyers among them, such as Frederick Loeber, William Kohlmann, Hugo A. Gabert, L. H. von Gehren, William E. Schuppert, H. P. Wahl, Charles Eckhardt, Charles Buck, Josiah Gross, and Leon Kahn, there were far more bakers, goldsmiths, machinists, stone masons, manufacturers, watchmakers, book binders, furniture and cabinet makers, architects, shoe manufacturers, gardeners, and domestics. Typical of a German organization of the city was the membership of the Liedertafel, a singing group, which was an accurate cross section of the occupations of many Germans. Of forty-eight members taken into its membership in November, 1881, twenty-five were salesmen, five bookhandlers, two lawyers, one dentist, one confectioneer, one planter, one drummer, one employee of the sheriff's office, one owner of a coffee house, two secretaries, one cashier in the sheriff's office, and a railroad clerk of the Morgan Railroad. [2]

There were capable farmers and gardeners among the Germans who had learned agriculture in their homeland. They turned to truck gardening, raising vegetables in the heavy soil and humid climate of New Orleans. Together with truck gardening, they operated dairy farms grazing their cattle in the wide open spaces around City Park and Gentilly. It was often said that the German farmer with his luxurious vegetables made living more enjoyable for New Orleanians since he offered his wares by peddling from house to house or occupying a stall at the French market on the banks of the Mississippi River. As the end of the century approached, many of these farmers were forced to sell out since they were being crowded by many Italians who also turned to truck farming and finally gained a monopoly in this particular field. In spite of this, a number of German gardeners continued, gradually turning their attention to raising flowers and ornamental shrubbery. Among them were C. W. Eichling, Henry Kraak, and E. A. Farley. The work was done not only by the man but by his helpful, sturdy wife and his numerous children. Hired help was seldom used. A goodly number also turned to the sugar fields

---

[1] Wittke, *Refugees of the Revolution*, 372.

[2] Minutes of the *Liedertafel*, November 5, 1881; New Orleans *Taegliche Deutsche Zeitung*, March 21, 1880; January 7, 1883; September 3, October 18, and November 24, 1889; *New Orleanser Deutsche Zeitung*, June 1, 8, 1898; Land, *Per Illustration of New Orleans-Its History, Commerce, Industry*, 128, 137; Myers, *The Israelites of Louisiana*, 120; *Souvenir of the Eightieth Anniversary of the German Society*, 45, 47, 55.

of Louisiana for employment, especially in time of the harvest. [1]

Another helpful source of employment was that of housework in the homes of the more wealthy Americans and Germans. Many a German girl found ready and profitable employment as a domestic. Proving themselves better workers than the ill-trained colored women of the city, they were in constant demand. [2]

Noteworthy was the development of two enterprises in the city that were monopolized by Germans. Both of these had their beginnings before the days of the civil conflict. One of them reached its brightest day in the early days of the mid-century, the other in the last two decades of the century. Both gave steady, although exacting, employment to a goodly number of German workers. These were the printing of German newspapers and the beer industry.

Joseph Cohn who conducted a German printing office on Poydras and Tchoupitoulas Streets, entered the journalistic field on August 1, 1848, by founding the New Orleans *Deutsche Zeitung.* [3] This event was the forerunner of a wave of journalistic efforts that flooded the New Orleans German newspaper market throughout the 1850's. On June 1, 1850, *Der Louisiana Zuschauer* made its appearance supporting the Whig cause. This German edition of the *Louisiana Spectator* was followed by a number of village papers, such as *Der Deutsche Courier, Die Lafayette Zeitung, New Orleanser Tageblatt, Das Kathmannsche Arbeiterblatt,* which was an organ of the *Allgemeiner Arbeiter Bund, Der Communist,* the *Deutsch-English Weekly,* the *Carrollton Journal,* and the Jefferson Parish *Waechter.* All of these papers were of a short duration with the exception of the *Deutsche Zeitung,* which had a life-span from 1848 to 1907, and the Louisiana *Staats-Zeitung,* which was founded on July 9, 1850, and continued until 1866. [4]

---

[1] New Orleans *Taegliche Deutsche Zeitung,* October 18, 1889; Minutes of the German Society, October 3, November 7, December 5, 1883, January 2, February 6, 1884; Deiler, *Zur Geschichte der deutschen Kirchengemeinden,* 108; interviews with numerous German people of New Orleans, especially with Mrs. Anna Altmann, who was born in New Orleans in 1858, on March 2, 1948; with Mrs. Anna F. Weidig, March 1, 1948; with Mrs. Anna Von Salzen, March 3, 1948; with Henry Kraak, May 30, 1953; with Mrs. L. Fremin, December 26, 1953.

[2] Minutes of the German Society, March 7, 1883, April 1, 1891, July 6, 1892. *Souvenir of Eightieth Anniversary of German Society of New Orleans,* 81.

[3] Rightor, (ed.), *Standard History of New Orleans,* 277. This newspaper had a continued existence throughout the last half of the 19th century.

[4] Deiler, *Geschichte der deutschen Presse,* 12, 30. While the *Deutsche Zeitung* changed its name twice during the century, it was popularly known as the *Deutsche*

Varied were the reasons for the appearances of these small German newspapers. More and more German immigrants were coming to the city and its environs, among whom was an expressive element of political refugees. These politically-minded reformers desired to acquaint their fellow Germans with happenings in the old homeland. This could best be done by the journalistic channel. Since the majority of the immigrants could not read the English newspapers, it became a necessity to publish German ones. When steady employment gave the immigrant a better living, which was the experience of the greater number of them, he always turned more avidly to newspaper reading for he could afford to buy one. At the same time those who had a little capital could find ready financial help to start a newspaper business. Finally, since the Germans lived in scattered places throughout the city, it was for a time profitable to publish village newspapers. After 1854, however, most of the small village papers died out. Even the *Staats-Zeitung* moved from the village to the center of town to insure its existence. [1]

In 1866, the Hassinger-Pfeiffer interests bought out the Louisiana *Staats-Zeitung*, thus giving a monopoly to their paper, the *Deutsche Zeitung*. The partnership of Hassinger and Pfeiffer did not last long, for in the same year in which the monopoly was established, Hassinger bought Pfeiffer's interest for the sum of $ 11,500.00 and a plot of real estate and became sole owner of the newspaper. Papers founded after this date had as their main objective the breaking of the Hassinger newspaper monopoly. [2] With this in mind, Sebastian Seiler and J. Kredell, the city editor of the *Deutsche Zeitung*, received support for the founding of a second New Orleans paper, the *New Orleans Journal*, and formed the New Orleans Journal Association with capital amounting to $ 25,000. The first board of directors consisted of Louis Schwarz, Charles Bendix, Leon Toll von Zincken, Salomon Marx, Georg Merz, and Fred Del Bondio. This association offered Hassinger $ 30,000.00 for his *Deutsche Zeitung*, but he wanted $ 32,500.00 and refused to

---

Zeitung. From 1848 to March, 1854, it was known as the *Deutsche Zeitung*; from March 1854 to 1890, as *Taegliche Deutsche Zeitung*; and from 1890 to 1907, as the *New Orleanser Deutsche Zeitung*.

[1] Deiler, *Geschichte der deutschen Presse*, 10-11.

[2] *Ibid.*, 21, 30-31. Jacob Hassinger was born in Rehborn, Rhenish Bavaria, in 1828. He arrived in New Orleans in 1841. He found employment in the printing office of the *Deutsche Zeitung* edited by Joseph Cohn. He finally became sole owner of the paper. *Official Text Book of the Twenty-Sixth American German Choral Union Festival*, 50-51; *Souvenir of the Eightieth Anniversary of the German Society*, 49.

bargain with the association. The *New Orleans Journal* brought M. F. Sibilski of the New York *Staats-Zeitung* and the printer, Georg Mueller, into its employ. These two men remained prominent in the field of printing and journalism after Civil War days, particularly, Georg Mueller. [1] In spite of the good start of the *Journal*, it discontinued publication after a little more than six months. [2]

Also opposing the monopoly of the *Deutsche Zeitung* was the appearance of the New Orleans *Deutsche Presse*, with Sibilski the publisher, and the New Orleans German Press Association with capital of $ 25,000 supporting the venture. Throughout 1868, Sibilski, Georg Foerster, and John P. Weichardt of the *Deutsche Presse* fought the *Deutsche Zeitung*, but in 1869, the *Deutsche Presse* went out of business. [3]

Efforts to have a second German newspaper did not cease with the death of the *Presse*. The man of perserverance behind the efforts was Georg Mueller. In April, 1872, Mueller's *Die Laterne*, a humorous-satirical weekly, made its appearance. It did not "shine" very long. [4] This weekly was followed by three other Mueller undertakings, the *Louisiana German Journal*, with a life span of one year during the presidential campaign of 1876, the *Narhalla*, a humorous-satirical organ of the Baerenclubs of which Mueller was a member, lasting through one edition only, and the *New Orleans Deutsches Familienjournal* with a supplement, *Unsere Lustigen Blaetter*, appearing for five months. [5]

Besides the Mueller enterprises, there were others. In January 1875, Fritz Ehren, seeing that the *Deutsche Zeitung* appeared every day except Monday, felt that another paper might fill in that gap. He therefore published the Louisiana *Staats-Zeitung*, named after the paper which disappeared in 1866. But by April of the same year, the venture died. [6]

Finally, in the 1890's appeared the last efforts to break the monopoly of the Hassinger interests. The first came in the spring of 1893. Journalist Hugo Lehmann, who had worked on various New Orleans newspapers,

---

[1] Georg Mueller, publisher, was born Georg Gumbel in Dienheim by Oppenheim on the Rhine, on March 21, 1839. He came to New Orleans in January, 1866. For thirty years he was engaged in the printing business in New Orleans. In 1897, he sold his business and moved to San Diego, California, where he died on December 19, 1898. Deiler, *Geschichte der deutschen Presse*, 39.

[2] Deiler, *Geschichte der deutschen Presse*, 30-31.

[3] *Ibid.*, 31-32, 34.

[4] *Ibid.*, 35.

[5] *Ibid.*, 35-37.

[6] *Ibid.*, 35.

came from Texas with a plan to publish a paper to interest German immigrants in coming to Louisiana due to the expansion of the Southern Pacific Railroad. Lehmann had gotten the support of C. C. and W. W. Duson of Crowley, Louisiana, to interest Germans to come there; and Georg Mueller, always eager to have a second newspaper for the Germans of New Orleans, welcomed him. [1] Thus appeared *Der Suedliche Pioneer*, which, however, ran only one edition for Lehmann lost the support of the Duson brothers.

The second attempt of the last decade came from Fritz Koelling, an insurance man of the city, who had been severely criticized by the *Deutsche Zeitung*. On June 22, 1896, Koelling, answering the criticism of the Hassinger paper, published *Unser Kaese Blaettchen*, which, after three issues, appeared under the name, *Der Deutsche Kritiker*. The first sixteen issues were printed by Paul J. Sendker, young German printer, who had his business on North Liberty Street between Bienville and Conti. After that Koelling sought the support of Georg Mueller and got it. At first the paper was read avidly, but the newness wore off and the interest of the reading·public waned. After one year the last effort to crack the monopoly of the *Deutsche Zeitung* failed. [2]

Throughout its history, the *Deutsche Zeitung* featured poetry, various editorials on general topics, jokes, stories, advertisements, reports, foreign and domestic news, full length novels in serials, local news, and varied articles. After 1890, pictures and jokes appeared in greater number. [3]

Throughout these turbulent decades, the "Big Three" in the German newspaper business—Hassinger, Mueller, and Cohn—gave profitable employment to many New Orleans Germans, which greatly assisted them in finding a happier life and in furthering their quest for economic independence.

The other industry, which was almost a monopoly of the Germans of the city, and which began prior to 1870, was the manufacture of beer.

---

[1] C. C. and W. W. Duson were sons of Cornelius D. McNaughton, a Scotch-Irish Canadian, who came to Saint Landry Parish, Louisiana after 1837. Cornelius C. Duson was the oldest of five children born August 31, 1846, and W. W. was born seven years later. Both of these brothers helped to develop the area now Crowley and Saint Landry Parish, to which place many Germans migrated after 1880; *Biographical and Historical Memoirs of Louisiana* (Chicago, 1892), II, 478-79; *Crowley* (Crowley, Louisiana 1906), 4.

[2] Deiler, *Geschichte der deutschen Presse*, 37-38.

[3] New Orleans *Taegliche Deutsche Zeitung*, 1883; New *Orleanser Deutsche Zeitung*, January 4, 1898.

German people have always been fond of drinking beer. With an increasing number coming to New Orleans after 1850, it was not at all surprising that the beer industry should thrive and should be owned and operated in greater part by Germans of the city.

Before 1852, the Germans of the city were drinking a home product, "city beer," which could not be shipped out of the town because it did not keep well. Many called it "a molasses brew and wormwood." In spite of its low grade it was drunk by most Germans since it was cheap. This caused the industry to thrive and breweries increased. Five breweries made the "stuff," and it was freely dispensed in all the popular beer taverns and family gardens. [1]

In October, 1851, the first lager beer was served in New Orleans by Christian Krost on Orleans Street. With this start, national companies began to ship their beer to the city. In 1854, Philadelphia's brewer, Engel and Wolf, shipped in beer. In 1858 came Milwaukee beer, and by 1859, *Culmbacher Waldschloesschen* and *Muenchener Bock* could be had from Germany. [2]

A red letter day in the city beer industry came on December 1, 1864, when Georg Merz, at the dedication of his *Erster Felsenkeller*, introduced the first New Orleans brewed lager beer. It proved, however, unsuccessful because of the high cost of ice sent from Maine, which also often melted before delivery. This difficulty, together with the simple manner with which cheap beer could be substituted for the lager beer without the customer knowing the difference, postponed the permanent arrival of brewed lager beer in the New Orleans area. [3]

In 1882, the age of lager beer and large breweries and the disappearance of the old "city beer" industry arrived. Southern Brewery was built on the site of the old Merz's establishment located on the corner of Villere and Toulouse Streets. [4] This was the first large brewery in the city owned and operated by Germans. Its officers were Peter Blaise, president; G. Faehnle, vice-president; and E. Pragst, secretary. H. H. Bierhorst was a member of the board of directors, while Fritz Gund was a brewmaster. As early as 1884, after operating only two years, the brewery received an award for making a fine beer from the World's Industrial

---

[1] Deiler, *Geschichte der deutschen Presse*, 25.
[2] *Ibid.*, 26.
[3] *Ibid.*, 26.
[4] *Official Text Book of the Twenty-Sixth American German Choral Union Festival,* rear page advertisement; New Orleans *Taegliche Deutsche Zeitung*, March 8, 1888.

and Cotton Exposition held in New Orleans that year. By 1890, it had an annual production capacity of 300,000 barrels or 93,000,000 bottles. [1] Drinking this product of fine lager beer, which was more readily available to the public, quickly ended the fraudulent practice of substituting the cheap "city beer" for lager. At the same time, less and less "city beer" was being manufactured since good beer was driving away the bad. [2]

About the time that the Southern Brewery started operations, another group of Germans led by P. W. Dielmann, Jacob Hassinger, and H. Engelhardt, built the Louisiana Brewery on the corner of Jackson Avenue and Tchoupitoulas Street. This organization had early success not only in the quantity of beer produced but also in the quality for it received three first prizes for the best beer in the South at the American Exposition in New Orleans from November 10, 1885 to March 31, 1886. [3]

These two breweries ushered in an era of brewery construction which lasted throughout the remainder of the century. In the year 1888, both the Weckerling and the Crescent breweries made their appearance. [4] It was J. J. Weckerling, an Alsatian German, who took the money he made in operating a modest shoe store on Elysian Fields and Decatur Streets, and invested it in a brewery by buying out an old "city beer" brewery located on Magazine Street in the uptown area. After four short years, however, Weckerling sold out to Peter Blaise of the Southern Brewery, who continued to operate the establishment. [5] In December, the Crescent Brewery was erected on the corner of Canal and Claiborne Streets. This was for the time the largest brewery with a daily production capacity of two hundred and fifty barrels. The refrigerating rooms had a storage capacity of 37,000 barrels, while the stables accommodated seventy horses. The malt bins held 13,000 bushels and the malt was handled

---

[1] *Ibid.*, advertisement, IX. Peter Blaise was born in Alsace-Lorraine, March 19, 1838. He came to New Orleans and identified himself with the beer industry of the city. He founded the old New Hope Brewery on South Prieur Street, the first steam brewery in the city. *Souvenir of the Eightieth Anniversary of the German Society*, 31.

[2] Interview, John Rettenmeier, December 29, 1952. John Rettenmeier came to New Orleans in October, 1885. He worked at several breweries and in 1898 became brewmaster of the Columbia Brewery. He has been associated with the business from 1885 to 1923. At the time of the interview he was 88 years of age and in exceptionally good health.

[3] New Orleans *Taegliche Deutsche Zeitung*, September 3, 1889; New Orleans *Daily Picayune*, November 10, 1885; March 31, 1886.

[4] Interview, John Rettenmeier, December 29, 1952.

[5] Interview with Mrs. J. J. Weckerling, wife of the founder of the Weckerling Brewery, April 6, 1953.

entirely by machinery. The bottling shop was located opposite the main
structure on Robertson and Customhouse Streets. Artesian water was
used for all purposes except for brewing. Two hundred and thirty stockholders, all consumers, gave a healthy financial status to the venture. [1]

The year 1889 saw three more breweries begin operation, all owned
by Germans of the city, the Belgian, the Pelican, and the Lafayette.
The Belgian and the Pelican, with capacities of one hundred barrels
a day each, were located in the downtown area of the city on Montegut
Street. The Lafayette, with the same capacity, did business on the corner
of Lafayette and Tchoupitoulas Streets. [2] With the opening of 1890,
there were seven breweries in operation, with the financial resources
and the productional know-how in the possession of a strong group of
New Orleans Germans.

The total production of these breweries soon exceeded the demand
for beer in the city and its immediate vicinity. Peter Blaise and others
seeing the need for a program of partial retrenchment spearheaded the
founding of the New Orleans Brewer's Association, which went into a
program of consolidation. The Lafayette and the Crescent breweries
were closed, and four of the six brewmasters were fired. It was noted
that each of the brewmasters fired had an annual salary of $ 3,000.
Even these early measures, however, did not bring a better day for the
Association. One brewery after another was lost, until the business of
the New Orleans Brewer's Association went into the hands of the
receivers. [3]

This did not mean, however, that the beer industry was suffering[3].
In spite of the reverses experienced by the New Orleans Brewer's Association, other ventures in the industry were exceptionally successful.
Tom Hofer, who was the Weckerling's brewmaster fired by the Association, helped to organize and start production at the Jackson Brewery by
the spring of 1891. [4] The building took in an entire square between
Jefferson, Decatur, Saint Peter, and Clay Streets and was a five story
brick and cement structure. At the turn of the century, outstanding
Germans of the city were members of its board of directors. Among them
were Laurence Fabacher, A. Dumser, Gus Oertling, Joseph Melcher,

---

[1] *New Orleans and the New South*, 67-68; interview with John Rettenmeier, December
29, 1952.

[2] Interview, John Rettenmeier, December 29, 1952.

[3] *Ibid.*

[4] *Ibid.*

Anton Frey, Albert Fabacher, Fritz Jahncke, John W. Fairfax, and Peter Fabacher. [1]

Another dismissed brewmaster, William Breisacher, formerly of the Crescent Brewery, assisted in the founding of the American Brewery about three months after the Jackson got under way. Buildings and operations were located on Conti Street between Royal and Bourbon. [2]

For the next several years no new breweries were constructed, but in 1896, the building fever again gripped the industry and the city. On the west bank of the river came the Security Brewing with a capital stock of $ 150,000 and a yearly production capacity of 40,000 barrels with forty-five regularly employed hands. Henry Reininger, brewmaster and superintendent, produced a beer that was hailed as a "brew of the amber-tinted nectar quite delicious." [3]

Not to be outdone, New Orleans offered sites for two more breweries before the end of the century. Peter Blaise, Henry Armbruster, Charles Wirth, and Charles H. Schenck pooled their resources and built the Standard Brewery in the uptown section of the city on Johnson Street, followed shortly after by Charles Krast, Gustav Paul, Charles Rieder. C.W. Scheurer, and Andrew Schlosser, who constructed the Columbia Brewing Company on Elysian Fields and Chartres Street. This latter group of Germans obtained valuable financial support for their venture from two enterprising Italians of the city, A. Monteleone and S. Pizzati. It was at the Columbia that John Rettenmeier was the mastermind of the brewing process, a trade he had learned in Friedrichshafen, Germany, and had brought with him when he came to New Orleans in 1885. [4]

The industry had grown from the humble production of the old "city beer" breweries to ten gigantic enterprises, the Southern, Security, Belgian, Pelican, Louisiana, Weckerling, Jackson, American, Standard, and Columbia. In 1885, the total production of beer was 125,000 barrels annually. By 1899, production had risen to 193,000 barrels, and in 1900, 236,000. Even then, the industry was just in its infancy. [5]

---

[1] *Jackson Brewing Company* (New Orleans, 1908), 3, 20. This pamphlet was published for distribution from their exhibit at the Manufacturer's Exhibition held in New Orleans from September 1 to 30, 1908.

[2] Interview, John Rettenmeier, December 29, 1952.

[3] William H. Seymour, *The Story of Algiers* (Algiers, 1896), 65.

[4] *New Orleanser Deutsche Zeitung*, August 16, November 19, 1898 interview, John Rettenmeier, December 29, 1952.

[5] Interview, John Rettenmeier, December 29, 1952. He kept these records in a personal account book, now in his possession.

Besides the production of beer, the industry also controlled, in large measure, the distribution and dispensing of the product. To insure the sale of their beer, all breweries bought suitable property sites for the location of bar rooms, saloons, and small restaurants, where their beer was to be sold exclusively. The Columbia Brewery was the first in this venture which proved very successful and was followed by all the others in the industry. To be more interested in the man who carried his beer home in a bucket or pitcher than in the "gentleman" who sipped his glass of "nectar" in an exclusive club in the Canal Street district proved a boon to the selling of the brew. Therefore, hundreds of bar rooms throughout the city were controlled directly by the breweries.

Hundreds of Germans found ready employment in this industry, either directly or indirectly. Besides the workers in the actual making of the beer, which was monopolized entirely by the Germans of the city, there were platform workers, drivers, salesmen, drummers, barkeepers, stable keepers, and ordinary laborers. The work was hard, the hours long, and the wages low. Nevertheless, a goodly number of those who were in the industry became prosperous and were numbered among the wealthier families of the city, even moving their domicile into the fashionable districts. The industry was good to many German people. [1]

---

[1] *Ibid.* John Rettenmeier was one of those Germans to whom the industry was good. Coming to New Orleans with less than seventy-five cents, he was able to retire and live on a very substantial income since 1923. He owns a beautiful home in the City Park area of the city, where he proudly displays his own formula of beer brewing, the very formula which made Columbia beer famous in the city of New Orleans before the days of prohibition.

CHAPTER V

THE NEW ORLEANS GERMAN AND HIS CHURCH, SCHOOL, LODGE, AND ELEEMOSYNARY INSTITUTION

In March, 1721, two hundred Germans arrived in Biloxi to continue their journey to the land concession of John Law, a notorious Scotch financier, located in the lower Arkansas river valley. After a little more than a year, these immigrants were joined by two hundred and fifty more of their countrymen. [1] While their lot in this region was hard and trying, their coming and settlement proved to be the beginning of German immigration to Louisiana and New Orleans, which by the mid-1830's had culminated in the establishment of a German colony within the city, numbering about 7,000. [2]

As far as religious persuasion was concerned, there were Catholics, Protestants, and free thinkers among these German immigrants. Within the Protestant element, Reformed, Evangelical, and Lutherans predominated, however, all were without any clear conception as to the distinctions among the three. This was the result of the spiritual condition in their homeland, largely the outcome of the Prussian Union of 1817. [3]

The establishment of the Prussian Union was an event of the first importance in the history of Protestantism in Germany. Two years earlier, the Congress of Vienna had deprived the German states of the right to determine the religion of their subjects. The adherents of all Christian creeds were placed on a footing of legal equality in all states. In some of them, which had been partly Lutheran and partly Reformed, this led to great confusion; and to end the confusion the government attempted to force a union of the two churches. In 1817, Fredrich William III decreed such a union for his kingdom of Prussia and issued, at the same time, a new liturgy for the use of all the congregations in the king-

---

[1] Deiler, *Geschichte der deutschen Presse*, 1; Martin, *History of Louisiana*, 140. Deiler stated that of the 1,200 Germans who left the Palatinate in 1721 only two hundred arrived in March of that year. One thousand of them died on board ship.

[2] Deiler, *Geschichte der deutschen Presse*, 2; Deiler, *Geschichte der deutschen Gesellschaft*, 41. The 1850 census of Louisiana showed that from 1820 to 1849 50,597 German immigrants landed in New Orleans. This compared with 68,854 from France and 50,656 from Great Britain.

[3] Kurtz, *Church History*, III, 178; Jacobs, *The Story of the Church*, 369-70; Qualben, *A History of the Christian Church*, 385.

dom. The example of Prussia was followed by other states. Only a few of the smaller states attempted to unite the Protestant churches, but practically all of them adopted the new method of church control. The state churches were placed under the direction of consistories, appointed by the rulers, and the rulers themselves became "ex officio" heads o' the churches. [1]

Circumstances favored this move. Both in the Lutheran and in the Reformed churches comparatively little stress was laid upon distinctive confessional doctrines; and the philosophies of Pietism and Rationalism, which preceded the era of the Prussian Union, had for different reasons taught the relative unimportance of dogma. Consequently, in Prussia and in many other German states an Evangelical national church with a common government and liturgy existed. This ecclesiastical body embraced three variant doctrinal viewpoints, a Lutheran, a Reformed which held to its distinctive doctrines though not regarding them as a cause of separation from this body, and an Evangelical which completely abandoned the points of difference seeking a real union church between the Lutherans and the Reformed. Squeezing these divergent viewpoints into one church organization, the Prussian Union became more and more identified with doctrinal indifference and the slighting of all church symbols. [2]

The greater number of Protestant German immigrants coming to New Orleans were by religious persuasion children of this merger in which doctrinal distinctiveness had been superseded by the effort at unity. While this feeling of outward unity among them led to the founding of the first German Protestant congregation in 1825, it also became the direct cause of strife, bitterness, and division in their early church life when it was seen that no true spirit of ecumenity existed among them. [3] Diversity of religious thought and conviction was the dominant factor in the origin of German congregations of many different denominations. [4] Those of Catholic faith also experienced strife and division in their churches

---

[1] Kurtz, *Church History*, III, 178-79; Jacobs, *Story of the Church*, 369-70.

[2] Kurtz, *Church History*, III, 178.

[3] *Hundred Years with St. Paul's 1840-1940* (New Orleans, n.d.), 4; W. Robinson Konrad, "The Diminishing Influences of German Culture in New Orleans Life Since 1865," (Master's Thesis, Tulane, 1940), 16-7; G. J. Wegener, *Kurzgefasste Geschichte der Deutschen Evangelisch-Lutherischen Kirche St. Paulus Gemeinde U.A.C. zu New Orleans, Louisiana* (St. Louis, 1890), 6.

[4] Konrad, "The Diminishing Influences of German Culture," 12: Deiler, *Zur Geschichte der deutschen Kirchengemeinden*, 63-7.

mainly because of the language question, yet not as intensely as among the Protestant element. They were a part of the dominant religious faction in the city and state under the jurisdiction of much higher and more united church officials. [1]

Prior to 1825, the Germans of the city had no church of their own which offered them spiritual solace in the language with which they were familiar. Catholic Germans worshiped either in Saint Patrick's Cathedral on Camp Street or in Saint Louis Cathedral at the *La Place D'Armes.* Protestants attended services either in Christ Church, the first Protestant congregation in Louisiana, on the corner of Canal and Bourbon Streets, or in the First Presbyterian Church and in the First Methodist Episcopal Church. [2] Eager to have the Word preached in their own language and being unable to understand too readily the preaching in a "foreign language," some Germans gathered for worship in a school house on Burgundy Street near Canal. By 1839, a church building was erected on Rampart Street which, however, was abandoned the very next year when this group moved into a new church structure on Clio Street between Saint Charles and Carondelet. The congregation gave itself the name of the Clio Street Church. [3]

The ensuing decades were propitious for the founding of German Protestant congregations, as well as those of the Catholic persuasion. In 1840, two Protestant churches were organized, one a Methodist, and one giving itself the name of the Deutsche Evangelische Orthodoxe Kirche in New Orleans. The former found a leader in Peter Schmucker, who in the winter of that year gathered a number of members placing Matthaeus Tautau in charge. The group rented a plot of ground on Erato Street between Camp and Magazine and built a small church. The latter was of a German-evangelical character but was not Lutheran. [4] Holding services in the fire engine house on Chartres Street, between Clouet and Louisa, and later in a private dwelling on the same street near Port, this congregation built a modest building on the corner of Port and Burgundy Streets, dedicating it on October 1, 1843. [5] Six years later, in 1849, the church

---

[1] *Ibid.*

[2] Letter of Bishop Blanc to the Trustees of the Saint Louis Cathedral, September 4, 1837; Deiler, *Zur Geschichte der deutschen Kirchengemeinden,* 20; Konrad, "The Diminishing Influences of German Culture," 28.

[3] Rightor (ed.), *Standard History of New Orleans,* 507.

[4] Deiler, *Zur Geschichte der deutschen Kirchengemeinden,* 29, 37. This congregation played a vital part in the history of the Lutheran church in Louisiana.

[5] *Ibid.,* 29; *Hundred Years with St. Paul's 1840-1940,* 8-10.

records revealed that one hundred and eighty-five baptisms were performed, ninety-seven weddings solemnized, and thirty-nine confirmants received into membership. [1] In March, 1872, the congregation adopted a more doctrinally conservative constitution and gave itself the name of the German Evangelical Lutheran Saint Paul's Congregation of New Orleans, Louisiana. [2]

Many Germans lived in the vicinity of Jackson Avenue and the river, known as the City of Lafayette, and among them were many of the Catholic faith. Warehouses, slaughter-houses, and other kinds of business had sprung up in that area which led to an increased population. The Germans living in that location had no church. The closest one to the neighborhood was the Church of Saint Therese. The attention of Bishop Blanc was directed to the situation, but being sorely in need of priests, especially German-speaking priests who could work among the many Catholic immigrants settling in and around the city, he was unable to begin work.

In 1836, the opportunity to start work in this area appeared. The Superior of the first Redemptorist order in the United States sent Father Czackert, then thirty-five years old, on a tour of the large cities of the country to collect funds for the Redemptorist Fathers' mission of Pennsylvania. Father Czackert came to New Orleans and was welcomed by Bishop Blanc, who gave him lodging at the episcopal residence, the old Ursuline convent on Chartres Street. The bishop was so impressed with the young Redemptorist that he asked him to remain for a time, at least, and do some work of gathering the Germans of Catholic faith at the Kaiser Hall, a popular dance hall located on Josephine Street and Chippewa. By paying a monthly rental Father Czackert was able to obtain permanent use of the hall from its Protestant owner. He fitted up the former dance hall as a church, and it became the center of religious activity for the City of Lafayette. He organized several catechism classes for children and adults, giving daily instructions, particularly to those of German birth, thus gradually building a German Catholic congregation about the makeshift dance-hall chapel. Bishop Blanc, noting the good work of Father Czackert and realizing the continued shortage of priests, was inspired to offer the work in the City of Lafayette to the Redemptorist Fathers. Accordingly, he wrote Father Passerat,

[1] Wegener, *Geschichte der St. Paulus Gemeinde*, 8-10.
[2] *Ibid.*, 19; G. J. Wegener, "Continued Progress of the Missouri Synod in the South-St. Paul's in New Orleans," *Southern District Bulletin*, VIII (1932-33), No. i, 1-2.

the Superior-General of the Redemptorists, who, moved by the bishop's plea, accepted the offer. In 1843, Bishop Blanc purchased two lots of ground on Josephine Street with the expressed intention "for a church to be built for the special use of the German Catholics living in Lafayette." [1]

Consequently, a church edifice was constructed which was blessed by the bishop on Sunday, April 14, 1844, and was called Saint Mary's Assumption Church. This was the first German Catholic Church not only in New Orleans but also in the state of Louisiana. [2] A frame structure, ninety by forty-five feet in dimensions, resting upon high pillars of brick, with a wide stairway leading into the interior, housed the first worshipers. [3]

The first Saint Mary's edifice served the congregation until 1858, when Father Anwander was successful in having the congregation venture upon building a second and more pretentious house of worship. The site chosen was right next to the original church. Parishioners worked hand in hand with the Fathers to erect the building. Even the women lent their aid carrying the bricks in their aprons from Jackson Avenue, since the deep mud permitted no traffic on Constance Street, then called Live Oak.

Of modified Gothic style, its beautiful majestic lines attracted attention and aroused enthusiasm from natives and visitors alike. As the years passed by, all that could enhance the beauty and the reverential atmosphere of the church was added. The gorgeous stained glass windows, the melodious bells, named "Mary-Joseph", weighing 4,000 pounds, and her companions, "Pius" and "Gabriel," and the great organ—all were installed as time went on. Finally, on Christmas Day, 1874, the high altar, made in Munich, Germany, which was one of the finest examples of the wood-carvers' art to be seen in this country, was solemnly dedicated. All which the church symbolized was a tribute to the pioneering Catholic Germans of the City of Lafayette. [4]

---

[1] Roger Baudier, *The Catholic Church in Louisiana* (New Orleans, 1939), 368-69.

[2] *Ibid.*; Deiler, *Zur Geschichte der deutschen Kirchengemeinden*, 39-41; *One Hundred Years in New Orleans, Louisiana*, 7-8. The first members of the Redemptorist Fathers, a German religious order, came to the United States in 1832 and worked among the Indians in Ohio and Michigan. In 1839, the Fathers took charge of a German congregation in Pittsburgh, and this event marked the beginning of their long apostolate among the Germans in various parts of the country. Pekari, "The German Catholics in the United States of America," *loc. cit.*, XXXVI (1925), No. 4, 352.

[3] *One Hundred Years in New Orleans, Louisiana*, 9.

[4] B. J. Krieger, *Seventy-Five Years of Service* (New Orleans, 1923), 53-6; *One Hundred Years in New Orleans, Louisiana*, 11-2.

Expansion of the church among the German Catholics of the city was very orderly, directed to take care of the Germans living in various sections of the city and its outlying areas. Just as the City of Lafayette attracted a goodly number of German immigrants, so also were the City of Carrollton and the Faubourg Marigny popular sections for the concentration of these people. In Carrollton preaching began in 1847 in a private home on Cambronne Street near Maple. A German priest from Saint Louis came at regular intervals to read the mass and give instructions, assisted by the priest of Saint Charles Borromeo, the little Red Church of Destrehan. Bishop Blanc realized that the Catholics of Carrollton consisting principally of German and French people, but including also Irish and American, should have a church with a resident pastor. In 1848, in compliance with the request of these Catholic people, he commissioned Father F. Zeller, a Lorrainian, to form a parish in Carrollton and to build a church. On May 2, of that year, Father Zeller bought three lots of ground upon which a church and a rectory were built. The dedication took place on September 8.

Preaching was carried on in German only. This angered the French and English speaking people of the congregation who plotted to burn down the church building. The threat brought out guards to protect the building but also the wise decision to preach in German, French, and English. This practice of preaching in three tongues was continued until 1861, when Father Franz Ceuppens, a Belgian priest, took charge of the congregation and discontinued German preaching since he could not speak the language. Discontent among the Germans resulted. In answer to their dissatisfaction, Father Anton Bicklmayer was sent as assistant to Father Ceuppens with instructions to work especially with the German-speaking people of the parish. All was well until the days of the Franco-Prussian War in 1870, at which time Father Ceuppens was in Europe. Bicklmayer was preaching in German only at that time, and the Germans, filled with patriotic fervor, were clamoring for their own church. With the return of Ceuppens, Father Bicklmayer was forced to leave to assume work in another parish and was ordered by his superiors "not to visit Carrollton under any circumstances." [1] Immediately the Germans of Carrollton went into action. They organized themselves into a congregation, bought a piece of ground measuring a hundred feet from the old church on the other side of Cambronne Street and built their own

---

[1] Deiler, *Zur Geschichte der deutschen Kirchengemeinden*, 70, 72-3.

building. Meant to serve the German Catholics of the area, it received its own pastor in Father Bicklmayer and its own name, German Mater Dolorosa Church. [1]

One section of the Faubourg Marigny was popularly known as "Little Saxony" because of the large number of Germans living in that area. Here the Catholic church concentrated its efforts to establish a congregation among them. Success was realized in 1847, when Father J. M. Masquelet founded Holy Trinity Catholic Church, erecting a small frame building at a cost of $ 3,000.00 on the corner of Saint Ferdinand and Dauphine Streets. The first church was blessed on July 18, 1848. Three years later, however, while Father Scheffer was pastor, the first church burnt. The members, all German Catholics, at once proceeded to rebuild and on the feast of the Holy Trinity, 1853, the new church was dedicated.

Misunderstanding on the part of the priest and the trustees and members of the congregation in regard to incorporation and proper assignment of the property as required by Bishop Blanc caused considerable confusion. For a time it seemed as if serious trouble would destroy the young parish entirely, but Father Scheffer carried on his ministrations and soon affairs were straightened out and settled. Holy Trinity rapidly forged ahead to become one of the outstanding parishes of the church in the city. [2] Its era of greatest achievement came during the pastorate of Father P. Leonhard Thevis, who served the parish from 1870 to 1893. [3] He was followed by J. B. Bogaerts

---

[1] Baudier, *Catholic Church in Louisiana*, 368; Deiler, *Zur Geschichte der deutschen Kirchengemeinden*, 70, 72-3; *New Orleanser Deutsche Zeitung*, May 1, 1898.

[2] Deiler, *Zur Geschichte der deutschen Kirchengemeinden*, 63; Baudier, *Catholic Church in Louisiana*, 367.

[3] Baudier, *Catholic Church in Louisiana*, 367; Rightor (ed.), *Standard History of New Orleans*, 492; Deiler, *Zur Geschichte der deutschen Kirchengemeinden*, 63, During the year 1867, Archbishop Odin was in Europe and there he met Father Thevis, inviting him to take up his work in his diocese in Louisiana. Father Thevis was a native of the Diocese of Cologne. The young priest accepted and came to New Orleans arriving during the yellow fever epidemic of 1867. He was assigned as assistant at Holy Trinity and at once plunged into the work of the parish. Seeing with dismay the toll of dead in the city, Father Thevis prayed to Saint Roch to intercede for the congregation among whom he labored. He promised Saint Roch that if the congregation were spared he would construct a shrine in honor of the saint with his own hands. Though many in Holy Trinity were stricken, there was not one death, according to Thevis. Keeping his promise, he visited mortuary chapels in Bavaria and Hungary to plan the one he had promised. He bought land in the rear of the parish and set to work alone to build the shrine. He directed all the work, laid the marble flooring and installed an altar and stained-glass windows. In the shrine he placed a statue of Saint Roch. The good priest himself led the congregation in procession to the shrine for its de-

from 1893 to 1898, and Anthony Bicklmayer from 1898 to 1900.[1]

Wherever German Catholics settled in any number, they always insisted upon a church of their own, where instruction, the Gospels, announcements, sermons, and catechism were given in the German language. Such feeling led directly to the founding of Saint Henry's Catholic Church on Berlin street between Constance and Magazine Streets in the year 1856; to the organization of Saint Boniface Catholic Church on Lapeyrouse and North Galvez Streets; and the chartering of Saint Joseph Catholic Church on the west bank of the river in Gretna, Louisiana.

Saint Henry's served the Germans living in the area known as Jefferson City, which was located between the City of Lafayette and the City of Carrollton. From 1870, when the parish received its first resident pastor, until 1900, the members received their spiritual guidance from four priests: Father M. Radamaerger from 1870 to 1871; Father J. Bogaerts from 1871 to 1872 and from 1874 to 1891; Father M. Radamaergerts from 1873 to 1874; and Father Louis Richen from 1891 to 1900.[2]

Saint Boniface was organized by Father Joseph Koergerl in 1869. He had been ordered by Archbishop Odin to establish a congregation among the Catholic Germans living in the area below Canal Street and in the rear of Holy Trinity German parish. These people had repeatedly petitioned the archbishop for a church of their own stating that the distance between their homes and Holy Trinity parish was too far and too difficult to traverse. In a rather short time Father Koergerl gathered about him a large flock, which grew in membership and included many French and Creoles who lived in the rear of the city.[3]

Saint Joseph had its beginning in 1859, after many German Catholics living on the west bank of the river in the vicinity of Gretna had been served for a number of years by priests coming from New Orleans parishes. In that year a church was built and dedicated. By 1870, the Germans of the city and its vicinity were able to worship in and work for five prosperous and growing churches of the Catholic faith.[4]

---

dication. The building is regarded as a masterpiece of Gothic architecture. It has become a favorite shrine in New Orleans and thousands visit it annually.

[1] Rightor (ed.), *Standard History of New Orleans*, 492.

[2] Deiler, *Zur Geschichte der deutschen Kirchengemeinden*, 90; Rightor (ed.), *Standard History of New Orleans*, 490, 493. Berlin Street was changed to General Pershing after World War I.

[3] Deiler, *Zur Geschichte der deutschen Kirchengemeinden*, 107-09; Baudier, *Catholic Church in Louisiana*, 415-16.

[4] Deiler, *Zur Geschichte der deutschen Kirchengemeinden*, 94.

Among the Protestant Germans church building and church organization were likewise going forward, with more individual congregations established than among the Catholic element. After the founding of the Clio Street Church, the First Methodist Church, and the Deutsche Evangelische Orthodoxe Kirche, Protestant groups mushroomed in all parts of the city. While a growing German population was one of the dominant reasons for the appearance of so many different church groups, the German as a religious individualist, the inability to obtain capable pastors, and the presence of dissentient elements within existing congregations were strong contributing factors. [1]

Germans who could not forget that they were children of the "Evangelical" movement in the fatherland were busy, soon after establishing their homes in the city and its outlying sections, in organizing their congregations. One of the earliest church groups assembled on September 21, 1845, in the home of Caspar Auch at Rousseau and Fourth Streets. There was great rejoicing when on August 16, 1846, the members, who had given much of their time and labor in the construction program, were privileged to dedicate a church building on the corner of Philip and Chippewa Streets. Since the location of the church was in the City of Lafayette, it was known as Lafayette Evangelical Church.

Strife and dissension plagued the congregation in its early history. The first pastor of the flock, C. A. Schramm, was dismissed for writing jocose sayings into the church records. [2] From 1849, the year of his dismissal, to 1864, the congregation was served by seven pastors, four of whom ministered only one year. The height of strife occurred in the year 1858, when Hermann Pressler, the pastor, was literally chased out of office by the women of the church wielding whips and unbrellas, and scattering salt, pepper, and sand. Pressler had made himself unbearable to a large number of his members by his belligerent attitude, first toward the teacher of the church school and then toward any and all who questioned his right as a clergyman. [3] Lasting peace came to the congregation, however, in 1864, when the Reverend Ludwig P. Heintz assumed the pastorate and served until 1900. [4] Under his guidance and inspired

---

[1] Konrad, "The Diminishing Influences of German Culture," 13.

[2] In the wedding register he wrote: *Similis simili gaudet* (like and like loves each others company); and in the death register he wrote: *Finis coronat opus* (All's well that ends well). Deiler, *Zur Geschichte der deutschen Kirchengemeinden,* 50.

[3] Deiler, *Zur Geschichte der deutschen Kirchengemeinden,* 51-3.

[4] Ludwig P. Heintz lived in New Orleans for fifty-one years. In 1864, he took charge of the German Evangelical Church in Lafayette, coming from the Carrollton Evangeli-

leadership a new house of worship was erected in 1875 on the corner of Jackson Avenue and Chippewa Street, which received the name of Jackson Avenue Evangelical Church. [1]

Another German Evangelical congregation was organized in the City of Carrollton on Zimple Street between Monroe and Leonidas Streets on April 22, 1849. Five years after the founding, at the time of the arrival of L. P. Heintz as pastor, a split occurred in the membership since some refused to stay with Heintz but followed the newly-arrived Basel preacher, Martin Otto. The result of this action was that from 1855 to 1884 there were two evangelical groups in the City of Carrollton, one known as the "Rooster Church" because of a cock adorning the tower, the other, the "Otto Church." They were within a few blocks of each other, the "Rooster Church" on Zimple Street and the "Otto Church" on Dante Street.

It was not a matter of faith or conscience but simple human selfishness and jealousy which kept the two apart. As early as 1878, an attempt at reunion was unsuccessful because the two groups could not decide which building to use. Finally, in 1884 when the two united, the "Otto Church" building housed the newly-merged group, named the German Evangelical Church of Carrollton 7th District of New Orleans; while the property of the "Rooster-Church" was sold to the Evangelical Lutheran Church-Missouri Synod for $ 600 and was used for the organization of a Negro mission. The old "Otto Church" structure did not, however, serve as the house of worship of the united group for any length of time, for during the year of the merger a new church building was erected on Dante Street near Elm Street. In 1890, the name of the congregation was changed to the German Evangelical Saint Matthew Church. [2]

An evangelical splinter was organized into a congregation by John H. Kleinhagen in 1854. After serving Clio Street Church and Zion Lutheran

---

cal Church where he had served since 1854. Besides being influential in the construction of a large new edifice on the corner of Jackson Avenue and Chippewa Street in 1875, he was instrumental in organizing the German Protestant Orphan Home in 1866. He was also active in masonry founding the Humboldt Lodge in 1858 and later identified himself with the Kosmos Lodge, both of which conducted their meetings in the medium of the German language. *Souvenir of the Eightieth Anniversary of the German Society,* 35.

[1] Deiler, *Zur Geschichte der deutschen Kirchengemeinden,* 49-52; Rightor (ed.), *Standard History of New Orleans,* 503.

[2] Deiler, *Zur Geschichte der deutschen Kirchengemeinden,* 57-60; Konrad, "The Diminishing Influences of German Culture," 18-9; Rightor (ed.), *Standard History of New Orleans,* 503.

Church, he started his own congregation by rallying around a small splinter group of evangelical Germans and, locating on Felicity Street, called it the German Evangelical Bethlehem Church. The organization remained in existence until the 1890's, when the group disbanded, selling its church building to a negro mission which moved it to Felicity Street and Claiborne Avenue. [1]

Two more evangelical congregations were organized among the Germans of the city before the close of the century. In Jefferson City a group of them led by Preacher J. J. Ungerer organized in 1862. For a while it seemed as if they would join the Lutheran church, being served for a time by ministers of that body. In 1864, however, a Reformed pastor, G. Dietz, was called, who immediately launched a building program by erecting a structure on Milan and Camp Streets, and who by 1877 was successful in placing the congregation in line with the Evangelical Synod of North America. This affiliation was made final in 1891 under the pastorate of Julius P. Quinius. [2] The other evangelical flock was gathered by Hermann Perpeet, who in 1879 left the Clio Street Church to form an independent congregation on North Derbigny Street. In this particular neighborhood Saint John's Church, a Protestant group with definite Lutheran leanings, was already active; and, after 1881, another church group, Emmanuel Lutheran, began activity in the same area. These conditions undermined the efforts of the independent church of Perpeet, which consequently disappeared in 1887. [3]

The Lutheran faith was a dominant one in the religious life of the German-speaking people. This was clearly reflected in the days when New Orleans Germans were laying the foundations of their church life in their adopted home. On September 12, 1847, J. H. Kleinhagen preached to a number of Germans in the Saint Marien Church on Gainie Street. [4] The effort led to the organization of Zion Evangelical Lutheran Church on July 2, 1848. While not possessing all the marks of a confessional Lutheran church body, the congregation was conscious of its heritage by incorpo-

---

[1] Konrad, "The Diminishing Influences of German Culture," 22; Deiler, *Zur Geschichte der deutschen Kirchengemeinden,* 89.

[2] Deiler, *Zur Geschichte der deutschen Kirchengemeinden,* 100-02; Konrad, "The Diminishing Influences of German Culture," 22.

[3] Deiler, *Zur Geschichte der deutschen Kirchengemeinden,* 120; Konrad, "The Diminishing Influences of German Culture," 18.

[4] Minutes of Zion Lutheran Church, August 26, 1849. Gainie Street has been changed to Saint Peters Street. John H. Kleinhagen had been pastor of the Clio Street Church.

rating the word "Lutheran" into its official name. During October and November, negotiations for the purchase of a piece of property on Euterpe Street were completed, and on March 18, 1849, the erection of the first church building was completed by contractor Friedrich Koch. [1] This group of Germans, together with Saint John's Church and the German Evangelical Lutheran Saint Paul's Congregation, was influential in bringing confessional Lutheranism to New Orleans during the early years of the 1850's. [2]

On January 18, 1852, a group of Germans organized a congregation on the corner of Customhouse and North Prieur Streets and gave it the name of Saint John Evangelical Lutheran Church. Brother J. H. Hollander was appointed the lay preacher in October of that year. Immediately after his appointment the members cast about for a trained spiritual leader, and it was soon evident that they would not be satisfied with any kind of pastor. On January 3, 1853, Pastor Press was recommended to them. Since he held to doctrines and practices not in accord with those of the congregation, he was not received. [3] About that time, C. F. W. Walther, president of a confessional Lutheran body with headquarters in Saint Louis known as the Evangelical Lutheran Synod of Missouri, Ohio, and Other States, heard of this congregation and its needs through the medium of a New Orleans daily newspaper. [4] He came to New Orleans accompanied by George Volk, a young candidate for the Lutheran ministry. Three days after, Volk was ordained and installed as Saint John Lutheran Church's first pastor. The rite was performed by Walther in the presence of a large gathering. [5] By this act the congregation came

---

[1] *Ibid.*, November 26, 1848; January 15, 21, 1848; April 15, 1849.

[2] Confessional Lutheranism subscribes to the symbolical books of the Evangelical Lutheran Church. These are: The three Ecumenical Creeds (the Apostles' Creed, the Nicene Creed, and the Athanasian Creed), the Unaltered Augsburg Confession, the Apology of the Augsburg Confession, the Smalcald Articles, the Large and Small Catechisms of Luther, and the Formula of Concord, 1580.

[3] Minutes of St. John Lutheran Church, May 21, 1853; January 3, 1853.

[4] J. W. Behnken, *The Missouri Synod in the South and Southwest* (St. Louis, 1922), 365-66. The Evangelical Lutheran Synod of Missouri, Ohio, and Other States was organized in the city of Chicago on April 26, 1847. Walther was its first president. H. Kowert, *The Organization of the Missouri Synod in 1847* (St. Louis, 1922), 95, 99. Carl Ferdinand Walther was born October 23, 1811, at Langenchursdorf, Saxony, Germany. He migrated with the Saxon Lutherans to America in 1839, and served as pastor of Trinity Lutheran Church in St. Louis from 1841 to 1850. He became professor at Concordia Seminary in St. Louis, where he remained until his death on May 7, 1887. Walter A. Baepler, *A Century of Grace* (St. Louis, 1947), 47-8.

[5] Minutes of St. John Lutheran Church, May 21, 1853.

into official membership of the Missouri Synod, which in time established more firmly the teachings and practices of this confessional body in the city of New Orleans. [1]

Germans of Zion Lutheran Church and of Saint John Lutheran Church, together with their pastors, participated in many joint efforts which created in both church groups the hope and desire to form a closer association with the Missouri Synod. As this spirit grew ,Kleinhagen, the pastor of Zion, became dissatisfied and consequently resigned. The leaderless congregation sent an urgent request for a pastor to the officials of the Synod and on December 3, 1854, received W. A. Fick in response to their call. The coming of Fick as pastor of Zion strengthened the tie between Saint John and Zion since both were served by ministers trained in the teachings and practices of the Missouri Synod of the Lutheran Church. By the beginning of 1855, through the combined work of the members of Saint John and Zion, Lutheranism was firmly established in the city of New Orleans. [2]

A consciousness of confessional Lutheranism gradually worked its way into the life of the members of the Deutsche Orthodoxe Kirche of New Orleans. In 1858, a new constitution was adopted in which it was stated that the congregation adheres "to all the symbolic books of the Evangelical Lutheran church, as the form and norm drawn from God's Word, according to which, since they have been taken from the Word of God, not only the doctrines taught in our church shall be proven or taught, but all eventual doctrinal and religious differences shall be judged and regulated. [3]" Finally, in the early years of the 1870's, the congregation, then known as The First Evangelical Lutheran Church of New Orleans, Louisiana, united in fellowship with Zion and Saint John. [4] At about the same time ,Lutheran churches among the Germans living in Algiers and Gretna were established. [5]

---

[1] The term "Missouri Synod" was the abbreviated form of the Evangelical Lutheran Synod of Missouri, Ohio, and Other States. In this thesis the abbreviated form has been used for this church body was known by this name throughout the world.

[2] Minutes of Zion Lutheran Church, May 21, June 1, 7, 9, 1854; Minutes of St. John Church, June 12, December 4,1854.

[3] The Constitution of the First Evangelical Lutheran Congregation of New Orleans, Louisiana, adopted December 19, 1858.

[4] G. J. Wegener, "Continued Progress of the Missouri Synod in the South-St. Paul's in New Orleans," loc. cit., VIII (1932-33), No. 1, 2.

[5] Minutes of Salem Presbyterian Church, November 6, 1871; New Orleans States, May 25, 1913; undated clipping, Algiers Herald, in possession of Trinity Lutheran Church, Algiers, Louisiana.

Germans of the city also affiliated themselves with congregations of the Presbyterian faith. Churches of this denomination among the Germans were usually the result of splits occurring in existing ecclesiastical organizations. In 1853, a number of members of the Lafayette Evangelical Church, because of the liberalism of its pastor who was in like mind with the Turners of the Forty-Eighters, left and founded a German Presbyterian church on First Street between Laurel and Annunciation Streets. From 1865 to 1878, it was affiliated with the Northern Presbyterium, because the pastors serving the congregation were in general closely associated with this conference of churches. In March, 1878, however, under the leadership of Professor Lesko Triest, the group returned to the Southern Presbyterium. Shortly thereafter, Candidate Louis Voss became the pastor, who served the church throughout the remainder of the century. He was a leading clergyman of the city who was not only interested in building the Kingdom but also in furthering German culture. During his ministry, the name, First German Presbyterian Church of New Orleans, was given the congregation. [1]

The Second German Presbyterian Church grew out of the Deutsche Orthodoxe Kirche on Port and Burgundy, where in 1861, strife broke out over the problem of changing from an Evangelical to an Evangelical Lutheran church. Dissatisfied members moved over to Saint Roch Street between Rampart and Saint Claude Streets to erect a modest building in 1863. Work was carried on at that location until 1867, when the congregation sold the Saint Roch site and relocated on Allen Street near North Claiborne Avenue, very close to the present location. At the time of the move, the group numbered one hundred and six members and was affiliated with the Northern Presbyterium. Two years later, however, under the strong leadership of the Reverend F. O. Koelle, which projected the congregation into an influential position in the city's religious life, the congregation returned to the Southern Presbyterium. [2]

---

[1] Louis Voss, *History of the First Street Presbyterian Church* (New Orleans, 1929), 1; Deiler, *Zur Geschichte der deutschen Kirchengemeinden*, 50, 85-88; New Orleans *Daily Picayune*, October 10, 1890; Rightor (ed.), *Standard History of New Orleans*, 502. Voss was born in Schleswig-Holstein, Germany, on March 7, 1856. In 1879, he graduated from the German Theological Seminary of Newark, New Jersey. He became pastor of the First German Presbyterian Church of New Orleans in October, 1880. He is the author of *The Beginnings of Presbyterianism in the Southwest, Louisiana's Invitation to German Settlers*, and *History of the German Society. Souvenir of the Eightieth Anniversary of the German Society*, 13.

[2] Deiler, *Zur Geschichte der deutschen Kirchengemeinden*, 97-8; *Celebrating the Seventy-fifth Anniversary-1863-1938* (New Orleans,1938),n.p.; Louis Voss,*Presbyteria-

In 1877, a number of the Milan Evangelical Church withdrew and organized a separate unit under the leadership of Owen Riedy. At the same time, the group joined the Northern Presbyterium. By 1880, the congregation took the name of Immanuel Presbyterian Church and purchased a suitable building for worship on Camp and Soniat Streets. It continued to serve a number of German people throughout the remaining years of the century. [1]

After the founding of the First German Methodist Church in 1840, Germans in the City of Carrollton organized a Methodist congregation during February, 1845, being ably led by N. Brickwaedel. The very next year the members received two building lots from Isaac T. Preston "to be held in trust for the benefit of the Germans in Carrollton." [2] In spite of this generous gift, the church was not incorporated until 1853 and did not erect a building in the area of Jefferson, Fourth, Leonidas, and Plum Streets until 1859. Such a struggle seemed to foretell the eventual fate of this Methodist group for in 1883 it closed the door of the church structure and sold all the property to a Negro congregation. [3]

There were several other ventures to organize Methodist German churches. One of the older and more successful ones was the Soraparu German Methodist Church, located in the City of Lafayette and organized in 1853. The congregation weathered several serious splits which were caused by the break that came in the Methodist church between the North and the South. In 1893, however, the group discontinued its services and disbanded. Another effort which achieved success was the founding of Felicity Street German Methodist Church in 1868. By 1871, the group had erected a building on Loyola and Saint Andrew Streets, shifted its activities to that location, and continued its work well into the years of the twentieth century. In the populous Third District of the city several Methodist German churches were organized. Perhaps, one

---

nism in New Orleans and Adjacent Points (New Orleans, 1931), 354; Konrad, "The Diminishing Influences of German Culture," 25; Rightor (ed.), Standard History of New Orleans, 503. Koelle was born in Elberfeld, Germany, April 19, 1839. He came to New Orleans in 1868. In April 1869, he was called to the pastorate of the Second German Presbyterian Church (now Claiborne Avenue Presbyterian Church) corner Claiborne and Allen. He was organizer and first president of the Protestant Home for the Aged on Magazine and Eleanore Streets. He founded the Protestant Bethany Home on Claiborne and Allen. Souvenir of the Eightieth Anniversary of the German Society, 33.

[1] Konrad, "The Diminishing Influences of German Culture," 25-6.
[2] Deiler, Zur Geschichte der deutschen Kirchengemeinden, 48.
[3] Ibid.

of the more successful was the dissentient faction of the Burgundy Street group which in 1874 established the Third German Methodist Church on North Rampart Street between Press and Saint Ferdinand Streets. This congregation prospered at that location until 1900. [1]

There were never many Baptists among New Orleans Germans. An attempt was made to have a branch of the Coliseum Place Baptist Church in the Third District. A piece of property was bought on Spain Street, but late in 1872, the venture was discontinued. [2]

With the heavy immigration from Germany in the 1840's, Jews settled in the city in considerable numbers and in family groups. Their coming was a boon to the congregation Shaarei Chesed, or Gates of Mercy, which had been organized in 1828 on North Rampart Street. By 1849, two hundred German members were affiliated with the Jewish church. Since it was found impracticable to unite all Israelites of New Orleans in one congregation, another group with the Portuguese ritual organized on August 21, 1846, under the name of Nefutsoth Jehudah, or Dispersed of Judah. Both of these congregations were fortunate to enter synagogues in 1850, the latter receiving the building located on Canal and Bourbon Streets as an outright gift from Judah Touro. [3] Pursuing separate ways for thirty-two more years, Shaarei Chesed and Nefutsoth Jehudah finally merged in the year 1882 under the name of Touro Synagogue, which at the time had its house of worship on Carondelet Street. Under the dynamic leadership of Rabbi J. L. Leucht, who became the spiritual leader of this congregation, a most beautiful house of worship was erected on the corner of Saint Charles Avenue and Berlin Street in 1892. [4]

In the town of Lafayette, lying along the river between Felicity and Toledano Streets and extending back to the "woods," a number of Jews,

---

[1] Deiler, *Zur Geschichte der deutschen Kirchengemeinden*, 84-5, 112. Konrad, "The Diminishing Influences of German Culture," 27-8.

[2] Deiler, *Zur Geschichte der deutschen Kirchengemeinden*, 92.

[3] Nathaniel S. Share, *One Hundredth Anniversary of Congregation of Gates of Prayer* (New Orleans, 1950), n.p. Heller, *Jubilee Souvenir of Temple Sinai*, 5; interview with Rabbi Nathaniel S. Share, pastor of Gates of Prayer since 1934, May 28, 1954. Judah Touro was a successful merchant of New Orleans who was remembered for his many deeds of charity.

[4] Myers, *The Israelites of Louisiana*, 42; Share, *One Hundredth Anniversary of Gates of Prayer*, n.p. Leucht was born in Darmstadt, Hesse, Germany, on January 25, 1844. He came to the United States in 1864 and to New Orleans in 1868 as assistant to Gutheim. He was a member of the state school board for two terms, president of the prisons and asylum commission, president of Kingsley House, first vice-president of Touro Infirmary and the Jewish Orphan's Home. Myers, *The Israelites of Louisiana*, 43, 69.

mostly Alsatian Germans, settled. From the very first, these newcomers had to depend largely on their own resources for the satisfaction of their religious needs because of the difficulty of getting into New Orleans. By 1848, about forty families considered the purchase of ground for a synagogue. In the same year officers were elected and the German ritual adopted .After a series of vicissitudes the work of organization was completed with the founding of the Congregation Shaarei Tefiloh, or Gates of Prayer, of the City of Lafayette. A house believed to have been on Washington Avenue was rented for a synagogue. When repeated attempts to unite with the congregation Shaarei Chesed failed, Shaarei Tefiloh worked toward obtaining its own church building, which was accomplished in 1855, when a two-room frame house was purchased. Four years later, a building site on Jackson Avenue and Chippewa Street was obtained. While the civil conflict interferred with the plans, the desire to erect a new edifice did not die but culminated in the dedication of an attractive synagogue on April 5, 1867. [1]

Toward the end of the 1860's, the reform movement was beginning to make itself felt in both of the German-Jewish congregations, Touro and Shaarei Tefiloh. In the latter congregation, reform was by evolution instead of revolution; while in the former some thirty members became impatient with conservatism and seceded to form Temple Sinai as a reform congregation. Rabbi James K. Gutheim ,who had served Shaarei Chesed on two different occassion, assumed the ministerial responsibility of this newly-organized reform group. [2] Temple Sinai was the only representative of Reform Judaism in the city. [3]

Around 1875, when the second generation of former German immigrants had been greatly influenced by the predominant power of the English language and consequently saw no necessity in continuing to preserve the German tongue, all German-preaching congregations of the city felt the first impacts of the use of the English langage. Every church introduced services in which the English language was used exclusively, although the German language remained the official one of the pulpit, the classroom, and the meeting room. Wherever a congrega-

---

[1] Share, *One Hundredth Anniversary of Gates of Prayer*, n.p.

[2] *Ibid.*; Heller, *Jubilee Souvenir of Temple Sinai*, 49-52. Gutheim was born in 1817 at Menne, District of Wartburg, Westphalia, Germany. He was trained at the Teachers' Seminary in Muenster but never followed this profession. He came to the United States and New Orleans in 1849 to serve Shaarei Chesed.

[3] Myers, *The Israelites of Louisiana*. 43, 69.

tion was too stubborn to introduce services in English, it soon noticed a drop in membership or a wave of dissatisfaction, which in several instances led to splits and the organization of churches in which the English language was used exclusively. [1] Prophetical were the words of Louis Voss:

> In the absence of German immigration the time cannot be far distant when German preaching will no longer be necessary and our German churches will cease to be German speaking churches. This does not imply that in that event they will have outlived their usefulness and must cease altogether, but the only means to prevent their extinction is their transformation into English speaking churches. [2]

The German language, however, survived in a measure in the church and school until 1939. [3]

Practically every German church, regardless of its membership and wealth, supported its own school for a longer or shorter period of time. [4] Christian Sans, organizer of Saint Paul's school, was the first to launch an educational program for the children of his congregation. Taking note of this event, one of the newspapers commented:

> Our particular attention has lately been called to the efforts of the Reverend C. Sans, pastor of the German Church of this city, to promote the cause of religion and education among his countrymen around him. It is estimated that there are upwards of 14,000 Germans, forming a large class of our most industrious and intelligent citizens. Among these, Mr. Sans, by great labor and perseverance, has formed a church and a large congregation. He has established two large schools containing in all nearly three hundred scholars. One of these schools is in the second municipality, corner of Race and Constance Streets, the other in the third municipality in Moreau Street. In each of these schools several assistants are employed, and sixteen branches taught after the Pestalozzian and Prussian Systems. [5]

---

[1] Minutes of Zion Lutheran Church, July 5, October 4, 1875; Minutes of St. John Lutheran Church, January 2. 1882; Minutes of Salem Lutheran Church, 1880; a letter addressed to First English Lutheran Church by St. Paul Lutheran Church, 1890, in which it was stated that "services in the English language have been conducted at St. Paul for the last seven years." This letter is in the possession of Wegener's family in New Orleans; Rightor (ed.), *Standard History of New Orleans*, 503; Share, *One Hundredth Anniversary of Gates of Prayer*, n.p.

[2] Konrad, "The Diminishing Influences of German Culture," 28.

[3] Interview with G. M. Kramer, Lutheran pastor of New Orleans, who preached the last German sermon at Zion Lutheran Church in New Orleans on April 7, 1939, December 10, 1947. Preaching in the German language is occasionally heard in a New Orleans church today.

[4] Deiler, *Zur Geschichte der deutschen Kirchengemeinden*. Histories of various Catholic, Protestant, and Jewish churches of New Orleans.

[5] *Lafayette City Advertiser*, January 29, 1842.

The purpose of their existence was manifold. The Germans' cherished theory of education in the nineteenth century was to give attention both to the intellectual and to the spiritual training of children. This principle, therefore, became the desired objective of all instruction in their schools. A thorough knowledge of the tenets of Christianity and of the subject matter fields, such as reading, writing, arithmetic, spelling, grammar, geography, and United States history or natural history for each child was the burden of every teacher of these schools. In this manner, it was believed, a child would be an upright member of the church and a "useful citizen of the United States.[1]" It was erroneous to suppose that the prime purpose of these schools was to teach and thus preserve the mother tongue of their native land. Although this was in a great measure accomplished, the schools continued to exist even after English became the medium of instruction. [2]

Unpopularity of the public school system in the state throughout the days of Reconstruction was undoubtedly a contributing factor to the appearance of so many church schools. In 1870, almost no white children were attending the public school system, while the church schools were generally filled to overflowing. [3] But the church schools continued to exist even after the number of public schools in the state increased to 2,276 in the year 1889. About that time, nineteen private schools sponsored by churches and related agencies had an enrollment of 2,835 pupils.[4]

These prosperous days were short-lived for in the 1890's one church school after another closed its doors because of the scarcity of funds and the inability to match the progress of the public school system. Two of the German church groups, however, held on tenaciously with their school system, that of the Catholic and Lutheran churches, whose schools continued in operation throughout the remaining years of the old century and into the days of the new. [5]

---

[1] L. Schweickhardt, *History of Saint Matthew Evangelical Church* (New Orleans, 1924), 29.

[2] Philip Vollmer, "What Germans Have Contributed to Our National Life," *Eightieth Anniversary of the German Society*, 42, 44.

[3] Richard Lineberger, *Zion Lutheran Church Centennial, 1847-1947* (New Orleans, 1947), n.p.; *Souvenir of the Diamond Jubilee of the St. John's Evangelical Lutheran Congregation, New Orleans, La.* (New Orleans, 1927), 7-8.

[4] "The History of Education in Louisiana," *United States Bureau of Education* (Washington, 1898), 107-09.

[5] Konrad, The Diminishing Influences of German Culture," 36; Hoffman, "German Education in Louisiana," 29-30. Catholic and Lutheran parochial schools are in operation in New Orleans.

Private schools were also conducted by individuals and secular organizations. One of the most successful private schools which had even more than a city-wide reputation was founded by John and Jacob Ueber. In 1850, after having taught for ten years in the city, these two brothers started their private school on North Rampart Street between Port and Saint Ferdinand Streets and for fifty-one years served as teachers for thousands of New Orleans children. The famous school differed from most in having no summer vacation. Except for the customary holidays, it continued the year round and at times had more students in the summer than in the winter. This was particularly true during the Civil War, when Federal authorities sought to intimidate the two brothers and demanded the teaching of Union songs in the school. The brothers replied that the only songs they would teach were Sunday School songs, and that they were rebels to the core. No effort was made to molest the school. At the time of Butler's authority in New Orleans, the Ueber school was crowded beyond its capacity, the attendance on one day, by actual count, reaching two hundred and seventy-nine. The average daily attendance during the winter was one hundred and fifty and during the summer seventy-five .Unlike other schools, the charges were not graded according to the classes but in consideration of the circumstances of the family. When the Ueber brothers celebrated their fiftieth anniversary of teaching in the year 1890, they had taught more than 3,000 pupils, of whom the greater number were of Teutonic origin. Among these were some who became prominent citizens of New Orleans, as, Captain Gustave Gersdorff, who became a well known bar pilot, L. A. Wiltz, one time governor of Louisiana, Professor Henry E. Chambers, Albert Winterhalder, manager of the *Times Democrat*, Ferdinand Dudenhefer, R. J. Whann, the Blum brothers, and many others. [1]

Another well known private school was conducted by the Turn-Verein of the city. [2] This school, known as the *Turn Schule*, was opened to some of the members and during the summer only gymnastics were taught.

---

[1] New Orleans *Daily Picayune*, March 22, 1906; Hoffman, "German Education in Louisiana," 47-8.

[2] The first Turngemeinde in the United States was organized in Cincinnati in October, 1848. In theory, the Turner endeavored to educate men physically, ethically, intellectually, and culturally. Their goal was more a "refined humanity" and their leaders regarded their organization as a vital education force for progress in culture and freedom and good citizenship. Much money went into libraries, singing societies, debating clubs, lectures, and dramatic performances. Wittke, *Refugees of the Revolution*, 148, 152.

During the winter, however, the course included foreign languages, history, mathematics, and singing. [1]

Textbooks used in the German schools were similar to those used in all public schools; and, although most of the German boys and girls in those days did not go any further than grammar school, those who wished to do so were prepared to enter the high schools and academies maintained by public tax funds or by the Catholic Diocese of Louisiana. [2] Public high schools were few and far between in the days of the nineteenth century. Only McDonogh High School and two high schools for girls under the direction of a Mrs. Lusher and Miss Marion Brown were included in the public school system. [3] The Catholic Church, however, maintained a very strong system of girls' academies and boys' high schools. Students of all denominations were welcomed, and many non-Catholics attended. [4]

Discipline was quite severe in the schools of that day. It was said of John Ueber that "he wielded the rod over unruly boys, taught sweet little girls their alphabet, coerced or persuaded boys to study and learn." [5] Nevertheless, the schools were looked upon with great pride not only by the Germans themselves but by all the citizens of New Orleans.

The non-Catholic Germans of the city responded enthusiastically to the American craze for lodges and secret societies. Among the more

---

[1] Laguaites, "The German Element in New Orleans", 33.

[2] Hoffman, "German Education in Louisiana," 32.

[3] Rightor (ed.), *Standard History of New Orleans*, 242.

[4] Roger Baudier, *Catholic History Collection*, files on Catholic Education in Louisiana. Replies to questionnaires by Religious Teaching Congregations, notes from Annals of Religious Congregations. Mr. Baudier stated that there were eleven girls' academies in New Orleans during the nineteenth century. The better known boys' schools were: College of the Immaculate Conception by the Jesuit Fathers, St. Aloysius College by the Brothers of the Sacred Heart, St. Mary's College of the Christian Brothers, 1851-1875, and Holy Cross College by the Congregation of the Holy Cross in 1878. "1954 Annual Catholic Directory," *Catholic Action of the South*, p. 32; *A Century of Service for the Sacred Heart in the United States, 1847-1947* (Brothers of Sacred Heart, 1946), n.p.; Angelus Gabriel, *The Christian Brothers in the United States* (New York, 1948), 472-73.

[5] New Orleans *Daily Picayune*, September 22, 1901; March 22, 1906. A. L. Rau, speaking of S. Speicher, teacher of the Evangelical church on Milan Street, says: "As a disciplinarian he was almost unequaled. The writer remembers distinctly the first Monday he made his appearance at school, and the fact that when he returned after his noon lunch, he had availed himself of the opportunity to purchase a good strong cowhide of which he made abundant use, as a number of scholars who read this can no doubt testify," A. L. Rau, *Some Interesting Facts Gathered from the Early Records of Our Church, The Echo* (n.p., 1904), 1.

successful German secret orders was the "Order of the Druids." It was founded in England in 1781 and introduced into the United States in 1832 but did not get well underway until 1839. The Order was a moral, social, and beneficial society. Its objects were to unite men together, irrespective of nationality, tongue or creed, for mutual protection and improvement; to assist socially and materially by timely counsel and instructive lessons; by encouragement in business and assistance to obtain employment for those in need; and to foster among its members the spirit of fraternity and good fellowship. [1] In 1856, the Magnolia *Hain* received its charter from the National *Hain* of the United States, bringing the first German Druid grove to the city. [2]

In quick succession came the formation of three more German groves, the Oak *Hain* Two and the Goethe *Hain* Four, both established in 1857, and the Mispel *Hain* Six, in 1859. Not until 1872 came the founding of the fifth Druid grove, the Louisiana *Hain* Thirteen. These five groves of Druids existed until 1880, during which time they enjoyed prosperous days. After this time, however, because of the decline in German immigration to the South, the membership of these organizations dwindled and consolidations became the order of the day. The Magnolia, Oak, and Goethe merged to form the Concordia *Hain* One, which continued until 1901, when it was forced to consolidate with the Louisiana *Hain* Thirteen. Through the remainder of the century, the Louisiana *Hain* Thirteen and the Louisiana Mispel *Hain* Six served those Germans of the City who desired to be affiliated with a Druid order. The motto of this society was appealing to the German mind for it called for "Unity, Peace, and Good Will." [3]

The work of the Masons was likewise attractive to the German immigrant of the city. As early as 1853, two German lodges of this secret organization were in existence, the Germania Lodge Twenty-Nine and the Germania Lodge Forty-Six. These two functioned separately until March 12, 1882, when a merger took place forming the Germania Free Mason Society. The first officers were J. H. Koehn, president; John Runte, vice-president; Philip Pfeffer, secretary; and J. G. Abry, treasurer. The purpose of the society was to help those in need and to offer a social opportunity for its members. Every German-speaking Free Mason

---

[1] *The Encyclopedia Americana* (New York, 1953), IX, 351.

[2] The English translation of the word *Hain* is Grove. This was the official name given each Druid group.

[3] *Program of the Third German Day*, n.p.

could become a member. The hall on Saint Louis Street, which had been the property of Germania Lodge Forty-Six, was used by the new order. In spite of the group's ups and downs, its headquarters was a regular rendezvous for Germans throughout the last decades of the century. [1]

Many other lodges existed among the Germans, particularly during the years before the 1880's. [2] Their purpose was to give aid to those in need, especially those who were members. To accomplish this end, most of these orders bought burial plots where their deceased members were placed at rest, paid funeral expenses, and gave a small insurance to the deceased member's closest kin. [3] This service, which was highly beneficial to many Germans because of their meager incomes, proved the very feature which not only insured the life of these societies but caused them to multiply even after the decrease of German immigration to New Orleans had set in. By 1897, more than twenty-five of such bene-volent associations were in existence and most of them were in very good condition as to membership and finances. [4]

Deeds of mercy were common among the New Orleans' Germans. [5] These were done for friend and foe alike, but especially for the unfortunate, the orphans, and the aged. The first German orphanage was founded in 1854. On the Feast of the Most Holy Redeemer, the cornerstone of Saint Joseph German Orphan Asylum was laid, and on December 28, its doors were opened. Ever since its beginning, the orphanage has annual-ly taken care of two hundred to three hundred children who, under the fostering care of the good Sisters, have been very happy and content. [6]

During the hectic days of Reconstruction, the Germans of the city organized two more orphanages which rendered great service throughout the remainder of the century. These were the German Protestant Orphan Home and the Bethlehem Lutheran Orphan Asylum. The spirit behind the founding of the former was Pastor Ludwig P. Heintz, minister of Jackson Avenue Evangelical Church. In the year 1866, Heintz had thirty-one orphans in a confirmation class of one hundred and fifteen. On Good

[1] New Orleans *Deutsche Zeitung*, May 26, 1853; *Program of the Third German Day*, n.p.

[2] New Orleans *Deutsche Zeitung*, May 26, 27, 1853; January 8, 1854.

[3] Minutes of the *Deutscher Verein Zweiter Distrikt*, August 3, 1884; *Program of the Third German Day*, n.p.

[4] *Program of the Franz Schubert Festival* (New Orleans, 1897), n.p.

[5] Deiler, *Geschichte der deutschen Gesellschaft*, 72-3.

[6] Krieger, *Seventy-Five Years of Service*, 47.

Friday of that year, he closed his sermon with the words: "Next year we must have an orphan home." [1] Consequently, a meeting was held on November 4, at which time those present elected the first directory of the home. [2]

This venture of mercy made rapid progress. After a sum of $ 4,000.00 was raised, it was decided to purchase a plot of ground on State Street at the cost of $ 18,000.00. The additional sum needed to purchase the lot was soon gathered and a building program was undertaken. While the building was in progress, additional ground was purchased for the sum of $ 5,000.00. There was great rejoicing on June 2, 1867, when the dedication rites of the ground and buildings were solemnized. At that time the organization had about four hundred active contributing members. Another wing was added to the building in 1869, and already in 1870, president Del Bondio was able to announce to the general assembly that the organization was debt free.

On January 16, 1871, the ladies auxiliary of the home was founded. The first officers were Wilhelmina Jackson, president; Dora Clerc, assistant chairman; Fannie Strohmeier, secretary; and Christine Kuhlmann, treasurer. With the help of the ladies the first general benefit for the home was scheduled and successfully carried out in the summer of 1847 at the New Orleans Fair Grounds. This event was the forerunner of annual benefit Volksfests which brought profit to the home and a good time to all who attended. After 1899, these affairs were held on the grounds of the home. Over the many years the home cared annually for seventy to one hundred children aged from one to sixteen years. [3]

Organizing an orphan home among the German Lutherans was the dream of the Reverend C. G. Moedinger, pastor of the Deutsche Orthodoxe Kirche. In 1866, a society for the support of needy orphans was organized. This association interested itself in the care of orphans, finding homes for them and supplying the needs for their physical well-

---

[1] *Program of the Third German Day*, n.p.

[2] Members of the first directory were: Jacob Nussloch, Jacob Hassinger, Fredrich Del Bondio, H. F. Stuerken, G. L. L. Mayer, F. Rickert, H. Zuberbier, George Strohmeier, H. F. Klump, J. G. Haas, G. Hufft, H. R. Gogreve, G. Spitzfaden, F. W. Haussler, T. Schorr, A. Bohne, Leon von Zinken, T. Pelle, N. Mueller, G. Gemming, A. Winkelmann, A. Goldmann, and C. Bornwasser. The first officers were: F. Del Bondio, president; F. Rickert, first vice -president; H. Zuberbier, second vice-president; G. Strohmeier, first secretary; H. F. Klumpp, second secretary; and J. G. Haas, treasurer.

[3] *Program of the Third German Day*, n.p.

being. The effort to secure a site for the building of its own home, however, was not successful. Seventeen years were to pass and two other German Lutheran churches were to join hands with the members of the Deutsche Orthodoxe Kirche, then known as Saint Paul Lutheran, before an old time, but well-preserved plantation house, a one story frame structure resting on brick pillars, located on the river front of the Mississippi river, became the Bethlehem Lutheran Orphan Asylum. [1] On November 15, 1881, Saint John and Zion congregations joined the Bethlehem Orphan Asylum Association, which had been incorporated by Saint Paul in June of that year; and with united action, the Association purchased the property for a home in 1883. [2] Since that time eight hundred orphans have been harbored in the safe retreat of "Bethlehem." [3]

While Germans of Catholic and Protestant faiths were erecting institutions of mercy through joint efforts of their churches, the German Jews were just as active and just as successful. November 25, 1854, was an epochal date for the Hebrew Benevolent Society. Under the leadership of J. K. Gutheim, rabbi, and Joseph Simon, president, a decision was reached at a mass meeting held in the Masonic Hall to create a home for widows and orphans. The following year the cornerstone was laid, and on January 8, 1856, the dedication took place. [4] The home was a blessing to many widows and orphans, and by 1886, it was found necessary to build a larger and more serviceable home. This new Jewish Orphan Home was built on Saint Charles Avenue and Peters Street. [5]

Two German Protestant Homes for the old and crippled were founded during the 1880's. Both of them were the results of the dynamic leadership of the Reverend F. Otto Koelle, pastor of the Second German Presbyterian Church. The first of these was organized in 1885, with Koelle assuming the presidency of the institution located on Magazine Street between State and Eleanore Streets. The work was supported by voluntary offerings and gifts, together with annual festivals which always netted good financial returns. [6]

[1] *Golden Anniversary-A Memorial of Fifty Years of Labor of Love-at Bethlehem Orphan Asylum, New Orleans, Louisiana* (New Orleans, 1931), 11.
[2] *Ibid.* The "Home" was bounded by North Peters, Flood, Andry, and Douglas Streets.
[3] Records of Admission, Bethlehem Orphan Asylum, New Orleans, Louisiana, 1883-1952.
[4] Heller, *Jubilee Souvenir of Temple Sinai*, 8.
[5] Myers, *The Israelites of Louisiana*, 50.
[6] Deiler, *Zur Geschichte der deutschen Kirchengemeinden*, 99; *New Orleanser Deutsche Zeitung*, May 24, 1898; New Orleans *Daily Picayune*, October 26, 1890.

The second institution for the care of the old and crippled resulted after Koelle withdrew his active interest in the home on Magazine Street. Seeing the need for administering to the poor and sick of his congregation in the downtown area of the city, he inspired the women of the church to do something about it. Consequently, on February 28, 1889, the women of the Second German Presbyterian Church conceived the idea of organizing a deaconess society to help with the poor and sick and to assist in spiritual work as well. As this work progressed, it was discovered that the greatest need was for a place to shelter the homeless and helpless aged Protestants. It was decided to expand the work and establish an institution dedicated to this purpose. On November 1, of the same year, the deaconess society developed into the German Bethany Home Society, and a piece of property on North Claiborne and Allen Streets was acquired for the sum of $ 4,500,00. The next year, 1890, the "home" was opened with five inmates. Under the loving solicitude of the members of the deaconess society, especially of the wife of the pastor of the congregation, the "home" prospered so that need for expansion was felt at the turn of the century. [1]

The Germans of New Orleans manifested their love for charity not only through the agency of their churches. During the turbulent days of the Civil War the Germans contributed through their various societies, such as the theater and the German Society, thousands of dollars for the relief and support of New Orleanian Confederate families. [2] This kind of activity continued throughout the decades as the many German benevolent and singing societies participated in innumerable benefits for charities and other worthy causes. [3]

A living monument to the Germans' sympathy for mankind's suffering was the work and labor which have gone into the building of one of the great hospitals of the city ,Touro Infirmary. This institution began operating as a charitable agency in May, 1854, in accordance with the will of Judah Touro, in the building located at the corner of Gaiennie and Celeste

---

[1] Louis Voss, *Presbyterianism in New Orleans and Adjacent Points*, 358; *Celebrating the Golden Anniversary of the Protestant Bethany Home* (n.p., n.d.), n.p.

[2] Robert T. Clark, Jr., "The New Orleans German Colony in the Civil War", *loc. cit.*, XX (1937), 1000. The German Society contributed $ 7,469.30 at one time, the proceeds of a huge Volksfest, while the city government voted only $ 2,000.00 to the support of families of Orleanians in the Confederate service.

[3] Minutes of the German *Liedertafel*, April 3, 1882; Minutes of the German *Quartette Club*, February 3, May 2, 1889, March 9, 1900.

Streets. [1] By 1880, Julius Weiss, then president of the Infirmary, saw the need for expansion; and with the ardent support of Doctor Frederick Loeber, who had been the house surgeon since 1869, had erected a new building on Prytania Street, the present site of the hospital. [2] This institution offered many Germans, particularly those of the Jewish faith, an opportunity to care for the sick. It was here that both Doctor Loeber and Doctor William Kohlman made outstanding records as surgeons and administrators which have lived in the memory of many New Orleanians. [3]

It was through church, school, lodge, and eleemosynary institution that the Germans of the city not only preserved their religious and cultural heritage but also contributed to the development of the ideals of the metropolis of the deep South. These ideals continued to live in the lives of many to come.

---

[1] John Nash, "Brief History of Touro Infirmary," (New Orleans, 1954), in possession of Dr. John MacKenzie, director of the hospital. Judah Touro was the individual who in 1840 donated $ 10,000.00 to complete the building of the Bunker Hill Monument and in his will left a sum of money to start the work of the Touro Infirmary. A typed copy of an article on the life of Judah Touro taken from Number 13 of the American Jewish Historical Society, in the private files of Dr. MacKenzie.

[2] M. J. Magruder, "Some Incidents in Connection with the Early History of Touro Infirmary," (New Orleans, 1936), in private file of Dr. MacKenzie, director of Touro Infirmary.

[3] Letter of A. J. Hockett to Mr. Thomas Ewing Dabney, November 30, 1936. In the private file of Dr. MacKenzie. Dr. William Kohlmann was born in Germany, June 6, 1863. In 1897, he became resident surgeon at Touro and then surgeon-in-chief until 1906. Fortier, *Louisiana*, III, 236.

CHAPTER VI

THE NEW ORLEANS GERMAN AND HIS THEATER, MUSIC, AND SONG

The Germans' attitude toward the legitimate stage was aptly expressed in an editorial of the *Deutsche Zeitung* which appeared on January 25, 1851:

> A theatre, when it is ably led, furnishes not only many pleasurable hours, but carries also the picture of the heart and spirit; with a word, it is a school for the people. [2]

To establish this folk institution among the Germans of New Orleans, a theater was built on Magazine Street near Delord Street in the year 1839, for the express purpose of offering German plays. Here the German drama was introduced on December 22 of the same year. [2] Announcing the opening of the theater, the *Daily Picayune* reported.:

> This new and handsome theater will open for the season on Sunday next 22nd instant, with a prologue, a favorite drama of Theodor Koerner, and an afterpiece by Kotzebue.

> A strong and effective company and an orchestra of well known artists have been engaged .... The manager has spared neither pain nor expense to render this theater worthy of the patronage of the German and American public in general. [3]

The theater was under the management of Felix Maxon. At first, performances were given twice a week, but audiences were small and the enterprise was soon abandoned. [4] In spite of the decided slump in the number of presentations of the German theater performances during the 1840's, as far as can be ascertained, New Orleans was the first city in the United States to have a presentation of "Faust" in the German language. New York, Philadelphia, Saint Louis, Milwaukee, Davenport, and Chicago, all of which were in the main circuit of tours made by traveling actors and actresses, showed no record of a "Faust" performance in the German

---

[1] New Orleans *Deutsche Zeitung*, January 25, 1851.
[2] Laguaites, "The German Element in New Orleans," 45.
[3] New Orleans *Daily Picayune*, December 15, 1839.
[4] J. S. Kendall, *The Golden Age of New Orleans Theater*, 600.

language earlier than the New Orleans showing, which was January 11, 1845. [1]

The fifties represented one of the most cultural periods of New Orleans German stage history. The quality of the plays and of the performers was outstanding. The Thielmanns, included among the country's best actors, came to New Orleans on their water-route circuit in 1851 and gave thirty-one performances. In 1853, the German Dilletanten Verein, a society of accomplished young Germans of the city, was active under the leadership of J. C. Meyer. [2] Then with the return of W. C. Adlersberg and his company from Cincinnati in 1854, having been in New Orleans during the slack season of the late 1840's, the German theater enjoyed a long and noteworthy season. [3] At that time the *True Delta*, a New Orleans newspaper, wrote:

> We have wondered why the large and respectable German population of this city did not fix up a theater where they might occasionally spend an agreeable evening during the winter months in hearing the best plays of German writers in a language perfectly familiar to them. Many attempts have been made for several years to introduce the German drama into our city but, until recently, without success. Whether the want of success was owing to a lack of artistic material or bad management or persons having control of matters, we are not prepared to say. We do know, however, that the intelligent sons and daughters of old Germania are excellent critics of matters appertaining to the German stage; and, while true merit receives from them all due praise, no person unworthy of applause receives it from them. We have now, however, a German theatre in our city which promises to be permanent, ably conducted and [a] successful place of amusement for such of our citizens as are able to appreciate the masterly productions of Schiller, Goethe, and other distinguished German writers in their own language. [4]

German plays presented during the course of the 1854-55 theatrical season included "Das Bemooste Haupt," Gutzkow's "Zopf und Schwert," and Schiller's "Die Räuber," "Wilhelm Tell," "Wallenstein's Tod," "Maria Stuart," "Die Karlsschüler," "Jungfrau von Orleans," and "Kabale und Liebe." [5]

---

[1] Arthur H. Moehlenbrock, "The German Drama on the New Orleans Stage," *Louisiana Historical Quarterly*, XXVI (1943), 382-83; Laguaites, "The German Element in New Orleans," 46-7.

[2] New Orleans *Deutsche Zeitung*, October 23, 1853; January 31, 1854.

[3] Laguaites, "The German Element in New Orleans," 47.

[4] New Orleans *True Delta*, October 28, 1854.

[5] New Orleans *Taegliche Deutsche Zeitung*, October 17, November 28, 29, and December 23, 1854; January 7, 16, and February 20, 1855.

In April, 1855, the German theater building burnt down. [1] Although another one was built in 1865 in the City of Lafayette, the "Deutsches Theater" in the meantime referred not to buildings but to the productions themselves which were offered in nearly all the theaters in the city at various times. The troupes gave their plays in whatever theater or hall they were able to rent. Consequently, advertisements for the German theater read, "Deutsches Theater in der neuen Saint Charles Opera Hall, Saint Charles strasse gegenueber Union." [2] Among the buildings leased regularly after 1855 were the "Turn-Halle," "American,""Pelican," "Orleans Ball-room," and the "Gaiety," with occasional presentations in a ball-room in Lafayette. [3] Later on, performances were staged in the "New American Theater Building," "Saint Charles Theater," "Placide," "Armory Hall" on Camp Street, "Deutsches Theater" (formerly the Concert-Hall) on Poydras Street, "Orleans," "Deutsches National Theater" at the corner of Saint Peter and Saint Claude Streets, and the "New Opera House" on Bourbon Street between Saint Louis and Toulouse. [4]

Professional performances were not the only offerings of the New Orleans German theater. The Liebhaber Theater and the Deutsche Philodramatische Gesellschaft were two of the more important amateur dramatic organizations. The former was organized in 1855, and the latter some time in 1857. Although their life span was ephemeral, these local societies sponsored appearances of guest actors and were very popular with the public. The repertory of the amateur theater was broad enough to include the favorites, "Die Räuber" and "Wilhelm Tell," and other plays of Germany's classical period of literature, as well as more recent works, both good and bad. To be sure, no theater could exist which gave only high and serious drama, and the largest part of any German-American theatrical repertory was necessarily composed of "potboilers," the farces of Kotzebue and comedies of Koerner. But when any company decided to perform a really great work, its liberal politics determined the choice with rare exceptions. Later dramatists of such high caliber as Kleist appeared only seldom, and one play of Grillparzer was performed from 1840 to 1860. [5]

---

[1] *Ibid.*, April 21, 1855.
[2] Konrad, "The Diminishing Influences of German Culture," 40.
[3] Laguaites, "The German Element in New Orleans," 52.
[4] Moehlenbrock, "The German Drama on the New Orleans Stage," *loc. cit.*, XXVI (1943), 375.
[5] Robert T. Clark, Jr., "The German Liberals in New Orleans," *loc. cit.*, XX (1937), 150.

According to the press, the middle fifties constituted the richest period of New Orleans' response to Schiller, whose dramas both preceded and outnumbered those of any other dramatist of literary merit whose plays were presented in the Crescent City. There were several reasons for this. The German Society of the city, organized in 1847, was building up a strong German consciousness, while the fifties experienced the greatest influx of immigrants from Germany. Added to this, New Orleans was prosperous for the time being and was hostess to a moneyed leisure class who came South to spend the winter. [1]

In the early years of the Civil War era other theaters had to cease operations, but the German stage continued to furnish entertainment for their own and other nationalities as well, even though many of the performances were of amateur quality. [2] The farces of Kotzebue, the comedies of Bendix, and the popular "lumpazi-Vagabunden" of Nestroy, with an occasional adventure into higher dramatic form, delighted the audiences. One performance of Goethe's "Faust" was staged, which, however, was bitterly criticized by the *Deutsche Zeitung* as an "unbearable travesty on the greatest German classic." [3] By 1865, activity in the theater increased again. In that year, some forty-one German plays were given. The upward trend continued, reaching its high water mark in the number of plays presented in the period from 1869 to 1871. One hundred and ninety-seven plays were staged during this period, and the New Orleans German theater was visited by one of the most famous actresses of the times, Fanny Janauscheck, who played with her troupe at the "Saint Charles Theater." One factor which may have attributed to the appearance of these many plays, particularly in 1871, when one hundred and twenty-eight different performances were given, was that by that time the news had reached the city of the defeat of the French and the founding of the German Empire. The popularity of the theater at this time did not, however, develop a richer quality in the plays presented. In fact, most of the plays were new in the sense that they had never been performed in the city; and the great number of plays resulted in the importation

---

[1] Moehlenbrock, "The German Drama on the New Orleans Stage," *loc. cit.*, XXVI (1943), 378-79.

[2] *Ibid.*, 374.

[3] Robert T. Clark, Jr., "The New Orleans German Colony in the Civil War," *loc. cit.*, XX (1937), 1006.

of many theatrical pieces by authors who had very little or no importance in the interpretation of culture. [1]

After 1871, the number of plays steadily decreased. In 1874, no plays were given except an opera and Schiller's "Wilhelm Tell." A number of interested Germans tried desperately to keep the professional stage alive but it never again achieved its earlier popularity. Although fifty-nine plays were given in 1878, each year thereafter very few were presented. From 1879 through 1890, the last year of the German theater in New Orleans, from none to eight plays were given annually. [2]

From 1871 it was evident that the German theater was dying. Besides the importation of a host of theatrical pieces from authors of very little or no importance, which hurt the cultural aspect of the theater, two other factors contributed to the death of the professional German stage in New Orleans. By the 1870's, a second and third generation of former German immigrants had been born and reared in the United States. These German-Americans did not possess the interest in the German culture and language as did their parents and grandparents, and therefore failed to support the German theater, preferring the staging of plays in the English language. [3] Perhaps, this shift of cultural interest was the most vital reason for the gradual disappearance of the German theater. Finally, the presence of too many musical comedies, thoroughly frivolous in nature, was not appealing to the German people of the city as a whole and therefore did not win their approval and support. [4]

The New Orleans German theater enjoyed the talents of the best actors whom the country could afford. Men and women who went on the

---

[1] Moehlenbrock "The German Drama on the New Orleans Stage," loc. cit., XXVI (1943), 374; Konrad, "The Diminishing Influences of German Culture " 41-2.

[2] Konrad, "The Diminishing Influences of German Culture " 41-2. German theater table of plays and the year.

1870	69	1878	59	1886	1
1871	128	1879	0	1887	3
1872	96	1880	0	1888	6
1873	68	1881	1	1889	7
1874	1	1882	1	1890	6
1875	16	1883	0		
1876	1	1884	8		
1877	40	1885	3		

[3] The same tendency was manifested in the German churches of the city which were experiencing a shift from the use of the German language to that of the English at this time.

[4] Moehlenbrock, "The German Drama on the New Orleans Stage," loc. cit., XXVI (1943), 374.

boards of the city's stages had performed in Vienna, Berlin, Prague, Munich, and other European cities, as well as New York, Cincinnati, Louisville, Saint Louis, and other cities in the United States. There were Felix Maxon, Adolph Icks, Julius Boetzow, Wetzlau Bidwell, Rudolph Riese, Madame Thielemann, Carl Ritter, Carl Stein, Otto Hayn from New York, Mollie Ziegler, Fräulein Touche, Minna Roth, Elizabeth von Stamwitz, and Fanny Janauscheck, "Queen of the German stage, supported by a company engaged by her in Europe," to mention only a few. [1]

The Germans of the city supported the theater movement with spirit and effort. A newspaper of the time reported:

> The Germans love the dramatic art, and when we attend the French or English Theatre, we find the house filled more with Germans than with American and French, although there is a foreign language spoken. [2]

Going to the theater was a gala occasion and affair for them. It offered a fine cultural experience and at the same time a social one since a regular feature of nearly every theater performance was the giving of a ball, which followed immediately after the stage play. It also gave an opportunity to satisfy the longing for *Gemütlichkeit*, for many of the theaters featured a bar and restaurant offering additional opportunity for relaxation and enjoyment. [3]

Support of the theater movement did not wane with the decline and ultimate disappearance of the professional stage in the city. In 1872, when the professional theater was at a low ebb, a group of spirited Germans organized the Dramatische Gesellschaft, an amateur theatrical group which sponsored plays in various theaters throughout the city. From that time on, other German cultural societies gave attention to the theatrical arts transferring the interest from the professional theater, which was being Americanized more and more, to the amateur theater which continued to live throughout the remaining decades of the century in the schools, churches, and cultural societies of the German people within the city. [4]

---

[1] *Ibid.*, 375-76.

[2] New Orleans *Deutsche Zeitung*, October 28, 1853.

[3] Laguaites, "The German Element in New Orleans," 56.

[4] Konrad, "The Diminishing Influences of German Culture," 42; *Program of the Third German Day*, n.p.; New Orleans *Taegliche Deutsche Zeitung*, February 13, 1884; February 19, 1888.

Centers of the amateur theater were concentrated in German clubs and schools, as the Turn-Verein, of which there were three associated in the city; the Frohsinn, a German singing society; Holy Trinity and Saint Mary's Catholic schools; and similar organizations and groups.[1] All of these supported amateur theatricals which developed the dramatic abilities of their members and furnished many an evening of delightful entertainment. Of special note in this effort were the German schools. Regular entertainments were given in which the German drama and song were featured so that the rising generation might become better acquainted with the German culture and the elders might be thoroughly entertained by them. [2]

One of the many German organizations which sponsored the German amateur theater with much enthusiasm was the Deutsche Company, a group of Jewish gentlemen, who organized themselves under the leadership of Solomon Marx in the early 1860's. The interest and purpose of this company was to foster sociability, patronize science and art, and promote fellowship. Especially active was the dramatic section of this group for the elders readily recalled in the 1890's the production of "Still Water Runs Deep," and Taylor's brilliant comedy, "Sweethearts and Wives," besides many other German comedies. [3] In this manner the Germans' love for the theater was satisfied and the art not entirely lost when, after 1871, the professional German theater began to wane and finally enter complete darkness.

Through the work of the amateur German theater sponsored by clubs, groups, fraternities, and schools, many an individual developed his

---

[1] *New Orleanser Deutsche Zeitung*, December 22, 1898; New Orleans *Taegliche Deutsche Zeitung*, February 19, 1888; New Orleans *Daily Picayune*, July 17 and 28, 1884; Laguaites, "The German Element in New Orleans," 59.

[2] The Turn-Verein halls were equipped with large stages utilized each Sunday for the production of amateur plays. A typical program of a German school during this period was the one offered by the pupils of Holy Trinity School on Royal and Saint Ferdinand Streets.

"Der kleine Rekrut," German song by chorus
"Ich bin ein Musikant," German song by chorus
"Der Schleifstein," a German drama
"So leb denn wohl du stilles Haus," German song by chorus
"Handy Andy," an Ethiopian drama
"My Little Mule and I," comic song by chorus
"Wanted a Male Cook," an English drama
"Grandfather's Clock," song by chorus. New Orleans *Daily Picayune*, July 28, 1884.

[3] Myers, *The Israelites of Louisiana*, 60-1.

talents in the art of speaking and acting. One of these amateur actors was Charles F. Buck, an eminent German citizən of the city, who, coming out of the ranks of the amateur German theater, made a name for himself in the amateur American dramatic societies and for a time enjoyed a brief career as a professional actor. [1] In the decade of the 1870's amateur dramatics had an extensive vogue in New Orleans among all, and a number of clubs featuring English plays were formed. Among these were the Shakespeare, Orleans Dramatics, the Histrionic, and the Varieties. These clubs secured the services of a leading professional actress and the members formed the remaining personnel of the companies. Buck was a member of two or more of these organizations and was usually the leading male actor in the performances which were given at the Varieties, later the Grand Opera House. He made an excellent Hamlet, Lear, or Iago, as well as other Shakespearean characters. As a Shakespearean scholar he was perhaps unsurpassed by any man in the South. He had a perfect command of French and German as well as English, and on one occasion he translated the German play, "Narciss," or "The Last Days of Pompadour," into English for the purpose of staging it by members of his dramatic society. [2]

The greatest and most important culture element fostered by the Germans of the city, however, was their love for music. A community's real love for it was not measured by its attendance at the concerts of world famed artists but by the musical activities in which the people themselves took part. The city which had its own choruses, its string quartette, its conservatory, or its orchestra was the city where the art really was appreciated. Such was the city of New Orleans, and much of its reputation in this respect was due to the Germans who lived there and fostered musical activities. [3]

The German's love for song and joy of living was expressed in his

[1] Interview with Ida Buck Henrigues, August 26, 1953. Mrs. Henrigues, daughter of Charles F. Buck, resided in New Orleans.

[2] New Orleans *Times Picayune*, January 20, 1918; interview with Ida Buck Henrigues, August 26, 1953. Prominent places of amusement in New Orleans, where German theater performances were offered were: The Academy of Music, St. Charles opposite Perdido Street; French Opera House, Bourbon and St. Louis Streets; Grand Opera House, Canal near Dauphine Street; Grunewald Hall, Baronne near Canal Street; St. Charles Theater, near The Academy of Music; and Werlein Hall, Baronne corner Perdido Street. Fountain and Christian, *Railway Guide to the City of New Orleans and Its Suburbs* (New Orleans, 1884), 33; New Orleans *Item* June 10, 1952.

[3] Faust, "Influences in American Life," *loc. cit.*, (1928), 14; Du Bois, *Germans in American Life*, 164-65.

particular singing club, of which there were a number formed in the city. [1]
The first of these came into existence with the founding of the German
Turn-Verein in November, 1851, at the home of Louis Stein on Orleans
Street. Forty charter members, realizing that the Turner movement
placed a strong emphasis not only on the physical education of the individual but also on his intellectual and cultural development, immediately
founded a singing society under the direction of a trained voice instructor, who rehearsed the singers at least once a week. The movement was
so well supported that less than two months later a second Turn-Verein
also sponsoring a singing group was started in the Second Municipality
near the city of Lafayette. By February, 1852, the original Turn-Verein
numbered one hundred and forty members. [2]

Stimulated by a growing German population, singing societies grew
in number throughout the period. Practically every German society
whether of a social, cultural, or benevolent nature sponsored a singing
group. But the singing societies which left their mark were the New Orleans Liedertafel, the Quartette Club, the Harugari Men's Glee Club,
the Turn-Verein Singing Society, the New Orleans Liederkranz, and the
New Orleans Frohsinn. [3]

While the Germans of the city kept singing throughout the days of
the civil conflict and the Reconstruction era, it was not until 1873 that
another city-wide singing organization was founded. This was the
Deutscher Maenner Gesangverein, which met in February of that year
with thirty charter members. Dr. F. Wilhoft was chosen president, and
Otto Weber was asked to be the music director. The number soon increased to over one hundred. In December, 1878, this group of singers
joined with the long-active New Orleans Liederkranz to form the organization known as the New Orleans Liedertafel, at that time New Orleans'
only German singing society exclusively given to German song. The
Carnival season of 1879 brought many new names to the membership
roll, including many ladies who joined a mixed choir. A large number of

---

[1] It is believed that New Orleans was the first city in the United States to have a
genuine German singing society for the record of the New Orleans German Liederkranz set the date as March 28, 1845. Laguaites, "The German Element in New Orleans,"
53-4; *New Orleanser Deutsche Zeitung*, January 9, 1898.

[2] Deiler, *Geschichte der deutschen Presse*, 27; Laguaites, "The German Element in
New Orleans," 54-5.

[3] Interview with Henry Drueding, musical director of the new New Orleans
Liederkranz, organized in 1896, and of the singing group of the Deutsches Haus,
June 13, 1953.

boys and girls who received a musical education at the expense of the society was also added so that by 1881, more than nine hundred belonged to the Liedertafel. [1]

The organization of the Quartette Club took place on August 8, 1882, the birthday of its founder, John Hanno Deiler. It was on January 29, 1872, that Deiler, who was to play the most conspicuous part in the preservation and development of German music and song in New Orleans, arrived from Munich, Germany, to become the teacher of the upper classes of Saint Boniface German school and organist of the church. In 1879, he accepted the appointment of professor at the University of Louisiana, later known as Tulane University, after which time he became extremely interested in all activities that engaged the Germans of the city. [2] As early as 1873, he had become a member of the Deutscher Maenner Gesangverein, whose director he became in 1874. When the New Orleans Liedertafel came into existence in 1879 and 1880, he organized the first German mixed chorus and directed it at Spanish Fort and West End upon the occasion of the opening of the Texas railroad. For the event the Liedertafel invited the Texas singing societies and held a three day festival during which two vocal and instrumental concerts were given, ending with a torchlight procession and a brilliant evening entertainment at the Grunewald Hall, in which the German Turners of New Orleans, the German Battalion, and the German Guards also participated.

Determined to participate with other singing organization throughout America by affiliating with the North American Saenger Bund, which the Liedertafel was not inclined to support, Deiler organized the New Orleans Quartette Club with seven other members, among whom were Friedrich Busch, Ludwig Mieg, and Mathieu Vonderbank. [3] He went with this group throughout the country, contacting German singing

---

[1] *A History of the Proceedings in the City of New Orleans on the Occasion of the Funeral Ceremonies in Honor of James Abram Garfield* (New Orleans, 1882), 202; New Orleans *Taegliche Deutsche Zeitung*, November 5, 1889; Minutes of the Liedertafel, 1879-1883; *Program of Twenty-Fifth Anniversary in Protokol of New Orleans German Quartette Club*, 1897.

[2] *Souvenir of the Eightieth Anniversary of the German Society*, n.p.; *New Orleanser Deutsche Zeitung*, December 10, 1897.

[3] The North American Saenger Bund was founded in the city of Cincinnati in 1849, where at the time the first German singing festival also took place with three societies represented, one from Cincinnati, one from Madison, Indiana, and one from Louisville. *Official Text Book of the Twenty-Sixth Saengerfest*, 6.

groups, advertising New Orleans and the South, and creating more and more interest in the German song. [1]

The fall of 1882 saw another singing group organized, the Harugari Men's Glee Club, having as its chief objective the preservation of German song. The director of music was professor A. J, Hoffmann, who regularly entertained with his singing organization at the German Volksfests and other benefits of a local and city-wide interest. [2] Before the decade closed two other singing clubs were founded, the New Orleans Frohsinn on January 16, 1885, and the Liederkreis of the Fourth District on February 18, 1889. [3] The former carried on its membership roll some of the best-known German citizens of the city, namely, Charles F. Buck, Joseph Voegtle, and A. G. Ricks. Carl Weiss, a noted musician, was the musical director of this group of enthusiast'c singers. [4]

These organizations continued to serve a multiple purpose in the lives of their members and friends. Each week at an evening hour, and at times more often, the singers gathered in a hall owned or rented by the group to rehearse a repertoire of songs which ranged from the classical to the religious. They were always under the direction of a master musician who had received his training in Germany. The air was filled with aria from various operas, well-known ballads and folk songs, and more serious numbers of a religious nature. Into every number went not only the voice of the singer but his heart. For that reason the stirring airs of "Deutschland, Deutschland, ueber alles," "Ich hatt' einen Kameraden," "Die Wacht am Rhein,"—all martial songs expressing one's love for the homeland—were sung with gusto and reverence. At the same time, since songs were also sung in the English language, the national, airs of their adopted land," America, the Beautiful," and "My Country, 'tis of Thee!" received the same respect and honor. Around Christmas time, voices were raised in the best-loved of Christmas carols, "Ihr Kinderlein kommet," "Gott ist die Liebe," "Der Christbaum ist der schoenste Baum." While the singing at times lacked quality, there was no want of enthusiasm, willingness, and volume of voices. [5]

---

[1] *Program of the Third German Day*, n.p.; *New Orleanser Deutsche Zeitung*, December 10, 1897.

[2] *Program of the Sixteenth Anniversary of the Founding of Harugari Men's Club* (New Orleans, 1898). This is in the Protokol of the Quartette Club, 1897-98, in the Deutsches Haus New Orleans, Louisiana. *Program of Third German Day*, n.p.

[3] *Official Text Book of the Twenty-Sixth American German Choral Union Festival*, 112, 125.

[4] *Ibid.*, 112.

[5] New Orleans *The Daily Picayune*, February 14, 1890; *New Orleanser Deutsche*

On innumerable occasions the singers appeared at public benefits and performances, assisting in entertaining and supporting worthwhile causes and charities. In this manner, the singing organizations provided an opportunity for their members to participate in many civic celebrations and in charitable endeavors, at the same time finding pleasure in entertaining others and themselves. [1]

After each weekly rehearsal hour, the singers enjoyed a period of sociability by indulging in eating and drinking their favorite brew, beer. Joy was also found in reminiscing over days spent in the fatherland, especially if a recent immigrant had just become a member of the group; or in telling a few ribald jokes and stories; or even in discussing more serious affairs such as, politics, the family, and work or business. [2]

Throughout the 1880's the groundwork was laid for the coming of the greatest event in the history of German singing in the deep South and the city of New Orleans. The promoter of this event was Deiler. Having organized the Quartette Club in 1882, he took its members as often as he could to the choral festival of the North American Saenger Bund and to other centers of the country which had German singing societies. In 1883, he took his group to Buffalo; and the year after, the club numbering twelve, he went to San Antonio. In 1886, a double-quartet of this club went to the festival of the Saenger Bund at Milwaukee, where the New Orleans German singers were called "the swallows from the South." All in all, Deiler and his singers were making an impression upon the Germans of the North, and he hoped it would culminate in the Saenger Bund accepting the invitation to come to New Orleans for their festival. In 1888, the Quartette Club and the newly-organized singing society, Frohsinn, sent forty men to Saint Louis to attend the Saenger Bund singing festival. After impressing the large gathering with their ability to sing, they extended an invitation to the North American Saenger Bund to hold its next event in New Orleans. The invitation was accepted. The date was set for the winter of 1890, and preparations were made

---

Zeitung, December 27, 1898; interview, Henry Drueding, director of the New Orleans Liederkranz, 1896-1900, June 13, 1953. The author of this dissertation has often attended the Thursday evening singing hour at the Deutsches Haus in New Orleans. This will offer one a taste of the singing groups of the late nineteenth century.

[1] New Orleans *Taegliche Deutsche Zeitung*, March 22, 1888; Minutes of the New Orleans Quartette Club, February 3, April 24, May 2, 1899; Minutes of the Liedertafel, April 3, 1882.

[2] Interview, Henry Drueding, June 13, 1953.

for the staging of the first Saenger Bund festival in the South, the twenty-sixth of the national organization. [1]

How were approximately 11,000 German-born New Orleanians with five active singing societies numbering from seventy-five to one hundred and twenty-five performers to entertain sixty-four singing societies representing about 1,700 singers? The answer was Deiler and the splendid cooperation given by the whole population of New Orleans, the press, the singers of the North American Saenger Bund, and the untiring efforts of every music-loving German of the city. [2]

After considering the staging of the festival at the Fair Grounds, at the popular lake resort at Spanish Fort Park, or at the Washington Artillery Hall, it was decided to build a wooden hall to seat 5,000 spectators and a stage accommodating 2,000 singers and orchestra. This hall was to be built at Lee Circle at a cost of $ 13,000 and was to be architecturally attractive. [3]

To raise the amount needed for the entertaining of the Twenty-Sixth Choral Festival of the North American Saenger Bund seemed insurmountable. However, a novel plan was introduced which not only raised the necessary funds but also assured a good attendance at every concert during the days of the festival. A bond company was organized with a capital of $ 50,000 and called the North American Saengerbund Limited. Bonds of twenty-five dollars each totaling 2,000 in number were issued. To encourage the purchase of bonds, every bondholder received two tickets for the festival. The plan realized a total sale of $ 34,425.00. That amount together with an additional $ 15,860.40, realized from

---

[1] *New Orleanser Deutsche Zeitung*, December 10, 1897; "Wie die Kosten fuer das Saengerfest in New Orleans aufgebracht wurden," *Lyra*, II (1898), n.p.

[2] *List of Stockholders of the Twenty-Sixth Saengerfest of the N.A.S. in New Orleans* (n.p., n.d.), 19; *Program of the Thirty-Eighth National Singing Festival* (St. Louis, 1934), 25. This copy is in possession of Flasdick. A planning and directing organization was formed shortly after the invitation was accepted. This important group consisted of Jacob Hassinger, president; Charles F. Buck, vice-president; J. Hanno Deiler, festival director; Maximilian Hermann, president of local festival committee; Reverend Max Heller, music committee. Besides these officers were R. H. Benners, second vice-president; Louis Grunewald, treasurer; Louis Leonhard, financial secretary; A. J. Hoffmann, corresponding secretary; Chas. J. A. Doerr, recording secretary; and R. Dietzins, acting corresponding secretary. *List of Stockholders of the Twenty-Sixth Saengerfest of the N.A.S. in New Orleans*, back page; New Orleans *The Daily Picayune*, February 13, 1890.

[3] "Wie die Kosten fuer das Saengerfest in New Orleans aufgebracht wurden," *loc. cit.*, II (1898), n.p.; New Orleans, *The Daily Picayune*, March 8, 1890.

various sources raised the total to $ 50,285.40, which assured the financial success of the undertaking. [1]

Work on the Saengerhalle was begun in the early fall of 1889. [2] Progress in building was good. The structure was quite massive, with a front of one hundred-fifty feet on St. Charles Street and a depth of two hundred feet. The tower of the building which faced the Lee monument was eighty feet in height including the lyre which crowned it. The double tower at the principal entrance on St. Charles Street was seventy feet high. The stage for the singers and the musicians was ninety-six feet wide and forty feet in height. The building had nine exits, two more than were required by the contract. Its seating capacity was approximately 6,400. [3]

While the building was being constructed, everything was being done to assure a record attendance at every concert. Deiler traveled 4,943 miles by rail into twenty states in the interest of the festival to encourage German singers to come to New Orleans in February, when the Saengerfest was to be held. Carl Weiss, who was to lead the opening chorus composed of singers from New Orleans, Mobile, and San Antonio, made an extended trip into Texas to create enthusiasm for the coming festival. Among the Germans of the city everything was buzzing. Committees were getting things in readiness, participating local German singing societies were rehearsing daily, even the women were busy to make the affair impressive, beautiful, and a high point of the city's social season. [4]

---

[1] *Ibid.*; *List of Stockholders of the Twenty-Sixth Saengerfest of the N.A.S. in New Orleans*, 16. The financial report as submitted by Louis Leonhard, financial secretary, was:

Cash received for 1377 shares of full paid stock.	$ 34,425.00
Cash received for entrance tickets at Music Hall.	10,159.50
Sale of sheet music	1,630.25
Membership dues	3,319.00
Cash received for souvenirs, programs, etc.	600.00
Sundries	151.65
Grand Total	$ 50,285.40

[2] *Official Text Book of the Twenty-Sixth American German Choral Union Festival*, 30-1; New Orleans *Taegliche Deutsche Zeitung*, October 8, 1889. Judge Howe's speech lauded the German's love for song. He said: "Every people has its particular characteristics. The Greeks had their art; the Romans their wars; the Phoenecians their commerce. ... But all these people are gone. But we ... have a better and more enduring heritage won by our song ..."

[3] *Ibid.*, 39.

[4] New Orleans *The Daily Picayune*, January 19, 1890; *New Orleanser Deutsche Zeitung*, September 26, 1899.

On Wednesday, February 12, 1890, at eight o'clock in the evening, the Twenty-Sixth North American Saenger Bund festival began. New Orleans was a city of roses and sunshine set to music. Thousands of people attended the first concert. These had a new experience in music in this city. It was the largest audience ever assembled at any musical festival in New Orleans, and it was the first time that New Orleans became thoroughly acquainted with German music and song. [1]

A capacity audience was on hand for the opening concert. It was a wonderful sight. [2] A city newspaper reporter described it.

> On the platform, rising tier above tier, were the singers. They seemed a sea of faces, of bearded masculine faces, and down in front of them on the same platform sat the orchestra and below, in the body of the hall, the prettily gowned and gracious sponsors were banked like beds of blooming roses.

> The hall is finely illuminated with gas and electric light, and over the platform is an arch of lights forming crescents in the center, with a lyre of blooms suspended above and huge stars of gas jets on each end. Across the arch the gas globes spell out the legend, 'North American Singers' Union. [3]

Every concert was attended by a large audience. [4] The majestic melodies echoed far beyond the audiences seated in the hall and stirred the thousands who remained on the streets either because they could not get in or did not have the price of admission. [5]

After six brilliant concert performances, the Saengerfest was history. Newspapers reported:

> This Saengerfest will go down in the annals of the South as one of the Greatest Successes of the Age.... It will be many years ere the city witnesses another such festival, but it should be held here again. Let it be even finer than it was in 1890. [6]

The event was both a cultural and a financial success. [7] Above all, the

---

[1] New Orleans *The Daily Picayune*, February 13, 1890; New Orleans *The Times-Democrat*, February 13, 1890.

[2] New Orleans *The Daily Picayune*, February 13, 1890.

[3] *Ibid.*

[4] *Ibid.* At the Friday, February 14th performance 8,000 people were crowded into Saenger hall. No other festival of any kind in New Orleans had ever had so large an audience. New Orleans *The Times-Democrat*, February 16, 1890.

[5] New Orleans *The Times-Democrat*, February 16, 1890; interview, John Rettenmeier who was one who sat outside to listen to the music because he did not have the price of admission, December 27, 1952.

[6] New Orleans, *The Times-Democrat*, February 16, 1890.

[7] The participating societies of New Orleans Germans were: The New Orleans Quartette Club with thirty active singers, the Harugari Men's Chorus with twenty active

Twenty-Sixth North American Saengerfest was an inspiration to the German singer and song of the city. The final decade of the nineteenth century found the Germans even more enthusiastic about their singing societies and about the entire movement of preserving German songs on a national scale. Several new societies were organized during these years. Henry Drueding, active in musical circles as teacher, director, and organist, gathered a group of singers in the downtown area of the city, to which the name New Orleans Liederkranz was given. [1] Anticipating the centennial of the birth of the world-renowned musician, Franz Schubert, in 1897, the Franz Schubert Singing Organization was founded on January 1, 1897. Under the direction of Joseph Engel this group met every Monday night at eight o'clock in the hall at 3718 Magazine Street. [2] In the same year, singers of the Quartette Club, the Frohsinn, the Harugari Men's Chorus, the newly-organized Liederkranz, and a singing group from the Turn-Verein joined efforts in the establishing of a United Singers' Association of New Orleans. After much hard work this mass chorus of over a hundred voices participated in the observance of the Franz Schubert Festival, staged in the hall of the Washington Artillery, on January 13, 1897. On this festive occasion the United Singers offered three selections, "Am Meer", "Wanderers Nachtlied," and "Taeuschung." [3] A most fitting climax to a half-century of German song and music in New Orleans came on June 29, 1899, when at the North American Saengerfest in Cincinnati, J. Hanno Deiler, the one figure most closely identified with the German element and its contributions to New Orleans and the South, was elected the president of this national organization of German singers.[4]

German music and song was fostered not only by the singing societies. The Germans of the city sang everywhere, in church, in school, and in their many places of entertainment. Wherever one encountered a group

---

singers, the Frohsinn with twenty-four active singers, the Liedertafel with thirty-two active singers, and the Liederkreis of the Fourth District with twelve active singers. *Ibid.*, 112, 125. Governor Nicholls, Mayor Shakespeare, and several local musicians of note attended. Even fashionable society attended in full force and all the musical people were present and deeply interested. Financially, after the final settlement of all affairs, the sum of four hundred dollars remained in the treasury. This undisposed sum was directed to the Ambulance Fund of the Charity Hospital of the city.

[1] *Program of the Third German Day*, n.p. The original Liederkranz amalgamated with the Deutscher Maenner Gesangverein to form the Liedertafel in 1878.

[2] *New Orleanser Deutsche Zeitung*, January 5, 1898.

[3] *New Orleanser Deutsche Zeitung*, January 2, 1898; Program in Protokol of Quartette Club found in Deutsches Haus, New Orleans.

[4] *Taegliches Cincinnatier Volksblatt*, June 29 1899.

of them, he was met with music and song. Their German bands often offered entertainment to the masses as they paraded on many festive occasions and gave concerts in many places throughout the city and in many of the amusement and resort centers around the area. [1] With their music and song they desired, as it were, to tell their fellow townsmen and fellow Americans that "bad men have no song." We have "soft feelings in our breast." It is our "desire to press the whole world to our heart!" [2]

The Germans of the city continued to act and to sing as they approached the coming of a new century. While troubles loomed ahead, which was evident from the lack of new immigration and the slow but determined influence of Americanization among the younger element especially, the Germans continued the work of preserving the German song and amateur theater, of sponsoring concerts and other festivities which were of a musical nature, and of fostering the fellowship of Germans which was greatly loved by all who had come from the Fatherland.

---

[1] Interviews with many old German citizens of the city who lived through the greater part of this period ,1950-1953.

[2] New Orleans *Taegliche Deutsche Zeitung*, October 8, 1889.

CHAPTER VII

THE NEW ORLEANS GERMAN AND HIS PLAY

Albert Bernhard Faust, in speaking of the contributions made by the German population to America, said that these could be summed up under four heads; blood, brain, brawn, and buoyancy. Buoyancy, he said, was a love of life and energy that appreciated the recreational aspects of living. [1] The Germans of New Orleans were of a lusty temperament, working hard and playing hard.

The home was the center of their play, for home life was held in high esteem by all Germans. [2] It was here that the humdrum and monotony of everyday life was occasionally broken by a neighborly and friendly visit, particularly on Sunday, and by the observance of a birthday, a betrothal, or a wedding .The casual visits of friends on a Sunday afternoon and evening found the men indulging in a game of cards and some beer drinking; while the women drank "Kaffee" and ate "Kuchen" as they gossiped. The children were there too but were only seen and never heard. The baptism of a newly-arrived member of the family, a birthday celebration, the announcement of an engagement, or the solemnizing of a wedding called for more elaborate festivities. On such occasions German men and women enjoyed themselves by eating and drinking, dancing and talking, into the early hours of the morning. No one was disappointed for it was at such times that the German housewife demonstrated her culinary art. All guests were served at well-laden tables, tables that groaned with pancakes with jam, apple tart, strawberry pastry, cold dishes such as goose liver, breaded veal cutlets, roast pork, sausages with mashed potatoes, stuffed goose, jugged hare, all kinds of sausages such as *Braunschweiger, Regensburger, Nuernberger, Leberwurst, Blutwurst,* also dumplings, macaroons in endless varieties, and things stewed, smoked, and baked. [3] No one left without having eaten and drunk well for beer and wine were also served liberally. If the family which entertained its friends could afford it, a lively German band was on hand to

---

[1] Dubois, *Germans in American Life*, 164.

[2] Philip Vollmer "What Germans Have Contributed to Our National Life " *loc. cit.,* (1927), 44.

[3] Dubois, *Germans in American Life*, 67-8.

play the familiar polkas for the dancing delight of the many guests. [1]

The home was the center also for the annual celebration of Christmas, Sylvester Abend, i.e., New Year's Eve, and Easter. The happiest time of the year for children and grown-ups was Christmas. The season of joy and merriment began about two weeks before Christmas Eve, when "Knecht Ruprecht," or "Pelsnickel," would make his appearance to threaten with the rod children who were bad and to bring nuts, apples, and cakes for those who were good. In some of the German homes of the city the Christmas season began with the first Sunday in Advent, at which time saucers filled with nuts, candies, and cakes were placed under the beds of the children. On awakening, the children found their saucers of goodies reminding them that "Knecht Ruprecht" and the "Christ Kind" would soon be on hand. At the same time, the parents restricted the children from going into the parlor. It was there that the presents were kept and the tree erected and decorated prior to the climax of the celebration on Christmas Eve. On Christmas Eve father and mother with the children gathered around the Christmas tree beautifully decorated with cookies, fruits, and candies and brilliantly glowing with many candle lights. Christmas songs were sung—"Ihr Kinderlein Kommet" and "Stille Nacht, Heilige Nacht." The father read the Bible and offered prayer, after which the mother jubilantly distributed to each member of the family a gift which had been placed under the tree. The remainder of the evening was passed in playing with toys around the Christmas tree. Friends and relatives might come in; however, this particular celebration was chiefly for members of the immediate family. [2]

The celebration continued through Christmas Day and the day after. By this time activities no longer centered around the home but shifted to the church and the many German societies and clubs throughout the city. [3] The Turn-Verein usually offered a Christmas party for its members and friends. These were well attended by young and old for it always was a time of fun and play. A newspaper reporter attending one of these German Christmas parties said:

---

[1] Interviews with numerous old New Orleans Germans, especially with Mrs. Anna Altmann, March 2, 1948; with Miss Clara Bauer, March 1, 1948; with Mrs. Anna Weidig, March 1, 1948; and Mrs. Anna Van Salzen, March 3, 1948.

[2] Interviews with many old German residents of the city; Dubois, *Germans in American Life*, 70-1.

[3] New Orleans *Taegliche Deutsche Zeitung*, December 25, 1889; *New Orleanser Deutsche Zeitung*, January 5, 1898.

There was a large attendance of the friends of this popular organization and everyone present had a most thoroughly enjoyable time.

The privileges of the floor were given exclusively to the little ones until 10 o'clock in the evening, when, in accordance with this time-honored custom, Santa Claus made his appearance and distributed toys among the children present. He chose as his conveyance last night a monster cannon, which he touched off just before his appearance, thus booming forth the announcement of his coming. When he had delighted the hearts of the children, he disappeared as he had come, and then the floor was given over to the older folks, who indulged in the pleasure of the dance until a late hour. [1]

It was a time for joy and pleasure which prompted also individuals to give Christmas parties to which many were invited. [2]

This season of celebrating affected the German churches in which special Christmas religious programs were offered to packed audiences. A typical celebration was annually scheduled at St. Paul's Lutheran Church. It was here that the first electrically illuminated Christmas tree in New Orleans was exhibited on Christmas Day, 1898 [3].

An immense crowd assembled to witness the joys and pleasures of the little ones and every seat in the large church, as well as standing room, was occupied. The church is a very handsome edifice and was neatly decorated inside. A large star formed of glass was placed at the entrance to represent the star of Bethlehem, which led the shepherds and the Magi to the manger which held the Christ child. The children assembled in the schoolroom under the church at 6 o'clock, but long before that time impatient boys and little girls congregated in the room and patiently (or rather impatiently) awaited the marching orders. At 6 o'clock they formed in a procession and marched upstairs into the church .... recitations and dialogues by the boys and girls of the Sunday school were delivered. A catechism appropriate to the services and the occasion was then recited by the children, interspersed with songs and Christmas carols ...

The children filed down into the schoolroom, where the gifts were placed in bundles and packages for each class. Then the children, each class led by its teacher, entered and distribution commenced. The little ones were very happy and the toys were soon all gone, and each one of the children received a present of toys and candies. [4]

Sylvester Abend was celebrated at home as well as at clubs, society gatherings, and at the many beer gardens that offered special amusement

---

[1] New Orleans *The Daily Picayune*, December 26, 1898.
[2] New Orleans *Taegliche Deutsche Zeitung*, December 23, 1864.
[3] New Orleans *The Daily Picayune* 26, 1898.
[4] *Ibid.*

on the last day of the old year. Large groups of Germans enjoyed dancing, playing cards, reading and exchanging New Year wishes, and indulged in much eating and drinking. [1]

While Sylvester Abend was generally a celebration for the adults, Easter was celebrated with an emphasis on enjoyment, fun, and play for the children. The Easter bunny and gorgeously colored eggs, ideas introduced to America by Germans, were the center of attraction. The German children were told that on the eve of Easter and only on that night, hares laid eggs and on Easter morning the children must go out to look for them. A goodly number of Easter egg hunts were sponsored by various German organizations, including the churches. [2]

The Germans of the city did not, however, restrict their play to these occasions alone. Sunday was perhaps the greatest day in the Germans' love of fun and play. In the summer months the great out-of-doors beckoned them. Milneburg, West End, and Spanish Fort were popular summer resorts visited frequently by the Germans of the city. Any Sunday many German families with well-stuffed picnic baskets were seen at the foot of Elysian Fields near the levee waiting for "Old Smokey" of the Pontchartrain road to carry them to Milneburg, an ancient but pretty town on the lake. The fare was very cheap, in reach of almost everyone, and the hours of train departure were frequent enough so that a family could travel to the resort almost any time of the day for an outing or a picnic. [3] Later in the century, Spanish Fort and West End became more popular than Milneburg. Steam trains carried passengers from Canal Street depots to the lake pleasure resorts. West End became a real Coney Island offering both relief from the city's heat and opportunities to swim and play, and at the same time to enjoy the orchestral concerts and operas that were regularly scheduled. [4]

Germans sought fun and play at more distant points from the city as time made them more prosperous. Clubs and societies sponsored outings to places across Lake Pontchartrain, which gave a greater number

[1] DuBois, *Germans in American Life*, 73-9.

[2] *Ibid.*, 75-6; interviews with numerous old Germans of the city.

[3] Excursions to the lake and back to the city on the same day was fifteen cents for adults and ten cents for the children.

[4] Fountain and Christian, *Street Railway Guide to the City of New Orleans and Its Suburbs*, 29. This copy is in the T. P. Thompson Collection, University of Alabama; James A. Renshaw, "The Lost City of Lafayette," *Louisiana Historical Quarterly*, II (1919), 54; New Orleans *Taegliche Deutsche Zeitung*, January 1, 1884; *New Orleanser Deutsche Zeitung*, May 14, 1898; New Orleans *The Daily Picayune*, August 5, 11, 1884.

the opportunity to leave town to seek the beauty of the pine country north of the lake. [1] One of the more popular places was the summer home of Paul Schreiber, a member of the New Orleans Quartette Club, at Covington. It was there that the annual birthday party of this singing group was celebrated.

> Already on the train the merriment began; at 7 A.M. the train reached Covington and many sweet ladies met the group to lead them to the villa Schreiber. Singing and swimming in Bayou *Falia* occupied much of their time. A dinner followed. It was a festive day also for many of the citizens of Covington. Fireworks were displayed at night which attracted even more people. A dance followed in which all took part. The German group stayed over night to continue the festivities on the morrow. [2]

The Germans were so fond of picnics and outings that it was not unusual for their newspapers to announce as many as five or more of these to be held on the same day. A day in April, 1883, promised picnics by the Harmony Club of Carrollton, together with a mammoth parade at the Carrollton Gardens; by the German Louisiana Women's Benevolent Association at Loeper's Park; by the German Military Group at Magnolia Gardens; by the Dairymen's Association in Oakland Park; and by the Volksfest committee on the grounds of the German Protestant Home. [3]

In the humid days of the summer, as well as in the rather mild days of winter, the Germans of the city sought fun and play in the many taverns and family beer gardens. Nearly every tavern and beer garden held regular "Familien-Baelle," for the Germans were fond of dancing. Before the Civil War hundreds of balls each year were sponsored, holding as many as six a night. Sunday was the popular night, especially for the young Germans, although Saturday night also attracted its many patrons. Orleans Street was the center of the German taverns during the 1850's and 1860's. After that time, a new German beer and tavern center developed on the uptown side of Canal Street near Common. Most popular places were the Kossuth House on Royal Street, Canterbury House on Chartres, Hatry on St. Louis, Hosch on Coliseum, Hambacher Schloss in Exchange Alley, Abel und Rochow on Carondelet, Kuester Mauesebach and Coelner Dom on South Rampart, and Seeliger at the St. Mary's

---

[1] Minutes of the New Orleans Quartette Club, August 3, 1897.

[2] Newspaper clipping, n.d. Found in the Minute Book of the New Orleans Quartette Club.

[3] New Orleans *Taegliche Deutsche Zeitung*, April 22, 1883.

Market. Later in the century Krost, Redwitz, Merz, and Kolb became famous. [1] At the same time taverns in the surrounding areas catered to the many Germans living there. Dances were held usually on Saturdays and Sundays at Rhaders, Beusel and Dirks, and Landborg and Munsch in Gretna, Schuettler in Freetown, Kraft at Algiers, and in taverns located in Jefferson City and Lafayette, as well as many other places. Here Germans congregated to eat, drink, talk, and read German newspapers which the proprietors ordered from larger cities which, because of their strong German population, printed German newspapers. [2]

It was the German beer gardens, however, which satisfied most fully the Germans' longing for *Gemütlichkeit*. In the area of the "Old Basin" the National and Tivoli, two of the finer beer gardens in the city, beckoned the Germans to enjoy an evening of genuine pleasure and relaxation. The Tivoli was the more aristocratic of the two and offered a genuine "Old World" atmosphere.

> A large yard shaded by trees, under which are numerous little rustic tables and benches separated by short intervals, and capable of accommodating two couples each; lampposts interspersed; shell walks; a bar with strong liquors and warm water at one extremity; beer-men with large baskets filled with beer jugs, which pop like champagne bottles and emit a frothy, yellow fluid, that will make you sleep before it makes you tipsy, and in the center the dance house—a circular building, the flooring surrounded by a balustrade, with a single door, and elevated on a platform, an orchestra of a dozen brazen instruments. The stars and stripes float in the breeze above the whole .... Five cents is paid by each male partner for the privilege of one waltz, which occupies nearly ten minutes. The 'frauen' pay nothing, heaven bless them! Often as many as twenty couples are whirling around at one time. Strangers and mere spectators crowd outside of the balustrade, gazing listlessly upon the waltzers. The Germans proper not engaged in the dance are seated upon the diminutive benches under the trees, gargling gutturals and beer. [3]

Taverns and beer gardens were, however, not the only places that offered hours of play to the Germans. Sharp-shooting contests, sponsored

---

[1] Deiler, *Geschichte der deutschen Presse*, 26-7, 57; interviews with numerous old Germans, particularly Fritz P. Schroeder, employee of Kolb's Restaurant and connected with the business since 1909. In New Orleans since 1890, he worked for Merz, who was owner of the restaurant before Kolb bought the business in 1898. New Orleans *Taegliche Deutsche Zeitung*, September 3, 1889.

[2] Deiler, *Geschichte der deutschen Presse*, 5-6; interviews with numerous old Germans of the city.

[3] "Stahl," *The New Orleans Sketch-Book* (Philadelphia, 1843), 84.

by many of the military organizations, were attended and participated in. These were usually scheduled for Sunday mornings. Here friends met to try their skill at shooting but also to talk about politics, business, and themselves, at the same time always enjoying a satisfying beer or two. From there a visit was made to the Turnhalle or to any of the many German clubs that existed to talk how best to help the Germans who were in need in the city or elsewhere. Before they returned home a stop was made at one's favorite tavern to take a bit of brew home. [1]

As was noted, drinking beer was a major pastime for most Germans. Nevertheless, it was said of them, "We Americans can learn from the Germans how to get real value out of life without getting drunk." Drinking to them was an art, as expressed in the verse used by one of the leading German restaurants in its advertising:

Das Trinken lernt der Mensch am ersten,
Spaeter dann das Essen;
Darum soll er auch aus Dankbarkeit
Das Trinken nicht vergessen. [2]

The Germans' love for sociability is clearly manifested in the purposes of their many and varied organizations. All singing groups, dramatic clubs, benevolent organizations again and again sponsored balls, plays, and banquets for the enjoyment of their members and friends. [3] One of the most significant of these affairs was the "Commers" Night celebrated on the 15th of February, 1890, the day after the conclusion of the Twenty Sixth Saengerfest of the North American Saenger Bund. [4] It was enjoyed in the Saengerhalle at Lee Circle. All the seats had been removed from the paraquette in the hall, and large tables around which sat the members of the various singing societies had been substituted. The evening was

---

[1] Louisiana *Staats-Zeitung*, July 25, 1855.

[2] Joseph Zimmermann, *Festival Writing of German American National Association* (New Orleans, 1911), n.p. This book is in possession of the Deutsches Haus.
    Man first learns to drink,
    Later then how to eat;
    Therefore out of gratitude he should.
    Not forget how to drink.

[3] New Orleans *Taegliche Deutsche Zeitung*, January 3, 4, 1880; January 1, 1884; October 27, 1889.

[4] "Commers" Night was a custom which was entirely new to the New Orleans people. It originated with the students of the universities of Germany and was taken up by the German-Americans and celebrated after every Saengerfest since the inauguration of these singing festivals in the United States. New Orleans *The Daily Picayune*, February 16, 1890.

spent in singing, speech-making, and drinking. A president was chosen who took charge of the entire affair, no man having the right to refuse any request the president might make. Sometimes a song was called for and sometimes a speech, but at the conclusion of either a glass of beer was drunk by every guest. This was called "salamander," the glasses being rattled upon the tables at the command of the president. Many toasts were given, each followed with the drinking of beer. All this was hilarious fun, and everyone enjoyed himself. The revels were kept up until a very late hour. [1]

Advantage was taken of any occasion which lent itself to banqueting since the Germans enjoyed eating, drinking, and much talking. This was demonstrated each time a German warship reached the port of New Orleans, particularly after the birth of the German Empire in 1871. [2] Members of all German societies marched to the river in festive procession and boarded the vessel where they were greeted by the officer in charge. After they made a brief inspection of the ship, the officers and men received an invitation to visit the various German societies of the city and to attend divine services at any of the numerous German churches. At the same time, the officers and men of the ship received an invitation to a special banquet to be celebrated in their honor. This affair was always the high mark of the entertainment shown the personnel of a German warship docking at New Orleans. The hall of a hotel or auditorium was readied for the banquet. German singing societies volunteered their services to furnish entertainment. Throughout the evening, singing and speech-making were very popular. Several dramatic presentations enlivened the program. [3] Above all, the delicious food delighted the palate of each banqueter. No cost was spared. On one occasion all were treated to a menu of tomato soup, pompano with new potatoes, turkey in sauce, filet of beef with champagne, pheasant with asparagus salad, omelet, cheese, dessert and coffee. Throughout the meal several wines and champagne were liberally served. The officers, in their brilliant uniforms, added a picturesqueness to the affair the like of which had never been seen in the city. [4] It was another opportunity to express and satisfy

---

[1] *Ibid.*

[2] *New Orleanser Deutsche Zeitung*, October 23, 1898.

[3] New Orleans *Item*, January 15, 1900; New Orleans, *The Daily Picayune*, January 15, 1900.

[4] *New Orleanser Deutsche Zeitung*, January 18, 1900; New Orleans *The Daily Picayune*, January 15, 1900; Minutes of the New Orleans Quartette Club, December 23, 1898; New Orleans *Item*, January 15, 1900.

the Germans' love for play in complete relaxation and enjoyment.

Because of their play, especially on Sundays, the Germans were often criticized by the English element of the town. This did not, however, deter them from enjoying the Sabbath as well as others. They felt that the fear of God and the sense of enjoyment together could do no harm, and that Sunday could be celebrated as both a holy day and a holiday. Germans of the city therefore were not friendly to any blue laws that threatened to rob them of their pleasure on that particular day. They likewise fought against license laws which were directed toward closing their beer houses. [1] While their Sabbath's "goings-on" were often referred to as the "Dutch carousals" in the earlier days, by 1890 the editor of the New Orleans *Times Democrat* stated:

> It is to the credit of our German fellow-citizens that the city has never been quieter, more orderly in every respect, than during the period of the Saenger-fest. [2]

Fellow citizens gradually understood the Germans' love for fun and play.

Perhaps, the most typical of all German institutions of play was the annual Volks-und-Schuetzenfest inaugurated early in the 1850's and continuing throughout the remainder of the century, even into the twentieth. On April 30, 1854, a large number of Germans representing a number of social and benevolent organizations, drawn up in parade formation, gathered on Canal Street. Led by banner carriers of the American flag, the black, red, and gold flag of the German people, and the Swiss flag, and paced by several bands playing stirring martial music, the marching crowd made its way to the Union Race Course, near Bayou Road. Later in the century these gala events were held at the Southern Park on the Bayou of St. John. The park was beautifully decorated with flags and bunting. Drinking bars and eating places invited the pleasure-seeking multitude. In spite of high prices and the manner in which the concessions were often handled, and the rude behavior of the festival marshalls who rode through the crowds on horseback, as they tried to keep order, the day was enjoyed by hundreds of persons. They participated in dancing and competitive games, such as bowling, rope and tree climbing, foot racing, sack racing, horse racing, and shooting for marks-

---

[1] New Orleans *Deutsche Zeitung*, February 1, 2, 5, 1853; New Orleans, *Taegliche Deutsche Zeitung*, October 18, 24, November 8, 9, 10, 1854; December 20, 1855; *New Orleanser Deutsche Zeitung*, January 18, 1900.

[2] New Orleans *Times-Democrat*, February 16, 1890.

manship. Prizes were awarded to the victors. Unforgettable was the occasion to those that renewed old friendships and made new ones. The day was thoroughly enjoyed by all so that a demand was made to make the affair a permanent one which the people promised to support. [1]

The profits derived from these annual Volksfests were divided either among the organizations which participated in staging the event or among eleemosynary groups in the city. In that way various organizations, such as the Howard Association, the German Society, and the German Protestant Orphan Home, received financial aid. At other times, if any of the German organizations needed financial assistance to meet deficits incurred in sponsoring city-wide celebrations for the German population, the officers of the Volksfest came to their aid with the money realized at the festival. In later years, the Turn-Verein sponsored the annual Volksfest for the benefit of the German Protestant Home exclusively. [2]

New Orleans Germans were also very fond of physical recreation. Physical development was considered essential for a "refined humanity," contributing to progress in culture and freedom and good citizenship. Considerable sums were spent on gymnasiums and gymnastic apparatus, and much energy was expended in calisthenics, acrobatic tumbling, and performances on the parallel bars, which men even in middle life thought essential to the maintenance of physical fitness. [3] The Turn-Verein, organized in 1851, sponsored physical culture throughout the years. Erecting a Turner Hall, first at Franklin Street, near Canal, and later on Clio Street, this organization conducted schools for boys and girls to build healthy and sturdy bodies through work in gymnastic and long hikes. Participating in many benefits throughout the city, the pupils excelled in dumbbell exercises, pyramid building, and folk dancing. [4] German soccer was introduced by the various organizations, particularly by the Turn-Verein. Young Germans organized teams and challenged sailors of German ships which were docked in the river harbor. This type of "football" was not very interesting to the Americans, as a sport either to play or to witness, but it was quite popular with the young Germans of the city. [5]

---

[1] Deiler, *Geschichte der deutschen Presse*, 18, 28; Louisiana *Staats-Zeitung*, May 17, 1855; May 25, 1855.

[2] Deiler, *Geschichte der deutschen Presse*, 28.

[3] Wittke, *Refugees of the Revolution*, 152.

[4] New Orleans *Taegliche Deutsche Zeitung*, October 24, 27, 1889.

[5] Interview with numerous old Germans of the city, who were members of the Turn-Verein, 1952-53.

Combining a spirit of loyalty to community and state with that of play, the Germans of the city organized volunteer military companies as early as 1842. As members of these companies the Germans were able to satisfy a love for parading in gaudy uniforms and for discharging firearms and cannons during military maneuvers. Among them were the German Fusiliers, (Captain Carl Fieska), the German Jaeger (Captain L. Autz), the Orleans Fusiliers (Captain H. H. Wagner), and Jaeger Company H (Captain Theodore Grabau). Others were added later, and all enjoyed a subsidy from the state during the early fifties. When the subsidy was discontinued, the companies began to break up, a fact bitterly deplored by the *Deutsche Zeitung*. After secession became a fact old companies were reorganized, notably the German Fusiliers and the German Jaeger. These companies were, however, discouraged by many political officials of the state. [1]

After Reconstruction some of these military organizations were revived. One of the more colorful groups at this time was the Deutsche Garde. This company was formed in March, 1878, and joined the German Battalion, which was organized the following year. The Garde remained with the Battalion as Company C until February, 1880, at which time the German Battalion joined the State National Guard. Company C took up its own independent organization under the name of the German Garde. Its uniforms were similar to that of the German Battalion. It was substantially that of the Prussian Imperial Guards; dark with red cuffs and collars; very dark gray pants with red stripes; helmets with horsehair plumes. The officers wore in addition white silver sashes and epaulettes. This was indeed a very showy uniform. [2] Their parades were just as colorful as the uniforms. Marching through the downtown and uptown streets of the city they evoked comment from every one who saw them. [3] A newspaper article of the time praised their marching.

> What is the most glittering revué held by a hundred thousand mercenaries of a European tyrant compared to the festive appearance of free men whose alliance has for its aim the protection of property? [4]

The achievement of these amateur soldiers, however, seemed to have

---

[1] Robert T. Clark, Jr., "The New Orleans German Colony in the Civil War," *loc. cit.*, XX (1937), 997-98; Wittke, *Refugees of the Revolution*, 282.

[2] *A History of Proceedings on the Occasion of the Funeral Ceremonies in Honor of James A. Garfield*, 181, 182, 188.

[3] New Orleans *Taegliche Deutsche Zeitung*, March 21, 1880.

[4] New Orleans *Deutsche Zeitung*, March 5, 1853.

been greatest at a banquet table and the bar instead of on the drill grounds. Eating and drinking were equally stressed with proficiency in the manual of arms. [1]

The military organizations experienced their ups and downs through the latter part of the century. Seemingly, all were disbanded by the early years of the 1890's. Toward the end of that decade, however, another call came to organize all Germans of the city who had seen military service in the German wars of 1864, 1866, 1870, and 1871. A meeting was called and held at the Vonderbank Cafe on December 18, 1898, under the inspiration of Josef Schuetzer. Those present set up an organization and elected a set of officers. Their chief purpose was to entertain, especially the personnel of German warships which came to the port of the city to remain for a time. [2] The original purpose for organizing these military companies, namely, to achieve "the common protection of the people from an inward as well as an outward foe, and the furtherance of peace and a stronger, virile spirit in all classes of our people," had therefore been lost sight of at this time. [3]

Volunteer fire companies likewise offered the Germans an opportunity for community service and for play. Many of these organizations had been founded prior to 1850 but remained very active until this service was incorporated into a municipal agency. By 1888, five German fire companies were still very active, besides others that remained active in name only. Possessing their own fire equipment, which they kept immaculately polished and shining, together with an excellently-trained stable of horses, these companies were ready not only to serve in time of distress but also to entertain the citizens by their parades which they staged often and which also gave them an opportunity to show off. Two of the companies which enjoyed many years of honorable service were the Louisiana Fire Company Number Ten, and the Jefferson Number Twenty. [4]

As the Germans of the city lived with their American neighbors, they soon adapted their form of play to theirs. While the crucible of the melting pot was at work Americanizing the German, it was also at work drawing

---

[1] Wittke, *Refugees of the Revolution*, 282.

[2] *Program of the Third German Day*, n.p.

[3] Laguaites, "The German Element in New Orleans," 46.

[4] New Orleans *Taegliche Deutsche Zeitung*, March 7, April 1, 1888; *A History of Proceedings on the Occasion of the Funeral Ceremonies in Honor of James A. Garfield*, 231-33.

the Germans into the orbit of New Orleans' play, fun, and relaxation. Most noticeable was the effect the annual Mardi Gras festival had upon the Germans' concept of play and amusement. [1]

While masked balls and street masking of a sort became features of the Mardi Gras celebration early in colonial times, they were at times de-emphasized after the territory became part of the United States. Street parades might have been held prior to 1838, when the first newspaper description of a street parade appeared. Following that, street parading became a regular event at the time of the festival. [2] Likewise Mardi Gras organizations which were to sponsor mammoth street parades and balls were founded. The first one was the Mistick Krewe of Comus, which staged its first street parade on the night of February 24, 1857. Fifteen years later, Rex, King of Carnival and Lord of Misrule, appeared, followed by the Knights of Momus. These were the three outstanding Carnival organizations until 1882, when the Krewe of Proteus, a god of sea and close friend of Neptune, joined their rank. [3]

The merrymaking of the Carnival season was to the liking of the buoyant spirit of the Germans. Quite early, various German societies introduced Carnival balls on the calendar of social events. These were generally festive occasions and were very well attended, offering the society an opportunity to provide pleasure for its membership and friends as well as to gather funds for a charitable endeavor. At such affairs it was very common that several hundred dollars were realized through paid admissions and the sale of food and drink. [4]

Not satisfied with staging carnival balls only, various groups participated in street parades. Wagons were rented and elaborate decorations transformed them into a moving "fairyland," filled with masquerading carnivalists, which paraded throughout the city. As time progressed, the German element identified itself more and more with the spirit of Mardi Gras, and great numbers looked forward to the time that they could

---

[1] Mardi Gras means Fat Tuesday in English and is the day immediately preceding Lent, or the forty days fast. On this day, for hundreds of years, in the Roman Catholic Countries of Europe the people tried to have as much enjoyment as could be crowded into twenty-four hours. Fountain and Christian, *Street Railway Guide to the City of New Orleans and Its Suburbs*, 39.

[2] New Orleans *City Guide*, 175.

[3] *Ibid.*, 177, 180, 182; Fountain and Christian, *Street Railway Guide to the City of New Orleans and Its Suburbs*, 39.

[4] Minutes of New Orleans Liedertafel, December 6, 1880.

masquerade and frolic up and down Canal and St. Charles Streets together with their American neighbors. [1]

The spirit of gambling, so prevalent in New Orleans, soon captivated the imagination of the German population. Undoubtedly, the Louisiana Lottery, founded by the legislature in 1866 during a period of financial crisis, had much to do with bringing the love of taking a chance into every home of the city, including that of the Germans. [2] To encourage the purchase of lottery tickets all German newspapers carried large advertisements of the prizes offered and the amount to be paid for tickets. Drawings took place in various large halls and auditoriums to accommodate the crowds which came to learn of their fortune and misfortune. These drawings were also advertised in the German newspapers for the Germans also desired to get a part of the millions of dollars that were distributed in prizes by this gambling syndicate. [3] Germans of the city were also urged to purchase lottery tickets of the Bavarian Government which was selling its tickets in this country. [4] With such incentives to win money many Germans of the city took a chance, or even more.

Although the German element did not take too kindly to professionalism in sports, they enjoyed horse racing and prize fighting as sports for spectators. Horse racing came to New Orleans quite early, for by 1850 races were being held at the Bingaman Course, later known as the Metairie Course. The purses offered were small, yet, patrons came out to see and wager on the races. Big time racing in the city started on April 13, 1872, when thousands of men and women gathered at Royal and Canal Streets, beneath the imposing statue of Henry Clay, to proceed to the site of the old Agricultural and Mechanical Fairs. This race course had been built by the Louisiana Jockey Club, headed by A. B. Breaux. The throng cheered as a chestnut gelding, named Templar, won the first race of the day and Monarchist, sired by the immortal Lexington, easily won the Grand Inaugural Post Stake. Surely, a number of Germans enjoyed the occasion and continued to support racing as long as it was staged in the city. [5]

Prize fighting as a spectator sport also became a favorite pastime

---

[1] *Ibid.*, May 23, June 25, 1881.
[2] New Orleans *Item*, June 10, 1952.
[3] New Orleans *Taegliche Deutsche Zeitung*, 1883; September 4, 1889.
[4] Louisiana *Staats-Zeitung*, May 8, 1855.
[5] New Orleans *The Daily Delta*, March 17, 1850; New Orleans *Item*. June 10, 1952.

for the Germans of the city. On February 18, 1890, the famous James J. Corbett fought the clever Jake Kilrain at the Southern Athletic Club. This contest, won by Corbett in six rounds, was seen by a goodly number of Germans. Again in 1892, when the heavy-weight crown was lifted off the brow of the great John L. Sullivan, and more than 10,000 spectators saw the brutal battle which lasted twenty-one rounds, many Germans of the city were there to cheer for their favorite contestant. [1] While they would not engage in boxing at their various Turn-Vereins as a physical exercise, the Germans enjoyed a boxing match as spectators and therefore supported the sport.

In many of the Germans' homes friendly games of cards were played with bets being made on every game. Often mutual friends met in their respective homes to enjoy a game of poker or some other game, which was always enlivened by the playing for some kind of a wager. Playing would continue into the early hours of the morning, generally interrupted by generous servings of food and drink by a gracious host or hostess. [2]

As some of the Germans through industry and thrift became prosperous, they also revealed another form of play which gave them many hours of joy and relaxation. This was the avocation of building and maintaining beautiful flower gardens. Wherever space permitted, the German raised a few flowers, if nowhere else but in a small flower pot or box. If, however, he had acquired a larger plot of ground, he spent many of his leisure hours in planting and tending trees, shrubs, and flowers. Some of their gardens were showplaces for the lover of flowers, like the garden of B. Ausemann on Saint Peter and Murat Streets, which was filled with blooming dahlias, camellias, chrysanthemums and roses. A number of the Germans with their love for greens and flowers were responsible for a part of New Orleans, to which a number of them moved after they became more wealthy, to be called "The Garden District." [3] Building by playing they, therefore, assisted in making New Orleans a more beautiful and attractive city.

Through his play the German also endeared himself to the many Americans living in the city, introducing some forms of play which he brought

---

[1] New Orleans *Daily Picayune*, February 18, 1890; New Orleans *Item*, June 10, 1952; interview with John Rettenmeier, December 23, 1952.

[2] Interview with John Rettenmeier, December 23, 1952.

[3] John S. Kendall, "Old New Orleans Houses and Some of the People Who Lived in Them," *Louisiana Historical Quarterly*, XX (1937), 810; New Orleans *Taegliche Deutsche Zeitung*, October 22, 1889; interview with Henry Drueding, June 10, 1953.

with him from abroad and borrowing some of the amusements taught him by his neighbor of the New World. Realizing that "All work and no play makes Jack a dull boy," he often played his way to health and into the hearts of fellow New Orleanians. By the end of the century he was working and playing side by side with all Americans.

CHAPTER VIII

THE NEW ORLEANS GERMANS OF NOTE

In this thriving port of the lower Mississippi River Valley, the Germans with their inborn sense of duty kept at their work, respected law and authority, and devoted themselves to the home, the school, the shop, and the church. As the city prospered, so did many of the Germans. This newly-found prosperity made a goodly number of them conscious also of their duty to the city and the state, readily accepting the responsibilities which their fellow citizens bestowed on them. [1] While a great number of the recently-arrived immigrants had to be encouraged to learn English and the functions of a democratic society, in order to participate in the political and economic life of the city, many, even the common laborers, were taking out citizenship papers and going to the polls to vote. [2]

Consequently, the 1880's and 1890's saw many German-born citizens of New Orleans rise to important positions in political, cultural, professional, and economic affairs. Perhaps, one of the most prominent individuals in politics was Charles F. Buck. He was born in Durrheim, Baden, near Fillingen, Germany, in the year 1841. [3] Arriving in New Orleans in December 1851, on his way to Missouri, he lost his parents in the fearful yellow fever epidemic of 1853. Forced to remain, he accepted his lot with determination and schooled himself carefully in the study of law. At the age of twenty-seven he became city attorney. [4] At the age of forty-

---

[1] Rightor (ed.), *Standard History of New Orleans,* 573-74; New Orleans *Item,* June 10, 1952.

[2] Faust, *The German Element in the United States,* 471; *Souvenir of the Eightieth Anniversary of the German Society of New Orleans.*

[3] Interview with Ida Buck Henrigues, daughter of Charles F. Buck, August 26, 1953. She related that little "Karl" lost every member of his family in the epidemic except his sister, Anne. He was educated in the High School system of the city and studied at Louisiana State Military Academy in Alexandria. During Civil War days he tried to enlist in the Confederate Army, but since the Yankees had already overrun the South, he returned to New Orleans. He studied law and worked in the office of Christian Roselius. After being admitted to the bar, he practised law for a while; but his love for dramatics forced him into a theatrical career for a time. He was a brilliant speaker often appearing as festival and after-dinner orator. He was a member of the Germania Lodge, Grand-master of the State, a Thirty-third degree Mason and a member of the Grand Council in Washington, D.C. He was a member of the German Turn-Verein and an excellent fencer and chess player.

[4] *Ibid.*

five he was offered the nomination of Representative from the Second
District to the United States Congress, but he graciously declined it. [1]
Eight years later, however, he accepted the nomination and was elected
in 1896. Twice he was a candidate in the mayoralty race, but was defeated
both times. [2] In the 1895 race, the local newspaper reported:

> In the late struggle whatever may be said of the merit of the question at
> issue, New Orleans witnessed the noble spectacle of two of her best men
> leading the forces to combat, neither of them seeking personal or selfish
> ends, but both acting on what they considered to be their duty and the
> best interests of the people, Walter C. Flowers, victorious, and Charles
> F. Buck, defeated. [3]

Buck's attitude and viewpoints on important political issues of the
day were courageously expressed in his numerous speeches. In them
he undoubtedly expressed the general point of view of the New Orleans
Germans since he was their spokesman on many occasions. Speaking
at a Fourth of July celebration he clearly expressed the sentiment of his
nationality toward the Declaration of Independence.

> The Declaration, 'All men are born free and equal,' came not as the catch-
> word of a prime minister or the craft of policy. It was the outburst of a
> conviction born through centuries of toil; one that had to contend against
> the prejudices of religion and education, one slow and difficult of develop-
> ment, because it assailed traditions, venerable in immemorial custom, ...
> It marks the beginning of a new civilization, the distinctive feature of
> which is the absolute independence, equality and sovereignty of the in-
> dividual man . . . . The excesses of communism, of socialism, of nihilism
> or whatever name the radical extremist may adopt, are threatened in a
> hundred varied shapes. There is strife immemorial. . . . These elements
> of contention must be met with the calmness of justice and the firmness
> of death. . . . If you and the youth and the men of the great land will heed
> the counsels of that pure and lofty promise which springs from the ambi-
> tion to sanctify your lives by devotion to duty, in the common cause of all,
> we need have no fear for the welfare of our country. [4]

As a member of the House of Representatives, Buck spoke courageously
on many controversial issues. The problem of immigration was disturbing

---

[1] The Second Congressional District included the parishes of Jefferson, Saint
Charles, Saint James, and Saint John the Baptist. Brief of Contested Election Case of
H. D. Coleman vs Charles F. Buck. This brief is in possession of Ida Buck Henrigues,
New Orleans.

[2] New Orleans *Times Picayune*, January 20, 1918.

[3] *Ibid.*, Undated clipping in possession of Ida Buck Henrigues, New Orleans,
Louisiana.

[4] Address of Charles F. Buck on July 4, 1884, to the students of Louisiana State
University. The copy of the address is in the possession of Ida Buck Henrigues.

the country because of the enormous number of foreigners pouring into the United States from Europe. Many in Congress desired exclusion of the immigrants, or, at best, the careful restriction of the number allowed to enter the country. [1] Buck queries, "Where is the danger?" Immediately he continued that "there is no danger because the principles upon which America and this American Government rest are the principles of all humanity; and every man who comes here comes to be an American, for to be an American is to be a citizen of the world." [2] When German-American citizens were said to be in favor of restricting immigration from Southern Europe, he charged that "if I were to utter a sentiment or make a stroke of the pen that would deny to the humblest lazzaroni in the streets of Venice the privileges and the benefits that I have acquired at the hands of the people and the institutions of this country, I would be ashamed of myself as a German-American citizen." [3] He believed that the man "who faithfully cleans the streets of Washington and is honest and honorable is as worthy as the man who cashes checks or keeps the Treasury of the United States of America. There is no prejudice in the heart of the Germanic races against the prosperity, much less against the aspirations, of any people." [4]

As a great humanitarian, Buck pleaded for the peoples of Cuba, who had suffered under the tyranny of Spain, to receive their independence and equal status with other free nations. In the halls of Congress he cried:

> Accord these people belligerent rights, yield to them the dignity, for the time being, of an equal nation upon earth, and light will come from them and go to them, and then it will be demonstrated whether they are right or whether they are wrong. If we are to be wrong, let us err on the side of humanity; let us err in pursuit of the principles which we advocate and teach. [5]

Undoubtedly, the name of Charles F. Buck was written large over the political horizon of New Orleans and Louisiana during the last two decades of the century and was instrumental in inspiring other German-Americans of the city to take their rightful place in the affairs of the Democracy. He advised

---

[1] Morison and Commager, *The Growth of the American Republic*, II, 184-86.
[2] Speech by Congressman Chas. F. Buck, in the House of Representatives, May 19, 1896, *Congressional Records* (Washington, 1896), XXVIII, Part VI, 5434.
[3] *Ibid.*
[4] *Ibid.*
[5] Speech by Congressman Charles F. Buck in the House of Representatives, April 4, 1896, *Congressional Records*, XXVIII, Part IV, 3590; *New Orleanser Deutsche Zeitung*, June 10, 1898.

> You know that there is no excellence without labor; no reward withou industry; no success without perseverance. You know that withou morality you cannot be respected; without virtue you cannot be honored; without justice you cannot be great. [1]

Perhaps the greatest exponent of progress, art, and learning—the cultural values of life—during the last decades of the century was J. Hanno Deiler. He was a man who combined the best qualities of the German and of the American, a man of many attainments, highly cultured in music, literature and historical research, ever ready to give and to do his best for the German people of New Orleans and elsewhere. [2] He was respected and loved by all citizens of the city and regarded as one of the most public-spirited individuals; [3] while the Germans voiced their high esteem for the man in the words, "Es gibt nur einen Hanno Deiler." [4]

Deiler was born on August 8, 1849, at Altoeting, Bavaria, Germany. His early training, particularly in music, was under the careful tutelage of his father, Konrad Deiler. In 1866, he entered the Royal Normal College at Freising which he left with highest distinction in music and in other disciplines. Entering government service as a teacher, he taught in various places including Munich. While there he attended the Royal Polytechnic Institute taking work in literature, aesthetics, and history.

In 1872, he came to New Orleans as principal and organist of Saint Boniface Church. Seven years later he assumed the position of professor of German language and literature at the University of Louisiana, which position he occupied throughout the remainder of the century. [5]

The very year Deiler arrived in New Orleans he became active in the life and culture of the Germans who had settled there. His chief interest was in preserving the customs and traditions of his people through the medium of the German song. He therefore associated himself with the German Maennergesangverein of which Otto Weber was the director. Being an excellent musician, Deiler soon assumed direction of the group. From that time on he was the most active and most enthusiastic exponent of the German song and of the benefits derived from preserving this

---

[1] Address of Charles F. Buck on July 4, 1884. In possession of Ida Buck Henrigues, New Orleans, Louisiana.

[2] *Souvenir of the Eightieth Anniversary of the German Society of New Orleans*, 86.

[3] New Orleans *Daily Picayune*, January 13, 1899.

[4] Minutes of the New Orleans Quartette Club, August 5, 1897. "There is only one Hanno Deiler."

[5] *Official Text Book of the Twenty-Sixth American German Choral Union Festival*, 53 *New Orleanser Deutsche Zeitung*, December 10, 1897.

heritage. In 1880, he became director of the New Orleans Liedertafel and founded the first German mixed chorus. In October of that year, he directed the grand concerts of the Liedertafel given at Spanish Fort and West End in honor of the Texas singers present to celebrate the opening of the railroad communication between New Orleans and Texas. His activities led to the founding of the New Orleans Quartette Club on August 8, 1882, bringing the Twenty-Sixth Saengerfest of the North American Saenger Bund to New Orleans, and being elected to the presidency of the Bund in convention at Cincinnati in June, 1899. These accomplishments were the high marks in the life of the man who did more to perserve and foster the culture of the Germans of the city than any other. [1]

His work received recognition also in the Fatherland for in January, 1899, the Kaiser of Germany, William II, conferred the Order of the Crown upon J. Hanno Deiler. The telegram from Holleben, German ambassador, to Baron von Mysenburg, German consul of New Orleans, read: "His majesty, the emperor of Germany, has conferred the Order of the Crown upon Professor J. Hanno Deiler and Doctor Frederick Loeber of New Orleans. [2]" The decoration was a medallion in the shape of a Maltese cross with white enameled bars and a center of Gobelin blue. On the one side was a crown of gold and the words, "Gott mit uns," while on the reverse side was the monogram of the older William, who established the Order, and the date of its founding, 1861, the time that William I became the monarch of Prussia. Taking note of the presentation of this honor, the New Orleans *Daily Picayune* commented that Deiler was acknowledged to be a leader in his chosen profession whose abilities were not confined to any creed or even nationality but given generously to thousands. [3]

Deiler was also the first author to undertake research and write histories of the German emigration into the southern states. Among his better known works are *Die ersten Deutschen am unteren Mississippi, Germany's Contribution to the Population of New Orleans With Census of German Schools, Geschichte der deutschen Gesellschaft, Geschichte der New Orleanser deutschen Presse, Louisiana Ein Heim fuer deutsche Ansiedler, The Settlement of the German Coast of Louisiana and the*

---

[1] *Official Text Book of the Twenty-Sixth American German Choral Union Festival,* 53; New Orleans *Daily Picayune,* January 13, 1899; *New Orleanser Deutsche Zeitung,* December 10, 1897; June 30, 1899.

[2] New Orleans *Daily Picayune,* January 13, 1899.

[3] *Ibid.*

Creole of German Descent, and *Zur Geschichte der deutschen Kirchen-gemeinden im Staate Louisiana.*[1] His work on the Germans of Louisiana was highly appreciated in Europe, where it was accepted as an original contribution to the history of the German race. [2] Being interested in preserving the history of the Germans of the city, he also encouraged the German Society of New Orleans to found an archives department for the purpose of gathering and preserving the documents and articles which dealt with the life and work of the Germans within the city and throughout the state. [3]

While the greater number of Germans were skilled artisans and fewer were trained in the professions, two Germans of the city, nevertheless, engraved their names indelibly upon the exacting and important profession of medicine. These were Frederick Loeber and William Kohlmann.

Frederick Loeber was one of the best known physicians in New Orleans. From 1869 until his death on October 18, 1901, he was house surgeon of the Touro Infirmary. Prior to 1869, he had been carefully trained in the schools of America, France, and Germany. At the time he became house surgeon, the Infirmary was located at the corner of Erato and South Peters Streets. Sensing and understanding the importance of this institution's future, he was instrumental in having the hospital moved to its present site on Prytania Street. As a physician and surgeon, he displayed rare skill and judgment, was a friend of the rich and the poor alike, and was honored and beloved by all whose good fortune it was to know him. [4] Members of his profession admired him and a number were greatly influenced by him. Doctor M. J. Magruder, recalling an operation performed by Loeber, reported:

> I recall one case in which I administered a pound and a half of chloroform during a single operation extending over four hours. This case was an old depressed fracture of the skull causing paralysis. The operation was performed by Dr. Loeber, assisted by Dr. Andrew Friedrichs, a dentist,

---

[1] All of these works are catalogued in the Howard-Tilton Memorial Library, Tulane University, New Orleans.

[2] New Orleans *Daily Picayune*, January 13, 1899.

[3] Interview with Henry Kraak, president of the Deutsches Haus, New Orleans, 1953, on April 15, 1953.

[4] M. J. Magruder, "Some Incidents in Connection with the Early History of Touro Infirmary." Letter of A. J. Hockett to Thomas Ewing Dabney, November 30, 1936. This letter is in the private files of Dr. Mackenzie; New Orleans *Daily Picayune*, January 13, 1899. Touro Infirmary began operating as a charitable institution in May, 1854, in accordance with the will of Judah [Joseph] Touro, in the building located at the corner of Gaiennie and Celeste Streets. See Dr. John Nash, "History of Touro Infirmary," n.p.

using a dental engine operated by foot, drilling hundreds of small holes around the margin of the fracture until the depressed portion, more than three inches in diameter, was finally removed. [1]

He was not only interested in his profession but gave much of himself to the preservation of that which was best in the German culture. He associated with the leaders of the Germans in their efforts to foster sociability and understanding through music and song. In 1890, he accompanied Paul Schreiber, a well-known German of the city, and Hanno Deiler to the German Saengerfest at Vienna. [2] For the services rendered to the community in which he lived a goodly-sized historical volume could be dedicated, but "any person who knows New Orleans, knows of Doctor Loeber and appreciates his services. "[3] A fitting recognition of his work came in the spring of 1899, when the German emperor conferred the Order of the Crown upon him. At that time he was acclaimed a benefactor of mankind by people not only of the western hemisphere but also of Europe. [4]

William Kohlmann became an associate of Loeber at the Touro Infirmary during the last decade of the century. While the greater part of his life's work was accomplished in the early decades of the twentieth century, he laid the foundations for his future renown in the last years of the nineteenth. Graduated from the medical department of the University of Heidelberg in 1889, and from the medical department of the University of Wuerzburg in 1890, he came to New Orleans in 1891. Although he experienced trying days in his effort to gain a foothold in his profession, he gradually occupied a position of prominence and leadership in the community. In 1897, he was appointed resident surgeon at the Infirmary. [5] It was largely as a result of his admirable labors that the

---

[1] M. J. Magruder, "Some Incidents in Connection with Early History of Touro Infirmary."

[2] New Orleans *Daily Picayune*, October 5, 1890.

[3] *Ibid.*, January 13, 1899.

[4] *Ibid.*

[5] Letter of A. J. Hockett to Thomas Ewing Dabney, November 30, 1936. Kohlmann was born in Reinpfalz, Germany, on June 6, 1863. He specialized in gynecology and abdominal surgery. He was professor of gynecology in the post-graduate school of Loyola University; he was the chief visiting surgeon in the Gynecological and Obstetrical Division of the Charity Hospital; the chief Gynecologist and Obstetrician of the Touro Infirmary, the consulting Gynecologist of the New Orleans Dispensary for Women and Children, and held membership in the New Orleans, the Southern, and the American Medical Associations and also in the Southern Surgical Association and the American College of Surgery. Fortier, *Louisiana*, III, 236; clipping from the *Jewish Ledger*, undated, in possession of Mrs. William Kohlmann, New Orleans. The author interviewed Mrs. Kohlmann in the summer of 1953.

hospital reached its later rating as one of the best in all the South. [1]

Besides his services to the Infirmary, he contributed many learned papers which were read to various medical bodies and published in the journals of the medical profession. A number of these were translated and reprinted abroad which made him well known to the clinics of Europe. [2] While not very active in the circle of the German element of the city, he was a member of the Harmony Club, which organization numbered several respected Germans among its members. [3]

The field of human endeavor receiving the greater share of the efforts and talents of the German element was the economic, embracing the commercial and business ventures of a growing and prosperous metropolis. Endowed with a tenacity of will, a loyalty to duty, and deep concern for efficiency and thrift, the German found himself at home in the business life of his adopted city and assisted in building its economic greatness and prosperity. [4] Among these Germans, without whom the history of the German people of New Orleans during the nineteenth century could not be told, were Jacob Hassinger, Fritz Jahncke, Gustav Seeger, A. G. Ricks, and Henry L. Frantz.

Jacob Hassinger was born at Rehborn, Rhenish Palatinate, Germany, on November 10, 1828, and belonged to one of the many families, who, discouraged by bad crops and other disadvantages, resolved to emigrate together. They took ship for New Orleans in the year 1841. After arriving, little Jacob, hardly more than a child, had to seek employment in order to contribute to the support of his family. He found permanent employment as an apprentice in the printing office of the *Deutsche Zeitung* edited at that time by Joseph Cohn. Not long after Hassinger completed his apprenticeship, the publisher of the paper, who was not making money

---

[1] *American Biography* (n.p., n.d.), I, 361.

[2] *Ibid.*, 362. Some of the published articles are: "Total Extirpation of the Urinary Bladder," *The Southern Medical Journal*; "Illeo-Cecal Adhesions," *The Southern Medical Journal*; "Interstitial Pregnancy," *New Orleans Medical and Surgical Journal*; "Radical Operation for Carcinoma of Uterus," *Pan-American Surgical and Medical Journal*; "The Treatment of Early Tubal Pregnancy, with Report of Cases," *New Orleans Medical and Surgical Journal*; "Pelvic Kidney-Pyonephrosis With Stones: A Case Report," *American Journal of Surgery*; "Abdominal Caesarian Section, with Report of Cases," *Pan-American Surgical and Medical Journal*; and "Radium in Carcinoma of the Uterus," *Surgery, Gynecology and Obstetrics.* All of these publications are in the possession of Mrs. William Kohlmann, New Orleans.

[3] Clipping from the *Jewish Ledger*, undated; S. B. Goodkind (ed.), *Distinguished Jews in America* (Toledo, 1918), 158.

[4] *New Orleanser Deutsche Zeitung*, August 31, 1902.

as fast as he wanted to, sold it to his printers, who continued it as a co-operative enterprise. One partner after another considered the enterprise a failure and gave it up. Finally, only Hassinger and another printer were left. Unable to agree on the conduct of the paper, Hassinger collected all of his available funds and bought out his partner, assuming sole charge of the paper.

Immigration continued. The German element gained a firm foothold in the city. With the development of the Germans the New Orleans *Deutsche Zeitung* entered upon prosperous days. Hassinger defined the task of the paper to be the vindication of the German character and the preservation of unity among the Germans. To this end, he employed editors, who, he was certain, would write from that standpoint and granted them full control. He devoted his time exclusively to the business direction of his paper. He employed traveling agents to secure an extended circulation through the Southeast and Texas, and in that manner he developed his publication into a great and lucrative enterprise. [1]

As his efforts were crowned with success, he turned to other business enterprises, particularly finance and banking. At the same time, he was closely identified with all undertakings of the Germans of the city, and in 1890 was honored with the presidency of the Twenty-Sixth American Saengerfest staged in February of that year. [2]

Fritz Jahncke has written his name in concrete and cement throughout the city as well as in other sections of the state. He was born in Lubtheen, Mecklenburg, Germany, on December 30, 1848, and received training in masonry while residing in his native town. As a young man, he served in the Prussian army during the Franco-Prussian War, in which he received recognition for bravery in the ranks. Immediately upon the close of the war he immigrated to the United States, landing in New York, where he received employment from John Schillinger. Schillinger was in the cement paving business and had made a fortune and a reputation in developing a concrete which could be finished in a manner that made walking safe for pedestrians.

In 1872, Jahncke was sent to New Orleans by Schillinger in connection with a paving contract. When he finished the particular job, he remained and began introducing the inhabitants of New Orleans to the Schillinger

---

[1] *Official Text Book of the Twenty-Sixth American German Choral Union Festival,* 48-51.

[2] *Ibid.,* 51; *Souvenir of the Eightieth Anniversary of the German Society,* 49; *New Orleanser Deutsche Zeitung,* August 3, 1898.

pavement, as it was popularly called. This pavement called for a mixture of sand, small gravel, and cement which lent itself well for sidewalk building which was desperately needed in the city. From 1876 to 1880, he confined himself to making sidewalk pavement and kindred work, but in the latter year he branched out into the general building material business.

At that time New Orleans was at the mercy of flood waters and mud. Of the five hundred miles of street, less than twenty miles were paved with cobblestones or wooden blocks. It was no uncommon sight to see the wooden blocks float away during rainstorms leaving the streets in a deep mire. The sidewalks were no better. Made of wooden boards or hardened dirt, they were quickly transformed into slippery and muddy walks which proved dangerous for pedestrian use.

The concrete mixture of sand, gravel, and cement, which was worked to a smooth top surface, was Jahncke's first step in convincing the residents of New Orleans that there was an escape from the mud sidewalks through which they sloshed daily. In the uptown area of the city, this type of sidewalk, more and more known by the name of Schillinger pavement, gradually became not only a necessity but also a mark of social distinction.

From Schillinger-paved sidewalks, other things followed as a natural consequence. Fritz Jahncke produced the spark that inspired community pride, which developed into a veritable conflagration. Having been shown that they could pull themselves out of the mud and mire, the citizens began to demand of public officials to put their shoulders to the wheel in an effort to pull them completely out of it. This agitation finally brought about the organization of the Sewerage and Water Board, which gave all of its time and effort in making the city a healthier and better place to live.

Fritz Jahncke also developed the New Basin Canal as a commercial waterway. Through this canal, into the heart of the then uptown section of the city, came his tugs towing barges loaded with sand, shell, and other building materials. On the banks of the canal, he established storage yards and business places from which these essential materials were sold and distributed.

Even the port of New Orleans profited greatly by the ingenuity and civic spirit of the German-born Jahncke. After the Illinois Central Railroad had built the Stuyvesant Docks along the foot of Louisiana Avenue, they could not maintain an adequate water channel along its front. They appealed to Jahncke for advice. He offered to dredge a channel which would be partially self-maintaining. He agreed to do all the work at his own expense until he had satisfied the railroad officials that he had succeeded in providing the kind of channel they wanted and needed. He was successful, and by reason of this venture, he gave impetus to port development thereafter. [1] Here, then, was a builder who could be favorably compared to any great American builder.

A goodly number of Germans rose from very humble circumstances to positions of economic power and prosperity. Typical of these were Gustav Seegers, A. G. Ricks, and Henry L. Frantz. Seegers became proprietor of a sewing machine repair shop on Canal Street and handled the sale of "New Home" Sewing Machines which gave him a virtual monopoly in this field during the last twenty years of the century. [2] Adolph Ricks, after serving valiantly the cause of the South in the Civil War, entered the business of handling hides and leather. By 1882, he had formed a company to which he gave the name of A. G. Ricks and Company. By 1885, it had become the largest manufacturer of boot, shoe, and gaiter uppers in the United States. Nearing the close of the century, he became involved in various financial undertakings, all of which proved very successful. In 1896, he was elected councilman-at-large from the fourth district of the city and served well. [3]

Henry L. Frantz was born in 1846 in Alsace-Lorraine and came to New Orleans in 1857. The immigrant family was practically destitute. They possessed not even a table, eating their frugal meals on the box which had held their small personal things as they traveled from Europe to America. Discouragement and futility were, however, far removed from their thinking. [4] With a cousin, Henry started a blacksmith and wagon shop in 1871, and three years later he and another German, Jacob Schoen, organized a profitable undertaking business. Hard work

---

[1] *Seventy-Fifth Anniversary-Jahncke Service-1875-1950* (New Orleans, 1950), 1-14; *Souvenir of the Eightieth Anniversary of the German Society*, 37; interview with Paul Jahncke, Jr., grandson of Fritz Jahncke, now director of Jahncke Services, New Orleans, March 23, 1954.

[2] New Orleans *Taegliche Deutsche Zeitung*, January 3, 1880; *The Artistic Almanac and Fund of Fact* (n.p., 1894), n.p. in T. P. Thompson Collection; *New Orleans and the New South*, 111.

[3] *The Times Democrat Almanac*, 1885, in the T. P. Thompson Collection; Fortier, *Louisiana*, III, 377; *Progressive New Orleans* (New Orleans, 1895), 30, in the T. P. Thompson Collection.

[4] His brother, William, also became a successful business man of the city. *Souvenir of the Eightieth Anniversary of the German Society*, 91.

and good management paid off. As the business prospered, Henry Frantz saw the value of investing in a company that would manufacture coffins. Consequently, he organized the Orleans Manufacturing Company, a venture which paid off handsomely. At the same time he interested himself in the Third District Building Association, serving as its first president and a regular member of the board of directors.

Successful in business, he devoted a great part of his time to political and civic enterprises. For two terms he was a member of the City Council and became the organizer of the City Park Commission. Blessed with material things, he found pleasure in works of charity, the Lutheran Bethlehem Orphan Asylum receiving a giant share of his generosity and love. [1]

These Germans, Hassinger, Jahncke, Seeger, Ricks, and Frantz, were symbolic of the many New Orleans Germans who have made lasting contributions to their adopted city and home, contributions which assisted in building a great city of the United States. It was no wonder, therefore, that the leading newspaper of the English-speaking public of the city of that day commented:

> The Germanic people of New Orleans are not only highly prosperous and full of business energy, but many of them are persons of culture and of the highest social worth, and they command the esteem and the large support in such an undertaking of the entire population of the city. [2]

---

[1] *Souvenir of the Eightieth Anniversary of the German Society*, 45; interview with G. J. Wegener, pastor of Saint Paul's Lutheran Church and pastor to the Frantz family, December 10, 1944.

[2] New Orleans *Daily Picayune*, February 13, 1890.

CONCLUSION

As the nineteenth century drew to a close, forces which contributed to the diminishing influence of German culture in the city of New Orleans became ever more apparent. "The great melting pot, God's crucible," wherein all the races of Europe were being fused and reformed to produce "the American," was also successful in molding the German element into an American one. Besides the German element decreased steadily after 1885. In fact, over a period of forty years, from 1860 to 1900, New Orleans lost twenty-three per cent of her German element in proportion to the total population. Reasons for this decrease were the material prosperity of Germany in the latter part of the century, which prompted many of her subjects to remain at home instead of seeking a fortune in America, and the disappearance of the frontier and cheap lands in the United States which rendered this country less attractive.

The producing of the "American" and the decrease of immigration had their effects upon the Germans and their culture in the city of New Orleans. The first effect was evident in the decrease of the German plays staged in the German theaters after 1875 and their ultimate disappearance, of which Arthur Moehlenbrock wrote "that the German theater is needed no longer as a separate entity in the cultural life of the populace. They were German-American; now they are American."

The second effect was visible in the church and school life of the Germans. It was here that pleas were heard for the use of the English language as the medium of teaching and preaching. Those congregations which dared to introduce services in which English was used found them so well attended that they continued the practice, while those which stubbornly refused had continued difficulty which even led to open hostility and eventual splits. Schools which had existed for the purpose of preserving the German language and culture were being closed.

The third effect centered about an apparent loss of patriotism for the fatherland. Deiler commented in 1898 that "the French and American will think" evilly of us "if we are not more patriotic." Because of growing laxity and indifference towards German-sponsored activities, it became increasingly necessary to give members of various German societies "pep talks" in the hope of reviving their waning interest.

Being mindful of these disturbing factors which contributed to the diminishing influences of the German culture, the *Deutsche Zeitung* directed a stirring plea to the German mothers and their sons and daughters.

> Do not forget your holy duty as mothers! Teach your little loved ones the true language which your mother spoke to you as you lay in her arms. Where does it give one that has so sweet and mild a tone for the heart? ... Encourage our youth for it and then they will come of their own accord and say, 'here we are, German children, who desire to learn German.'
>
> And you, sons and daughters of German parents, who can understand German, keep what you have and become more expert in your language. Be proud of it that you know two languages. Many an English tongue envies you; they also would like to speak German, but unfortunately they cannot unless they work hard at it. [1]

At the same time, some of New Orleans' best known and best loved Germans—Hassinger, Deiler, and Buck—participated in the attempt to check these symptons with stirring speeches and appeals. Nothing seemed to hinder, however, the process of the eventual disappearance of the German, as a German, in the city of his adoption.

In spite of all, J. Hanno Deiler could honestly say in 1898, on the occasion of the visit of the German cruiser *Geier*, to the city:

> You say that we here in New Orleans still have the German spirit, German customs, and German ideals. Even though our powers are weak, our determination and loyalty will never fail. [2]

The *German People of New Orleans, 1850 to 1900*, is the history of this German determination and loyalty. These outstanding characteristics made lasting contributions to the building of New Orleans as a city of many cultures, least of which were not the cultural achievements of the German immigrants. To read the history of New Orleans and Louisiana aright, it is important to consider carefully the part played by the German element of the city in molding the culture and life of this American city.

Even though the energy of German culture weakened as the dawn of the twentieth century broke, the determination and loyalty of the German people, which had motivated them to build so well in the former century, continued to inspire them. This was apparent in the continuation of their churches, schools, and singing and benevolent societies, as well as in their businesses and industries, many of which continue operation

---

[1] New Orleans *Deutsche Zeitung*, October 13, 1889.
[2] *Ibid.*, October 23, 1898.

to this very day. It is possible in 1954 in the land of crawfish bisque and créole shrimp and gumbo to find the German *Gemütlichkeit*, to dine on German foods at Kolb's restaurant and to drink beer made by a German-trained brewmaster, to attend a church and a school founded by German people in the past century, and to enjoy German songs by visiting the Deutsches Haus on a Thursday evening, where husky yet loyal voices give their all in singing *Lieder*. The influence of the German upon the city of New Orleans still lives, while his contributions to the building of the city of his adoption are visible on every hand.

BIOGRAPHY

The author was born on October 8, 1910, in Nagercoil, British India, the son of a Lutheran missionary. At the age of four, his parents took him to Germany, where he lived through the years of the First World War up to 1921. His formal schooling began while a resident of Germany.

In 1921, he came to the United States in the company of his parents and three brothers and three sisters. After a brief stay in Ohio, his family moved to New Orleans, Louisiana, in the late spring of the same year. He attended St. John Lutheran Parochial School, from which he graduated in 1925. That same summer, he departed with his parents to Greensboro, North Carolina. He attended Greensboro High School for one year and then entered Concordia College of Conover, North Carolina, to prepare for the ministry in the Lutheran church. He finished his work at Concordia College in the spring of 1930 and entered Concordia Seminary, St. Louis, Missouri, in the fall of the same year. From 1932 to 1934, he served as assistant pastor of Salem Evangelical Lutheran Church of Buffalo, New York, and in 1935 taught at Immanuel Lutheran College of Greensboro, North Carolina. He completed his studies at Concordia Seminary in the spring of 1936.

After teaching at Immanuel Lutheran College for another year, he accepted the call of Christ Evangelical Lutheran Church of Pascagoula, Mississippi. He served this congregation for three and a half years. In 1939, he married Johanna Leonora Hasenkampf of New Orleans, Louisiana. He is the father of three children, John (Jr.), Henry, and Carolyn.

Redeemer Evangelical Lutheran Church of New Orleans, Louisiana, extended a call in 1940 which he readily accepted. While serving this congregation, he studied at Tulane University, receiving the degree of Master of Arts in History in the spring of 1948.

At the same time, he accepted the pastorate of Messiah and Holy Trinity Evangelical Lutheran congregations of Columbia, South Carolina. In the fall of 1948, he enrolled in the Graduate School of the University of South Carolina to continue his studies leading toward a doctor's degree. Four years later, after completing all residence requirements for the degree, he accepted a teaching position with Mississippi Southern College, Hattiesburg, Mississippi. He received the Doctor of Philosophy degree in History from the University of South Carolina in 1954. At present he is professor of history and chairman of the Department of Religion and Philosophy.

BIBLIOGRAPHY

I. RECORDS, MINUTES AND ARTICLES OF CONGREGATIONS, SOCIETIES, AND INSTITUTIONS OF THE CITY OF NEW ORLEANS, LOUISIANA:

Berichte der deutschen Gesellschaft von New Orleans, 1883-1895. This portfolio is in the archives of the Deutsches Haus, 200 S. Galvez Street, New Orleans, Louisiana.

Bethlehem Evangelical Lutheran Orphan Asylum. Records of Admissions of the Bethlehem Evangelical Lutheran Orphan Asylum of New Orleans, Louisiana, 1883-1952. This record is in the possession of the Bethlehem Evangelical Lutheran Orphan Asylum, 5413 N. Peters Street, New Orleans, Louisiana.

Catholic History Collection by Roger Baudier, Official Chronicler of the Archdiocese of New Orleans. Files on Catholic Education in Louisiana. Replies to questionnaires by Religious Teaching Congregations. Notes from Annals of Religious Congregations. These records are in the possession of the Archbishop's Chancery, 7854 Walmsley Avenue, New Orleans, Louisiana.

Deutscher Verein Zweiter Distrikt. Minutes of the Deutscher Verein Zweiter Distrikt. Meetings held in New Orleans, 1884. These records are in the archives of the Deutsches Haus, 200 S. Galvez Street, New Orleans, Louisiana.

Ellis Diary in Samuel Lang's "The First Century of Tulane University of Louisiana." Excerpts from this diary are in the possession of Samuel Lang, 6034 Hurst Street, New Orleans, Louisiana.

First Evangelical Lutheran Congregation, New Orleans, Louisiana. The Constitution of First Evangelical Lutheran Congregation of New Orleans, Louisiana, adopted on December 19, 1858. This constitution is in the possession of Saint Paul's Lutheran Church, Port and Burgundy Streets, New Orleans, Louisiana.

New Orleans German Society. Minutes of the German Society of New Orleans for the years 1850 to 1863, 1883 to 1885, 1887 to 1892, and 1895. These minutes are in the archives of the Deutsches Haus, 200 S. Galvez Street, New Orleans, Louisiana.

——, Liedertafel Singing Society. Minutes of the Meetings of this organization for the years 1879 to 1883. These minutes are in the archives of the Deutsches Haus, 200 S. Galvez Street, New Orleans, Louisiana.

——, Quartette Club. Minutes of the Meetings of this organization for the years 1887, 1897 to 1900. These minutes are in the archives of the Deutsches Haus, 200 S. Galvez Street ,New Orleans, Louisiana.

Saint John Evangelical Lutheran Church, New Orleans, Louisiana. Accessions of Saint John Evangelical Lutheran Church of New Orleans, Louisiana, 1853 to 1880. These records are in the possession of Saint John Evangelical Lutheran Church, 3937 Canal Street, New Orleans, Louisiana.

——, The Baptismal and Confirmation Records of Saint John Evangelical Lutheran Church of New Orleans, Louisiana, 1853 to 1878. These records are in the possession of Saint John Evangelical Lutheran Church, 3937 Canal Street, New Orleans, Louisiana.

——, The Financial Reports of Saint John Evangelical Lutheran Church of New Orleans, Louisiana, 1860 to 1867. These records are in the possession of Saint John Evangelical Lutheran Church, 3937 Canal Street, New Orleans, Louisiana.

——, Minutes of the Congregational Meetings of Saint John Evangelical Lutheran Church of New Orleans Louisiana. These records are in the possession of Saint John Evangelical Lutheran Church, 3937 Canal Street, New Orleans, Louisiana.

——, The Monthly Financial Reports of Saint John Evangelical Lutheran Church of New Orleans, Louisiana, 1872 to 1873. These records are in the possession of Saint John Evangelical Lutheran Church, 3937 Canal Street, New Orleans, Louisiana.

Salem Evangelical Lutheran Church of Gretna, Louisiana. Minutes of the Congregational Meetings of the Salem Evangelical Lutheran Church of Gretna, Louisiana, 1880. These records are in the possession of Gretna Evangelical Lutheran Church, 418 Amelia Street, Gretna, Louisiana.

Salem Evangelical Lutheran Church of Gretna, Louisiana. Presbyterian Church of Gretna, Louisiana. Minutes of the Congregational Meetings of the Salem Presbyterian Church of Gretna, Louisiana, 1871 to 1880. These records are in the possession of Salem Evangelical Lutheran Church, 418 Amelia Street, Gretna, Louisiana.

Zion Evangelical Lutheran Church, New Orleans, Louisiana. Minutes of the Meetings of Zion Evangelical Lutheran Church of New Orleans, Louisiana, 1848 to 1849, 1854, 1860 to 1864, 1875. These minutes are in the possession of Zion Evangelical Lutheran Church, 1924 Saint Charles Avenue, New Orleans, Louisiana.

——, Records of Baptisms and Confirmations of Zion Evangelical Lutheran Church, New Orleans, Louisiana, 1847 to 1880. These records are in the possession of Zion Evangelical Lutheran Church, 1924 Saint Charles Avenue, New Orleans, Louisiana.

II. OFFICIAL DOCUMENTS:

Buck, Charles F. Speech in the House of Representatives, April 4, 1896. 54th Congress, First Session. *Congressional Records* (Washington, 1896), XXVIII, Part IV, 3590.

——, Speech in the House of Representatives, May 19, 1896. 54th Congress, First Session. *Congressional Records* (Washington, 1896), XXVIII, Part. VI, 5434.

III. LETTERS AND PRIVATELY OWNED DOCUMENTS:

Blanc, Bishop, to the Trustees of the Saint Louis Cathedral, September 4, 1837. This letter is in the possession of the Archbishop's Chancery, 7854 Walmsley Avenue, New Orleans, Louisiana.

Brief of Contested Election Case of H. D. Coleman vs Charles F. Buck. This brief is in the private possession of Ida Buck Henrigues, New Orleans, Louisiana.

Buck Charles F. Address to the students of Louisiana State University on July 4, 1884. This address is in the private possession of Ida Buck Henrigues. New Orleans, Louisiana.

Hockett, A. J., to Thomas Ewing Dabney, November 30, 1936. This letter is in the private files of Dr. John MacKenzie, director of the Touro Infirmary, New Orleans, Louisiana.

Magruder, M. J., "Some Incidents in Connection with the Early History of Touro Infirmary," April 30, 1936. This mimeographed article is in the private files of Dr. John MacKenzie, director of the Touro Infirmary, New Orleans, La.

Nash, John, "Brief History of Touro Infirmary," February 5, 1954. This mimeographed history is in the private files of Dr. John MacKenzie, director of the Touro Infirmary, New Orleans, Louisiana.

Saint Paul Evangelical Lutheran Church to First English Evangelical Lutheran Church, 1890. This letter is in the private possession of the G. J. Wegener family, New Orleans, Louisiana.

Touro, Judah. A typed copy of an article on the life of Judah Touro taken from Number 13 of the American Jewish Historical Society (n.p., n.d.). This copy is in the private files of Dr. John MacKenzie, director of the Touro Infirmary, New Orleans, Louisiana.

IV. NEWSPAPERS:

Algiers *Herald*, undated clipping in possession of Trinity Evangelical Lutheran Church of Algiers, Louisiana.

Lafayette *City Advertiser*, 1837.

Louisiana *Staats-Zeitung*, 1854-56, 1858.

New Orleans *Daily Picayune*, 1839, 1853, 1872, 1884-1886, 1889-1890, 1898-1901, 1906.

——, *Delta*, 1860.

——, *Deutsche Zeitung*, 1847-1848, March 1850, 1853.

——, *Item*, 1900, 1952.

——, *States*, 1913.

——, *Taegliche Deutsche Zeitung*, April 1854-1856, 1862, 1864-1865, 1880, 1883-1884, 1888-1889.

New Orleans, *The Daily Delta*, 1850.

——, *The Times Democrat*, 1890.

——, *Times Picayune*, 1918, 1937.

——, *Times Picayune*, undated. This newspaper clipping is in the private possession of Ida Buck Henrigues, New Orleans, Louisiana.

——, *True Delta*, 1854.

New Orleanser Deutsche Zeitung, 1897-1900, 1902.

Taegliches Cincinnatier Volksblatt, 1899.

Undated miscellaneous newspaper clippings in the Minute Book of the New Orleans Quartette Club in the archives of the Deutsches Haus, 200 S. Galvez Street, New Orleans, Louisiana.

——, Miscellaneous clippings in the private Scrap Book of Philip Werlein Company, Canal Street, New Orleans, Louisiana.

——, Newspaper clipping from the *Jewish Ledger* in the private possession of Mrs. William Kohlmann, New Orleans, Louisiana.

V. PAMPHLETS:

A Century of Service for the Sacred Heart in the United States, 1847-1947 (Brothers of Sacred Heart, 1947).

Celebrating the Golden Anniversary of the Protestant Bethany Home (n.p., n.d.).

Celebrating the Seventy-Fifth Anniversary, 1863-1938-Claiborne Avenue Presbyterian Church, New Orleans, Louisiana (New Orleans, 1938).

Golden Anniversary-A Memorial of Fifty Years of Labor of Love-Bethlehem Orphan Asylum, New Orleans, Louisiana (New Orleans, 1931).

Hahn, Michael, *What is Unconditional Unionism?* (New Orleans, 1863). This speech was delivered before the Union Association at Lyceum Hall, New Orleans, Louisiana, on November 14, 1863. Copy of the speech is in pamphlet form in the T. P. Thompson Collection, University of Alabama.

Hundred Years with Saint Paul's ,1840-1940 (New Orleans, 1940).

Jackson Brewing Company (New Orleans, 1908). This pamphlet is in the T. P. Thompson Collection, University of Alabama.

Land, John E., *Per Illustration of New Orleans-Its History, Commerce, Industry, 1881-1882* (New Orleans, 1882). This pamphlet is in the T. P. Thompson Collection, University of Alabama.

Lineberger, Richard, *Zion Lutheran Church Centennial, 1847-1947* (New Orleans, 1947).

List of Stockholders of the Twenty-Sixth Saengerfest of the North American Saengerbund (New Orleans, 1890).

Louisiana. Its Builders and Its Industries (Louisiana, 1924).

New Orleans and the New South (New Orleans, 1888). This pamphlet is in the T. P. Thompson Collection, University of Alabama.

Progressive New Orleans (New Orleans, 1895). Published by the Young Men's Business League. This pamphlet is in the T. P. Thompson Collection, University of Alabama.

Souvenir of the Diamond Jubilee of the St. John's Evangelical Lutheran Congregation, New Orleans, Louisiana (New Orleans, 1927).

The Epidemic Summer List of Interments in all the Cemeteries of New Orleans from the First of May to the First of November, 1853. Published by the proprietor of the *True Delta*, New Orleans, 1853. This pamphlet is in the T. P. Thompson Collection, University of Alabama.

The Tribune Tracts Number One, "New Orleans Riot." Published in the New York *Tribune*, 1866. This tract is in the T. P. Thompson Collection, University of Alabama.

VI. PROGRAMS:

Bengston, W. H. *Golden Jubilee Program of the Protestant Home for the Aged, New Orleans, Louisiana* (New Orleans, 1937).

Program of the Franz Schubert Festival (New Orleans, 1897).

Program of the Sixteenth Anniversary of the Founding of the Harugari Men's Club (New Orleans, 1898). This program is in the Protokol of the New Orleans Quartette, Club, 1897-1898, in the archives of the Deutsches Haus, 200 S. Galvez Street, New Orleans, Louisiana.

Program of the Third German Day Festival-October 6 (New Orleans, 1912). This program is in the private possession of Adolph Flasdick, member of the Deutsches Haus, New Orleans, Louisiana.

Program of Thirty-Eighth National Singing Festival (St. Louis, 1934). This program is in the private possession of Adolph Flasdick.

Program of Twenty-Fifth Anniversary of the Quartette Club, 1907 (New Orleans, 1907). This program is pasted into the Protokol of the New Orleans German Quartette Club, 1897, in the archives of the Deutsches Haus, 200 S. Galvez Street, New Orleans, Louisiana.

VII. INTERVIEWS:

Altmann, Anna, life time member of Zion Evangelical Lutheran Church, New Orleans, Louisiana, born in New Orleans in 1858, on March 2, 1948.

Bauer, Clara, old member of the Lutheran Church of New Orleans, Louisiana, on March 1, 1948.

Drueding, Henry, director of music and organist of Saint Boniface Catholic Church and a member of German singing societies, especially the New Orleans *Liederkranz* of which he was the founder, on June 11 and 13, 1953.

Fremin, Mrs. L., of Bogalusa, Louisiana, formerly a resident of New Orleans, Louisiana, whose people were known to a number of old German gardeners and dairymen in the Gentilly area, on December 26, 1953.

Henrigues, Ida Buck, daughter of Charles F. Buck, eminent German of New Orleans, Louisiana, in the latter part of the nineteenth century, on August 26, 1953.

Jahncke, Sr., Paul, son of Fritz Jahncke, founder of Jahncke Services, New Orleans, Louisiana, on May 15, 1954.

Jahncke, Jr., Paul, grandson of Fritz Jahncke, founder of Jahncke Services, on March 23, and May 9, 1954.

Kohlmann, Mrs. William, wife of Dr. William Kohlmann, well-known surgeon of New Orleans and the Touro Infirmary, on July 14, 1953.

Kraak, Henry, German florist of New Orleans, Louisiana, a member and past president of the Deutsches Haus, New Orleans, Louisiana, on April 15, May 30, and June 13, 1953.

Kramer, G. M., Lutheran pastor of New Orleans and superintendent of the Lutheran Mission among the Colored, on December 10, 1947, and December 10, 1948.

Kuss, E. W., pastor of New Orleans, Louisiana, since 1888 and presently pastor of Gloria Dei Evangelical Lutheran Church, New Orleans, Louisiana, on February 29, 1948.

Nuhrah, Arthur G., instructor of History at Tulane University, who in writing a history of Tulane University found valuable material on Christian Roselius, on June 10, 1951.

Rettenmeier, John, old time resident of New Orleans since 1885, on December 29, 1951; December 23 and 29, 1952; and January 15, 1954.

Salzen, Anna von, old member of the Lutheran church of New Orleans, Louisiana, on March 3, 1948.

Schroeder, Fritz P., employee of Kolb's Restaurant, New Orleans, Louisiana, January 15, 1954.

Share, Nathaniel S., rabbi of New Orleans Temple Gates of Prayer Congregation, New Orleans, Louisiana, on May 28, 1954.

Weckerling, Mrs. J. J., wife of the founder of the Weckerling Brewery Company, New Orleans, Louisiana, on April 6, 1953.

Wegener, G. J., pastor of Saint Paul Evangelical Lutheran Church, New Orleans, Louisiana, from 1887 to 1946, and well-known historian of the Lutheran Church in the South, on September 30, 1943.

Weiding, Mrs. Anna F., old member of the Lutheran church of New Orleans, Louisiana, on March 1, 1948.

VIII. GENERAL WORKS AND MONOGRAPHS:

A History of the Proceedings in the City of New Orleans on the Occasion of the Funeral Ceremonies in Honor of James Abram Garfield. New Orleans: A. W. Hyatt, 1882.

Altamira, Rafael, *A History of Spain-From the Beginning to the Present Day.* New York: Van Nostrand Company, 1949.

American Biography, 2 vols. n.p.: [?], n.d.

Artz, Frederick B., *Reaction and Revolution, 1814-1832.* New York: Harper and Brothers, 1934.

Baepler, Walter A., *A Century of Grace.* St. Louis: Concordia Publishing House, 1947.

Baldwin, Leland D., *The Stream of American History*, 2 vols. New York: American Book Company, 1952.

Baudier, Roger, *The Catholic Church in Louisiana.* New Orleans: A. W. Hyatt, 1939.

Behnken, J. W., *The Missouri Synod in the South and South-west.* St. Louis: Concordia Publishing House, 1922.

Behruemte Deutsche Vorkaempfer fuer Fortschritt, Freiheit, und Friede in Nord-Amerika. Cleveland: [?], 1889.

Binkley, Robert C., *Realism and Nationalism, 1852-1871.* New York: Harper and Brothers, 1935.

Biographical and Historical Memoirs of Louisiana, 2 vols. Chicago: The Goodspeed Publishing Company, 1892.

Bismark the Man and The Statesman, The Reflections and Reminiscences of Otto, Prince von Bismark, translated under supervision of A. J. Butler, 2 vols. New York: Harper and Brothers, 1899.

Booth, Andrew B., *Records of Louisiana Confederate Soldiers and Louisiana Confederate Commands*, 3 vols. New Orleans: [?], 1920.

Bragg, Jefferson Davis, *Louisiana in the Confederacy*. Baton Rouge: Louisiana State University Press, 1941.

Burns, Edward McNall, *Western Civilization*. New York: W. W. Norton and Company, Inc., 1949.

Cable, George W., *Dr. Sevier*. Boston: J. R. Osgood and Company, 1885.

Crowley, Crowley: [?], 1906.

Dabney, Thomas Ewing, *One Hundred Great Years*. Baton Rouge: Louisiana State University Press, 1944.

De Bow, J. D. B., *The Eighth Census of the United States*. Washington: Tucker, 1864.

——, *The Seventh Census of the United States*. Washington: Tucker, 1853.

Deiler, J. Hanno, *Die ersten Deutschen am unteren Missisippi*. New Orleans: [?], 1910.

——, *Die Europaeische Einwanderung nach den Vereinigten Staaten*. New Orleans: Deutsche Zeitung, 1897.

——, *European Immigration 1820-1900*. New Orleans: [?], 1907.

——, *Germany's Contribution to Population of New Orleans with Census of German Schools*. New Orleans: [?], 1886.

——, *Germany's Contribution to the Present Population of New Orleans*. New Orleans: [?], 1886.

——, *Geschichte der deutschen Gesellschaft*. New Orleans: Deutsche Zeitung, 1897.

——, *Geschichte der New Orleanser deutschen Presse*. New Orleans: Paul J. Sendker Co., Ltd., 1901.

——, *Zur Geschichte der Deutschen am unteren Mississippi*. New Orleans: Tulane University Press, 1901.

——, *Zur Geschichte der deutschen Kirchengemeinden im Staate Louisiana*. New Orleans: Georg Mueller, 1894.

Dowler, Bennet, *A Tableau of the Yellow Fever of 1853 with Topographical, Chronological, and Historical Sketches of the Epidemics of New Orleans Since Their Origin in 1796*. New Orleans: Office of the *Picayune*, 1854.

Faust, Albert Bernhardt, *The German Element in the United States*, 2 vols. New York: Houghton Mifflin Company, 1909.

Ficklen, John Rose, *History of Reconstruction in Louisiana*. Baltimore: The Johns Hopkins Press, 1910.

Fortier, Alcee, *A History of Louisiana*, 4 vols. New York: Goupil and Company of Paris, Manzi, Joyant and Company, successors, 1904.

——, *Louisiana*, 2 vols. with a supplementary volume of contemporary biography. Madison: Century Historical Association, 1914.

Fountain and Christian, *Street Railway Guide to the City of New Orleans and Its Suburbs*. New Orleans [?], 1884.

Gabriel, Angelus, *The Christian Brothers in the United States*. New York: McMullan Publishing Company, 1948.

Gayarre, Charles, *History of Louisiana*, 4 vols. New Orleans: A. Hawkins, 1885.

Goethes Werke, 14 vols. Hamburg: Christian Wegner Verlag, 1948.

Goodkind, S. B., (ed.), *Distinguished Jews in America*. Toledo: [?], 1918.

Hall, Walter Phelps, and Davis, William Stearns, *The Course of Europe Since Waterloo*. New York: D. Appleton Century Company, 1947.

Hayes, Carlton J. H., *A Generation of Materialism, 1871-1900*. New York: Harper and Brothers, 1941.

——, *Modern Europe to 1870*. New York: Macmillan Company, 1953.

Heller, Maximillian, *Jubilee Souvenir of Temple Sinai 1872-1922*. New Orleans: American Printing Company, 1922.

Hesseltine, William B., *A History of the South, 1607-1936*. New York: Prentice-Hall, Inc., 1936.

Hoppe, Anne, *Negro Slavery*. St. Louis: R. Volkening, 1935.

Index to Executive Documents. Washington: United States Government Press, 1850.

Jacobs, Charles M., *The Story of the Church*. Philadelphia: The United Lutheran Publication House, 1925.

Johnson, Thomas C., *Life and Letters of Benjamin Morgan Palmer*. Richmond: Presbyterian committee of publication, 1906.

Kendall, John S., *History of New Orleans*, 3 vols. New York: The Lewis Publishing Company, 1922.

—— *The Golden Age of the New Orleans Theatre*. Baton Rouge: Louisiana State University Press, 1952.

King, Grace, and Ficklen, John R., *A History of Louisiana*. New Orleans: L. Graham and Son, 1893.

Kowert, H., *The Organization of the Missouri Synod in 1847*. St. Louis: Concordia Publishing House, 1922.

Krieger, B. J., *Seventy-Five Years of Service*. New Orleans: Redemptorist Fathers, 1923.

Kurtz, John Henry, *Church History*, 3 vols. New York: Funk and Wagnall's, 1890.

Lonn, Ella, *Foreigners in the Confederacy*. Chapel Hill: The University of North Carolina Press, 1940.

——, *Reconstruction in Louisiana After 1868*. New York: G. P. Putnam's Sons, 1918.

Martin, François-Xavier, *The History of Louisiana*. New Orleans: J. A. Gresham, 1882.

Merriam, William R., *Abstract of the Twelfth Census of the United States 1900*. Washington: Government Printing Office, 1902.

——, *Twelfth Census of the United States 1900* Part I and Part II. Washington: Government Printing Office, 1901.

Morison, Samuel Eliot, and Commager, Henry Steele, *The Growth of the American Republic*, 2 vols. New York: Oxford University Press, 1937.

——, *The Growth of the American Republic*, 2 vols. New York: Oxford University Press, 1942.

Myers, W. E., *The Israelites of Louisiana-Their Religious, Civic, Charitable and Patriotic Life*. New Orleans: Meyer, 1904.

New Orleans City Guide. Boston: Houghton Mifflin Company, 1938.

Official Text Book and Programmes of the Twenty-Sixth Saengerfest of the North-American Saengerbund. New Orleans: The Crescent Publishing Company, 1890.

One Hundred Years in New Orleans, Louisiana, Centenary Souvenir-Redemptorist Fathers. New Orleans: [?], 1944.

Orth, Samuel P., *Our Foreigners*. New Haven: Yale University Press, 1921.

Overdyke, W. Darrell. *The Know-Nothing Party in the South*. Baton Rouge: Louisiana State University Press, 1950.

Phelps, Edith M., (compiler), *Restriction of Immigration*, 2 vols. New York: The H. W. Wilson Company, 1924.

Porter, Robert P., *Report on Population of United States at Eleventh Census*. Washington: Government Printing Office, 1895.

Qualben, Lars P., *A History of the Christian Church*. New York: T. Nelson and Sons, 1936.

Rau, A. L., *Some Interesting Facts Gathered from the Early Records of Our Church*, *The Echo*. n.p.: [?], 1904.

Rightor, Henry, (ed.), *Standard History of New Orleans, Louisiana*. Chicago: The Lewis Publishing Company, 1900.

Ross, Edward Alsworth, *The Old World in the New-The significance of past and present immigration to the American People*. New York: The Century Company, 1914.

Schevill, Ferdinand, *A History of Europe-from the Reformation to the Present*. New York: Harcourt, Brace and Company, 1947.

Simkins, Francis Butler, *A History of the South*. New York: Alfred A. Knopf, 1953.

Schurz, Carl, *Abraham Lincoln*. New York: Houghton Mifflin Company, 1888.

——, *The Reminiscences of Carl Schurz*, 3 vols. New York: Doubleday, Page and Company, 1909.

Schweickhardt, L., *History of Saint Matthew Evangelical Church*, New Orleans: Jones, 1924.

Schweppe, Rachel Davis DuBois Emma, *The Germans in American Life*. New York: T. Nelson and Sons, 1936.

Seventy-Fifth Anniversary-Jahncke Service 1875-1950. New Orleans: Searcy and Pfaff Ltd., 1950.

Seymour, William H., *The Story of Algiers*. Algiers: Algiers Democrat Printing Company, 1896.

Share, Nathaniel S., *One Hundredth Anniversary of Congregation of Gates of Prayer*. New Orleans: Ben M. Wolf, 1950.

Souvenir of the Eightieth Anniversary of the German Society of New Orleans. New Orleans: Sendker Printing Service, Inc., 1927.

Swain, Joseph Ward, *The Ancient World-Empires and City States of the Ancient Orient and Greece Before 334 B.C.*, 2 vols. New York: Harper and Brothers, 1950.

The Artistic Almanac and Fund of Fact. n.p.: [?], 1894. This book is in the T. P. Thompson Collection, University of Alabama.

The Encyclopedia Americana, 30 vols. New York: American Book-Stratford Press, Inc., 1953.

The Times Democratic Almanac. New Orleans: [?], 1885. This book is in the T. P. Thompson Collection, University of Alabama.

Voss, Louis ,*Die Deutschen in Louisiana*. Detroit: Concord Society of America, 1929.

——, *History of the First Street Presbyterian Church*. New Orleans: The Presbyterian Board of Publication of the Synod of Louisiana, 1929.

——, *History of the German Society*. New Orleans: Sendker Printing Service, Inc., 1927.

——, *Presbyterianism in New Orleans and Adjacent Points*. New Orleans: The Presbyterian Board of Publication of the Synod of Louisiana, 1931.

Walker, Francis A., *The Statistics of the Population of the United States Compiled from the Original Returns of the Ninth Census*. Washington: Government Printing Office, 1872.

Waring, George E., *Report on the Social Statistics of Cities* Part I and Part II. Washington: Government Printing Office, 1887.

Wegener, G. J., *Geschichte der St. Paulus Gemeinde*. St. Louis: Concordia Publishing House, 1890.

——, *Kurzgefasste Geschichte der Deutschen Evangelish-Lutherischen Kirche St. Paulus Gemeinde U.A.C. zu New Orleans, Louisiana*. St. Louis: Concordia Publishing House, 1890.

W. E. H. v. W., *Sechs Monate in Amerika*. Oppeln: [?], 1869.

Wharton, George M., "Stahl" [pseud.], *The New Orleans Skech-Book*. Philadelphia: A. Hart, 1853.

Wittke, Carl, *Refugees of Revolution-The German Forty-Eighters in America*. Philadelphia: University of Pennsylvania Press, 1952.

World Book Encyclopedia, 19 vols. Chicago: Field Enterprises, Inc., 1953.

Zimmerman, Joseph, *Festival Writing of German American National Association*. New Orleans: Hofeline and Adams, 1911. This book is in the archives of the Deutsches Haus, 200 S. Galvez Street, New Orleans, Louisiana.

IX. MAGAZINES AND PERIODICALS:

Arndt, Karl J. R., "A Bavarian's Journey to New Orleans and Nacogdoches in 1853-54," *Louisiana Historical Quarterly*, XXIII (1940), 485-500.

Briede, Kathryn C., "A History of Lafayette," *Louisiana Historical Quarterly*, XX (1937), 895-964.

Clark, Jr., Robert T., "Reconstruction and the New Orleans German Colony," *Louisiana Historical Quarterly*, XXIII (1940), 501-524.

——, "The German Liberals in New Orleans 1840-1860," *Louisiana Historical Quarterly*, XX (1937), 137-151.

——, "The New Orleans German Colony in the Civil War," *Louisiana Historical Quarterly*, XX (1937), 990-1015.

Dabney, Thomas Ewing, "The Butler Regime in Louisiana," *Louisiana Historical Quarterly*, XXVII (1944), 487-526.

Elder, Mrs. S. B. ,"The Germans in Louisiana History-Their Splendid Work in Colonization," *Souvenir of the Eightieth Anniversary of the German Society of New Orleans*, (1927), 48-73.

Faust, Albert B., "German Culture Influences in American Life," "*The Concord Society of American Year Book 1928*, (1929), 6-16.

Kendall, John S., "Old New Orleans Houses and Some of the People Who Lived in Them," *Louisiana Historical Quarterly*, XX (1937), 794-820.

Moehlenbrock, Arthur H., "The German Drama on the New Orleans Stage," *Louisiana Historical Quarterly*, XXVI (1943), 361-627.

"1954 Annual Catholic Directory," *Catholic Action of the South*, (1954), 32.

Pekari, Matthew A., "The German Catholics in the United States of America," *Records of the American Historical Society*, XXXVI (1925), 347-365.

Renshaw, James A., "The Lost City of Lafayette," *Louisiana Historical Quarterly*, II (1919), 47-55.

Roselius, Christian, "Collegiate Education," *The Louisiana Book*, Mc Caleb (ed.), 149-151.

"The History of Education in Louisiana," *United States Bureau of Education*, (Washington, 1898), 100-125.

"Tulane vs Tropics," *Newsweek*, (August 3, 1953), 46-51.

Vollmer, Philip, "What Germans Have Contributed to Our National Life," *Souvenir of the Eightieth Anniversary of the German Society of New Orleans*, (1927), 38-47.

Voss, Louis, "Die Letzten Sechzig Jahren," *The Concord Society of American Year Book 1928* (1929) 51-54.

Wegener, G. J., "Continued Progress of the Missouri Synod in the South-St. Paul's in New Orleans," *Southern District Bulletin*, VIII (1932-33) 1-2.

"Wie die Kosten fuer das Saengerfest in New Orleans aufgebracht wurden," *Lyra*, II (1898).

X. THESES:

Burke, Martin H., "Discipline in the New Orleans Public Schools," Master's Thesis, Tulane University, 1941.

Forster, Walter O., "Settlement of the Saxon Lutherans in Missouri, 1839-1847," PH. D. Dissertation, Washington University, 1942.

Hoffman, Beryl M., "German Education in Louisiana," Master's Thesis, Tulane University, 1939.

Kaiser, Thais Emelda, "Yellow Fever in 19th Century New Orleans," Master's Thesis, Tulane University, 1941.

Konrad, Robinson, "The Diminishing Influences of German Culture in New Orleans Life Since 1865," Master's Thesis, Tulane University, 1940.

Laguaites, Jeanette K., "The German Element in New Orleans, 1820-1860," Master's Thesis, Tulane University, 1940.